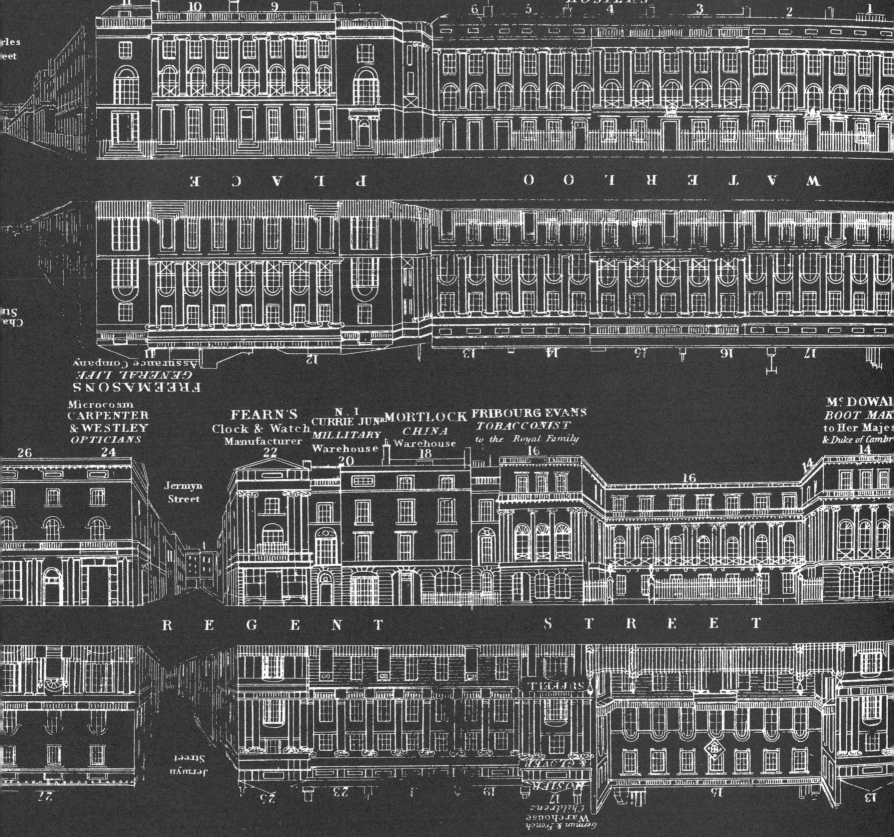
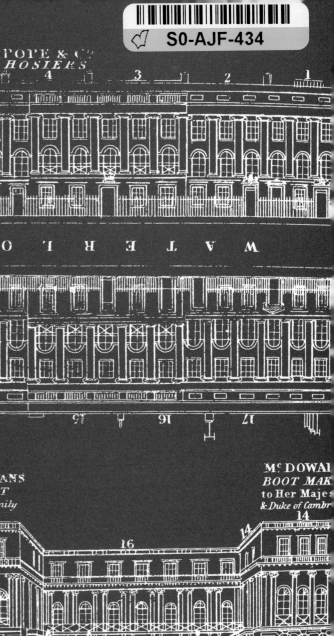

JOHN NASH

JOHN NASH

A complete catalogue

Photographs and text by
MICHAEL MANSBRIDGE

Introduction by John Summerson ·

PHAIDON · OXFORD

To the memory of Ben,
an Irish water-spaniel and
a good companion

Phaidon Press Limited
140 Kensington Church Street, London, W8 4BN
First published in 1991

© 1991 by Phaidon Press Limited
Text and photographs, other than those acknowledged elsewhere,
© 1991 by the estate of Michael Mansbridge
Introduction © 1991 by John Summerson

ISBN 0 7148 2678 2

A CIP catalogue record for this book is available from the British Library

Designed by Tim Higgins

Typeset in Linotype Fournier
by Wyvern Typesetting Limited, Bristol
Printed and bound in Singapore

Title-page spread: Luscombe Castle, Devon (see No. 67)

CONTENTS

Gloucester Terrace (see No. 249): the terrace is set back from the road and protected by a belt of trees

PREFACE

THE FIRST SCHOLARLY CATALOGUE of John Nash's works was compiled by Wyatt Papworth for the *Dictionary of Architecture*, which he edited for the Architectural Publication Society between 1852 and 1892. This formed the basis of the list in John Summerson's pioneer biography, *John Nash: Architect to George IV* (1935). This list was, in turn, the basis of the Nash entry in H. M. Colvin's *A Biographical Dictionary of English Architects, 1660–1840* (1954), the second edition of which was reissued, in expanded form, as *A Biographical Dictionary of British Architects, 1660–1840* (1978). Neither Papworth's nor Colvin's work was illustrated, and Summerson's biography contained only fifty-eight illustrations. The late Terence Davis's *The Architecture of John Nash* (1960) and *John Nash: The Prince Regent's Architect* (1966) both improved on this, with 194 and 91 illustrations respectively, and Summerson's rewritten version of his biography, *The Life and Work of John Nash, Architect* (1980), has 107. Until now, however, a full corpus of illustrations has not been attempted, and that is the primary object of the present work.

In attempting an inventory of all the works by or attributed to Nash, together with some that are at present only loosely associated with his name, I have consulted many sources. In addition to the books already referred to, the following have been of special value: Ann Saunders, *Regent's Park* (1969); Hermione Hobhouse, *Regent Street* (1973); F. Ladd, *Architects of Corsham Court* (1978); Nigel Temple, *John Nash and the Village Picturesque* (1979); John Dinkel, *The Royal Pavilion* (1983); and Thomas Lloyd, *The Lost Houses of Wales* (1986). References to these and other sources are made under the individual catalogue entries. Full titles of books referred to in shortened form, as well as other abbreviations used in the captions, are given on page 34. For full descriptions of Nash's several careers, his achievements and his personal life history, John Summerson's *The Life and Work of John Nash* is indispensable.

I am especially grateful to the owners of Nash's extant buildings for allowing me to visit and photograph them. To Sir John Summerson, Dr Nigel Temple, Thomas Lloyd and J. A. K. Dean I am indebted for the advice and information they have freely given me from their unpublished researches. I am also grateful to the staffs of libraries, museums, galleries and record offices throughout the British Isles and Eire and to the many private owners of material I have been allowed to use.

I also thank Phaidon Press and Simon Haviland for their help and especially Jenny Haviland, who diligently carried out the editing, Tim Higgins, who designed the book, and John Conaway of Darkroom Associates, who printed many of my photographs. I am also most grateful for the advice and encouragement given to me by Sally Reckert, who also typed my manuscript, Alison Vaspe and Nicholas Reckert and finally to Daphne for her patience and understanding spread over many years.

East Molesey, September 1990   M. M.

The author died a few days after returning the corrected galley-proofs of the text

INTRODUCTION

John Summerson

WHEN JOHN NASH DIED in his castle at East Cowes in 1835, few kind things were said about him. The general view was that he had built a great deal of very questionable architecture, had been hand-in-glove with a monarch whom nobody greatly revered, had made a lot of money for himself and now deserved only to be forgotten. Such is the readiness of posterity to believe the worst of a public figure that in all the remaining decades of the nineteenth century and the first three of the twentieth, Nash's reputation was under a cloud. I remember as a student in the twenties being snubbed for enquiring why the history lectures contained nothing about Regent Street or Regent's Park. In the early thirties, when I proposed to write a biography of Nash, I was firmly told by the curator of the Soane Museum (an able but not unprejudiced scholar) that I was wasting my time; that Nash was an ignorant rogue in whom no artistic excellence was to be found. Sir Reginald Blomfield, just then rebuilding the Quadrant, endorsed the view. Nevertheless I wrote the book and it came out in 1935, the centenary year of its subject's death. It was not a very satisfactory book; it bore the marks of youth, inexperience and impatience, but it was received with acclamation and widely reviewed. People looked at Nash with new eyes. Forty years later, becoming conscience-stricken about the book's inadequacy, I rewrote it from beginning to end. The new version, called *The Life and Work of John Nash* (Allen and Unwin), appeared in 1980. By that time the tide had turned. Regency architecture was loved and preserved and Nash esteemed as one of its heroes.

The second version of my book contains a list of Nash's works incorporating discoveries made by myself, Howard Colvin and others, but does not claim to be complete. The loss of nearly all Nash's papers puts completeness out of the question, but I was always aware that a thorough search of archival sources up and down the country would bring to light more houses and perhaps more forgotten London buildings as well. This has proved to be the case and Mr Mansbridge's inventory puts Nash's *opus* on a broader basis than it has so far been. My book, with only 107 illustrations, is underillustrated. Mr Mansbridge, with 720, has made a point of including every work of which a representation can be found – photographs where possible and prints or drawings of buildings which have been lost. Thus we have here the best possible basis for an appreciation of Nash's enormous output and of his lively variety of styles.

My book of 1980 does, I think, bring together in narrative form all the biographical information at present available, including discoveries made by myself and others since 1935, and omitting only a few minor finds made since publication. The two books together may claim to present a picture of Nash's life and work which future students may take as a platform of departure. Mr Mansbridge's inventory is in itself a major contribution to the history of architecture in Britain.

One thing must be said about this inventory; it is very generous – in my view rather too generous – with unproven attributions. Mr Mansbridge was apt to take printed attributions at their face value, especially if the building concerned had for him a Nash-like look. His sudden death in 1990 put an end to the possibility of seeking conclusive authority for every item and the fruits of his twelve years research, travel and photography seemed too valuable to be delayed and eroded by the endless process of scholarly enquiry. My own contribution to the work consists, therefore, solely of the summary biographical entry which follows. This should help the reader to see Nash's life and work in perspective. It is followed by a brief note on style. References to the catalogue are given throughout. The biographical summary is not annotated and I must refer the reader in search of sources to my book of 1980, of which what follows is a brief synopsis.

NASH: A BIOGRAPHICAL SUMMARY

Nash's life of eighty-three years can conveniently be divided into four periods. (1) The forty years which took him from obscurity in Lambeth to eminence in Wales and thence to celebrity in London. (2) The period of about twenty years during which, though based in London, he was a fashionable country-house architect in England and Ireland. (3) The Regency period, 1811–20, when he was principally concerned with the planning and execution of Regent's Park and Regent Street, but parallel with these working for the Regent at Carlton House and Windsor as his private architect. (4) A period of fifteen years during which, as the King's architect, he converted Buckingham House into Buckingham Palace, simultaneously extending the Regent Street plan to Charing Cross. Overshadowed by attacks on his professional conduct and personal integrity, the period ends with his death in 1835.

(1) THE FIRST FORTY YEARS (1752–92). John Nash was born in 1752, the son of a Welsh millwright working in Lambeth but retaining connections with his native country. His father dying in 1758, young Nash was apprenticed to Sir Robert Taylor,

Miniature of Nash aged about 46. Artist unknown. Collection of Mr Peter Laing

sculptor and architect. He left Taylor in about 1774 and in 1775 he married Jane Elizabeth Kerr, a surgeon's daughter by whom he had two sons. Also in 1775 he entered on a speculative enterprise on the property of Sir John Rushout (later Lord Northwick) in Bloomsbury Square, London. This failed and he was declared bankrupt in 1783. Divorce proceedings against his extravagant (and perhaps mentally unstable) wife failed, and in 1784 Nash left London for Wales, where he mixed on a social equality with the local squirearchy and, about 1789, started an architectural practice, rapidly acquiring local fame for his gaols at Carmarthen and Cardigan and his houses for the Welsh gentry.

(2) THE COUNTRY-HOUSE ARCHITECT (1793–1810; age 41–58). When completing Carmarthen Gaol in 1792 Nash already had a new London address in Duke Street, St James's Square. He continued his Welsh connections, however, building Castle House, Aberystwyth (No. 38) for Sir Uvedale Price, who initiated him into the theory of the 'Picturesque'. He also got to know Price's friend, Richard Payne Knight, and was attracted by the 'castle' style of his house, Downton, Herefordshire (No. 4). By 1798 he had acquired a leasehold in Dover Street, London. Here he built a strikingly original stucco-fronted house, no. 29 (destroyed 1941), where he lived and practised till 1820. Also in 1798 he started building, for himself, East Cowes Castle in the Isle of Wight (No. 59) and married as his second wife (the first being presumably deceased) Mary Anne Bradley, daughter of a coal-merchant of Abingdon Street, Westminster. Also at this time he formed a partnership with Humphry Repton, the rising landscape-gardener: this resulted in valuable commissions for estate buildings and sometimes for rebuilding or enlarging the houses themselves, as well as in an introduction to George, Prince of Wales, who was employing Repton at Brighton.

In 1802 a disagreement with Repton resulted in the dissolution of the partnership but Nash was now well established as one of the leading country-house architects. Villas near London and grand country houses and castles in many parts of England and Ireland belong to this period and, in addition, cottages in a personal version of the English vernacular as exemplified in the 'village' on the Blaise Castle estate, near Bristol (No. 133). In 1806 Nash accepted the office of architect to the Commissioners for Crown Lands, possibly with the foreknowledge of the Commissioners' intention to build on the Marylebone Park estate when the freehold should revert to the Crown.

(3) METROPOLITAN IMPROVEMENTS (1811–20; age 59–68). The Prince of Wales was made Regent in March 1811 and the greater part of Marylebone Park, on lease to the Duke of Portland, reverted to the Crown a month later. As architect to the Office of Woods and Forests Nash was instructed to submit plans and a report on the development of the park as a residential area. Thomas Leverton, surveyor to the Office of Land Revenues, was likewise required to submit plans. Both architects,

moreover, were to report on the formation of a new highway from Regent's Park to Charing Cross. Leverton's submissions were old-fashioned and half-hearted; Nash's, profoundly original and accompanied by a brilliant report, were recommended to the Treasury. The Prince Regent was impressed by Nash's vision of street and park ('it will quite eclipse Napoleon') and Nash became his confidential adviser, not only on architecture but even on political issues; he tried, though unsuccessfully, to enter Parliament. Work started on the Park in 1812 but was delayed by the failure of the builder who undertook the southern half of the circus (now Park Crescent) at the junction of the Park with Portland Place. The Street had to await the passage of the New Street Act through Parliament; the measure received the Royal Assent in 1813, from which date demolition and clearance proceeded rapidly, builders taking the new sites from 1814. The construction of the Quadrant (see No. 102) presented a problem because a building on a continuous curve had necessarily to be built as a single undertaking and no builder could willingly bargain for curved blocks on that scale; Nash cut the knot by taking all the house-lots in his own name and forming a consortium of building tradesmen, bricklayers, masons, paviors, plasterers and iron-founders who would agree to accept remuneration in terms of 99-year leases of the houses they were building. The Quadrant was completed in 1819 and the whole street opened for traffic in the following year.

Nash at the age of 72. Portrait by Sir Thomas Lawrence, begun in 1824. Canvas, 54 x 43½ in. Jesus College, Oxford

Parallel with this work in the Park and the Street, Nash was acting in this period as private architect to the Prince, turning an old house in Windsor Park into the so-called 'cottage' (in fact, a very spacious house but with a thatched roof; No. 137) and rearranging the basement of Carlton House as a suite of richly decorated rooms, one of them Gothic (No. 143). At Brighton he started in 1815 to convert the Pavilion which Henry Holland had designed for the Prince in 1786–7 into an Oriental fantasy (No. 165), with five Indian domes providing a silhouette and with interiors in a Chinese taste.

(4) Architect to King George IV: Buckingham Palace (1820–35; age 68–83). The old King dying in 1820, the Regent ascended the throne as George IV. The question of an appropriate royal residence at once arose and Parliament resolved to restore Windsor Castle and to convert Buckingham House, in St James's Park, into a metropolitan palace, Nash being entrusted with the latter. He was to conduct the work as the Sovereign's private architect, while being at the same time accountable to the Treasury, a difficult position to maintain without either giving offence to the King or disobeying Treasury orders. Nash started on Buckingham House (No. 235) in 1825 and continued without interruption till the King's death in 1830. In 1828 the rising building met with severe criticism and was admitted by Nash himself to have serious shortcomings which could only be remedied by demolition. A Select Committee, set up to consider the state of public works in general and the

expenditure they involved, sat in the same year and Nash's evidence raised doubts about his professional competence. Another Select Committee, in 1829, went further in questioning his professional integrity; this was in the matter of leases on Crown land which was being developed by the Office of Woods, Forests and Land Revenues, the MP for Worcester accusing Nash of taking, as a private individual, land which he had valued at a low rate as an officer of the Crown. From this enquiry Nash emerged unscathed and his accusers were humiliated.

The King thought this the right moment to make Nash a baronet but the intention was opposed by the Duke of Wellington, as Prime Minister, chiefly on the grounds that the accounts for Buckingham Palace were not yet settled and might disclose some inconvenient facts – which they did. Nash, preferring to obey the King's commands rather than to conform to the restrictions on expenditure ordered by the Treasury, had overspent the parliamentary allowance by a large amount. This led to the appointment of another Select Committee to enquire more specifically into Nash's conduct of the Palace works. The committee sat in 1830. George IV died in January of that year and Nash's enemies were at last free to trounce him ('make a hash of Nash', in Wellington's words). His commission at the Palace was withdrawn and he was dismissed from his office as architect to the Board of Works.

Nash formally retired from practice in 1834, moving from the Regent Street mansion he had occupied since 1821 to East Cowes Castle and taking with him his gallery, which was re-erected in the long conservatory at the Castle. Although facing financial difficulties, chiefly because of a recession in property values, his last years were spent in comfort and serenity at East Cowes. Nothing is known of the lives of the two sons he had by his first wife. By his second wife he had no children and nearly the whole of his estate was left to her. His health deteriorated after a stroke in 1830 and he died on 3 May 1835. He was buried at the foot of the west tower of the church he built at East Cowes. His debts, amounting to £15,000, were paid in full in 1841.

THE QUESTION OF STYLE:
NEO-CLASSICISM AND THE PICTURESQUE

The style of architecture which prevailed in Britain, indeed throughout Europe, during the period of Nash's professional life was the style which, in our time, has come to be called Neo-classicism. This is a severe and sometimes pedantic form of classical designing based on antique prototypes. It was the style most often adopted for public buildings and for the urban scene in general. Introduced in Britain by two great masters, Sir William Chambers and Robert Adam, the Neo-classical passed through two distinct phases. Nash's career belongs to the second though his roots are in the first. His primary loyalty was to Chambers, and the façade of the pair of houses in Bloomsbury Square is a humble imitation of Chambers' Somerset House front to the

Strand then recently completed. Forty years later the park front of Cumberland Terrace (No. 241) is a dramatic re-enactment of the river front of the same building. Nash also borrowed from Adam, a notable derivation, often repeated, being the tripartite window with a radial-fluted tympanum introduced by Adam in his Royal Society of Arts building in the Adelphi and used by Nash in many instances from Southgate Grove (No. 51) to Piccadilly Circus. A more powerful influence than either of the two English masters was the classical school of Paris. Nash's design for a County Hall at Stafford (No. 25) is an early example of the square-cut model with a saucer dome and inset columns which was typical of French academic design. Versailles is reflected in the pavilions of Cumberland Terrace (1824), and the twin Carlton House Terraces (begun 1825; No. 256) are very obviously inspired by Gabriel's twin palaces on the Place de la Concorde.

The second phase of Neo-classicism in England developed after 1790, in a peculiar context – the 'Picturesque'. This started as a landscape cult; equally hostile to the old-fashioned formal layouts and to the smooth and conventional irregularities of Lancelot (Capability) Brown, it claimed a more imaginative and romantic interpretation of landscape values. The promoters of the Picturesque were Sir Uvedale Price, Payne Knight and Humphry Repton, the latter of whom, as we have seen, had joined Nash in a partnership. The Picturesque mood swept the country between 1794 and 1815. Nash was friendly with Price and Knight and soon became the leading architect of the movement. His country houses were often in the Picturesque spirit, especially the 'castles' with their clustering towers, embattled in the style of Warwick or Windsor (e.g. Caerhays, 1808; No. 117), or the smaller villas (e.g. Cronkhill, 1802; No. 72) imitating the buildings in a Claude landscape.

The Picturesque legitimized and encouraged the use of styles other than the Greek or Roman and Nash made considerable play with this new stylistic eclecticism. He interested himself in Gothic, Tudor, Chinese and Indian. His earliest houses were mostly classical but at Corsham (1793) he built a Gothic gallery with a drawing-room limb in the style of Henry VII's chapel at Westminster. His house plans were adaptable to any style. He could explode the symmetrical Palladian villa into an irregular pattern with a Gothic silhouette (e.g. Luscombe); or he could make a plan with an impressive spinal gallery in the Gothic (as at Ravensworth, 1808; No. 111), or in the Classical (e.g. Witley, 1805; No. 86) mode, the latter bringing him to the noble gallery plan of Buckingham Palace (1824–33).

With the 'Indian style' (an arbitrary amalgam of Hindu and Islamic based on the pictorial evidence), Nash achieved, against all the odds, a real triumph at the Brighton Pavilion (No. 165), lifting Henry Holland's modest Neo-classical villa into an extravaganza of domes and pinnacles, with interiors more Chinese than Indian and perhaps more Soaneian than either. At Windsor, the Prince Regent's 'cottage' (No. 137) took a different direction again: the English countryside vernacular with a conspicuous

Stone bust of Nash in the portico of All Souls, Langham Place, by Cecil Thomas. Modern copy of marble bust by William Behnes, 1831

NASHIONAL TASTE !!!
(Dedicated without permission to the Church Commissioners —
Providence sends meat,   Parliament sends Funds —
The Devil sends cooks.   But who sends the Architects, ? —

Caricature of Nash impaled on the steeple of All Souls, Langham Place, by 'Q in the corner'. Published 7 April 1824 by G. Humphrey

thatched roof. The vernacular had a strong attraction for Nash and his cottage designs are among the most inventive and carefully detailed of his works (Blaise Hamlet, near Bristol, 1811, is the outstanding group).

If the Picturesque manifests itself most readily in his country-house work it does so in a less obvious but ultimately dramatic way in his London parks and streets. Regent's Park was from the first a picturesque conception, with its scattered villas and scenic terraces; but the great new street had to go through two stages of invention. As first designed it consisted of straight lines, colonnades and formal vistas. Only when this was found unworkable did Nash see how the Picturesque would solve his London problem – by turning the whole conception from prose to poetry. He took Oxford's High Street as his model – an acknowledged masterpiece of the urban Picturesque. Like its prototype, in which historical accident played the principal role, Regent Street would bend, the bends being calculated, however, to provide picturesque scenes as well as to solve problems of convenience and viability (No. 102).

NASH AND TECHNOLOGY

From the earliest days of practice Nash was a great experimenter with new materials and new devices. In Bloomsbury Square in 1783 he had been one of the first to use the Adams's patent stucco. His single-span iron bridge at Stanford on Teme (1795) was a brave affair; the first bridge collapsed but he rebuilt it and the second bridge, a single arch of cast-iron voussoirs bolted together, was in good shape a century later (No. 40). The Royal Pavilion at Brighton he made an opportunity for experiment with iron columns invisibly carrying his Indian domes over the roofs of Holland's drawing-rooms. The staircases were made of cast-iron; the flat roofs were sealed with newly invented mastic and the Indian ornaments modelled in a patent stucco. At Buckingham Palace he carried the floors of the State Apartments on iron girders; they were much criticised at the time, but they still do their work.

Nash was the last English architect to consider himself not only an architect but an engineer. He built the great brick sewer under Regent Street and formed the canyon bridged by Highgate Archway without any specialist advice. He was an able financier who, bankrupt at 30, learnt how to play dangerous games without going over the edge. He was immensely courageous and fought his way through years of opposition and criticism; and he was as intensely loyal to his beloved Prince and Sovereign as his Prince and Sovereign was to him.

BIOGRAPHICAL OUTLINE

1752 — Born of Welsh parents almost certainly in London

c.1766–c.1774 — Works in office of the architect Sir Robert Taylor (1714–88)

1775 — Marries Jane Elizabeth Kerr; first son born 1776

1777 — Builds 17 Bloomsbury Square and 66–71 Great Russell Street; lives with family at 66 Great Russell Street

1783 — Declared bankrupt

1784 — Moves to Carmarthen, Wales

c.1785–9 — Builds minor works locally; James Morgan joins office

1789–92 — Builds first public works: St David's Cathedral restoration and Carmarthen Gaol

1790 — Introduced to Humphry Repton (1752–1818)

1791–7 — Develops interest in cast iron and bridge-building

c.1792 — Auguste Charles de Pugin joins his office

1793 — War with France

1795 — Indoctrinated in the Picturesque by Sir Uvedale Price at Castle House, Aberystwyth

First commission in England: Kentchurch Court

1796 — Forms partnership with Humphry Repton, whose son John Adey joins the office

Exhibits at Royal Academy for first time

1797 — Moves back to London and lives first at 28 Duke Street, St James's, then at 28 Dover Street

1798 — Introduced to the Prince of Wales; makes first design for him ('A Conservatory')

Marries Mary Anne Bradley; moves to 29 Dover Street

c.1800 — Partnership with Humphry Repton dissolved

1802 — Builds Cronkhill (first Claudean villa)

George Stanley Repton (1786–1858) replaces his brother John Adey in the office after John's departure in 1799

1806 — Appointed as salaried architect to Office of Woods and Forests, with James Morgan as partner

1810 — Instructed to prepare plans for Marylebone (Regent's) Park and the New (Regent) Street

1811 — The Prince of Wales becomes Regent

Takes over promotion and management of Regent's Canal

1811–20 — Designs the Royal Lodge, Windsor, and suite of rooms at Carlton House for the Prince Regent

1814 — Designs temporary buildings in St James's Park and Green Park to celebrate peace with France

Appointed, together with John Soane (1753–1837) and Robert Smirke (1781–1867), as Attached Architect to the Board of Works

Makes first recorded visit to France

1815 — Begins reconstructing the Royal Pavilion, Brighton

1818 — Makes second recorded visit to France

1820 — Accession of the Prince Regent to the throne as George IV

1820–1 — Builds 14–16 Regent Street for himself and his cousin John Edwards

1825 — Begins rebuilding Buckingham House (Palace)

1827 — Plans St James's Park

1829 — Called before Parliamentary Select Committee and exonerated from accusations of professional misconduct

1830 — Death of George IV; dismissed as architect to Buckingham Palace

1834 — Retires; James Pennethorne (1801–71) succeeds to practice

1835 — Dies at East Cowes Castle, buried at St James's Church, East Cowes, Isle of Wight

1 The Dairy at Luscombe Castle, Dawlish, Devonshire (No. 67)

2 The Warrens, Bramshaw, Hampshire (No. 65)

3 Sandridge Park, Stoke Gabriel, Devonshire (No. 90)

4 The Clock Tower at Longner Hall, Atcham, Shropshire (No. 77)

5 The Orangery at Barnsley Park, Barnsley, Gloucestershire (No. 101)

6 Parnham House, Beaminster, Dorsetshire (No. 109)

7 Knepp Castle, West Grinstead, Sussex (No. 122)

8 Blaise Hamlet, Henbury, Gloucestershire (No. 133)

9 Regent's Park, London, with Cumberland Terrace in the background (No. 123)

10 The Music Room at the Royal Pavilion, Brighton, Sussex (No. 165)

11   The Banqueting Room at the Royal Pavilion, Brighton, Sussex (No. 165)

12 The east elevation of the Royal Pavilion, Brighton, Sussex (No. 165)

13 Park Village West, Regent's Park,
London (No. 221)

14 York Terrace, Regent's Park, London (No. 200)

15 St James's Park, London (No. 161)

16 Cumberland Terrace, Regent's Park,
London (No. 241)

CATALOGUE

ABBREVIATIONS

Abbreviations and full names of books and references used

J. B. Burke,
*A Visitation of Seats
and Arms*

John Bernard Burke, *A Visitation of the Seats and
Arms of the Noblemen and Gentlemen of Great Britain*,
2 vols, 1852–3; 2nd series, 2 vols, 1854–5

Davis 1960

Terence Davis, *The Architecture of John Nash*,
London, 1960

Davis 1966

Terence Davis, *John Nash: The Prince Regent's
Architect*, London, 1966

Elmes,
*Metropolitan
Improvements*, 1827

J. Elmes, *Metropolitan Improvements; or London in the
Nineteenth Century: Displayed in a Series of Engravings
of the New Buildings, Improvements, &c. by the Most
Eminent Artists, from Original Drawings, taken from the
Objects Themselves expressly for this Work, by Mr. Thos.
H. Shepherd*, 1827

HMB

Historic Monuments and Buildings Branch,
Department of the Environment, Northern Ireland

King's Works, vi, 1973

H. M. Colvin (ed.), *The History of the King's Works*,
6 vols, 1963 etc

Nash Sale Catalogue,
1835

*A Catalogue of the valuable architectural and
miscellaneous prints and drawings, of the late John Nash,
Esq.* The sale took place 15–20 July 1835 in Pall
Mall. There are copies of the catalogue in the
British Museum and the Sir John Soane Museum

NLW

National Library of Wales

NMR Wales

National Monuments Record for Wales

J. P. Neale,
Views of Seats

J. P. Neale, *Views of the Seats of Noblemen and
Gentlemen in England, Wales, Scotland and Ireland*,
6 vols, 1818–23

Repton,
Brighton Sketchbook

George Repton's sketchbook, unpublished, now in
the Royal Pavilion, Art Gallery and Museums,
Brighton

Repton,
RIBA Sketchbook

George Repton's sketchbook, unpublished, now in
the British Architectural Library Drawings
Collection, Royal Institute of British Architects.

RCHME

Royal Commission on the Historical Monuments of
England

Shide Hill Ledger

The only surviving account book of Nash, found in
a house lived in by the Pennethorne family, Shide
Hill, Isle of Wight

Summerson 1935

John Summerson, *John Nash: Architect to King
George IV*, London, 1935 (2nd edn 1949)

Summerson 1980

John Summerson, *The Life and Work of John Nash,
Architect*, London, 1980

Survey of London

Survey of London, London, 1900–

N. Temple,
Hants Society, 1988

Nigel Temple, 'Pages from an Architect's
Notebook. George Stanley Repton: his drawings
for a house and a greenhouse for George Eyre, of
Warrens, Bramshaw, Hampshire', *Proceedings of the
Hampshire Field Club and Archaeological Society*,
1988

N. Temple,
*Records of
Huntingdonshire*, 1986

Nigel Temple, 'Pages from an Architect's
Notebook. Lady Olivia Sparrow and John Nash',
Records of Huntingdonshire, 2, 1986

N. Temple,
IOW Society, 1987

Nigel Temple, 'Pages from an Architect's
Notebook. Some minor buildings in the Isle of
Wight. Part 1', *Proceedings of the Isle of Wight
Natural History and Archaeological Society*, 8 (2),
1987

N. Temple,
IOW Society, 1988

Nigel Temple, 'Pages from an Architect's
Notebook. Some minor buildings in the Isle of
Wight. Part 2', *Proceedings of the Isle of Wight
Natural History and Archaeological Society*, 8 (3),
1988

N. Temple,
Society of Cymmrodorion,
1985

Nigel Temple, 'Pages from an Architect's
Notebook. John Nash: some minor buildings in
Wales', *Transactions of the Honourable Society of
Cymmrodorion*, 1985

*Victoria County History:
Hampshire*

*The Victoria History of the Counties of England:
Hampshire and the Isle of Wight*, 5 vols and index,
1900–1914

*Victoria County History:
Oxfordshire*

*The Victoria History of the Counties of England:
Oxfordshire*, 11 vols, 1907–

I

16–17 BLOOMSBURY SQUARE *and* 66–71 GREAT RUSSELL STREET

London

1777–1778

On leaving Robert Taylor's office, Nash bought this Bloomsbury property as a speculation. Acting as architect and developer, roles he was to combine many times in the future, he built two large classical mansions on Bloomsbury Square, each with three storeys and a basement. The rusticated ground floors support Corinthian pilasters facing the square, with full entablature and blocking course to both fronts. The attic floors and projecting porches are later additions.

In Great Russell Street Nash built a row of six small houses for letting, early examples – perhaps the first – of stucco finish being applied overall. The original dentilled cornice has been removed. Nash, together with his first wife and small son, lived in No. 71 Great Russell Street for three years. The remaining houses failed to let; Nash was bankrupted, and retreated to Wales.

Summerson 1980

ABOVE Bloomsbury Square: the top storey and porch are later additions
BELOW Great Russell Street: Nash and his first wife and family lived in the corner house

2

ST PETER AND
ST PAUL

Farningham, Kent

1778

The mausoleum built in the churchyard of St Peter and St Paul at Farningham contains the remains of Thomas Nash, possibly a rich uncle of John Nash. John is thought to have planned the tomb before Thomas's death. In 1988 the Georgian Group made a donation towards the repair and upkeep of the tomb, noting that it was possibly designed by John Nash.

Georgian Group Journal, 1988
N. Pevsner, *Buildings of England: Kent*, 1976

The mausoleum of Thomas Nash in the churchyard of St Peter and St Paul

3

ST PETER'S CHURCH

Carmarthen, Carmarthenshire

1785

St Peter's dates from the twelfth century. It was the largest and most important church in Carmarthen, and the acceptance of the estimate of six hundred guineas to replace the roof and ceiling, made by Nash and Samuel Saxon, resulted in Nash's name becoming known to the important people of Carmarthen. Part of the ceiling collapsed in 1860.

Summerson 1980

4

DOWNTON CASTLE

Leintwardine, Herefordshire

1773–1778

Downton Castle was the first deliberately planned asymmetrical house – the earlier house, Strawberry Hill, owned by Walpole, had simply evolved over several years. Downton Castle was designed and built by Richard Payne Knight, according to the precepts of the Picturesque movement. Knight and Uvedale Price of Foxley were the leaders of a coterie of Hereford squires, including Cornewall of

Moccas, Matthews of Belmont and Peploe of Garnstone, all of whom employed Nash to embellish their estates. The interiors of Downton were classical, yet 'it is hard to credit Knight with the assured yet brash interiors' (Rowan). It is recorded that Knight consulted a cousin in the building trade named Nash, and Rowan also points out that the prominent octagonal tower was altered between 1782 and 1805 with a particular form of machicolation that later became a trademark of Nash's castles. Therefore it is probable that Nash originated this feature instead of, as previously thought, copying it.

A. Rowan, 'Downton Castle', *The Country Seat*, 1970 (eds Colvin and Harris)

5

GREEN GARDENS

Carmarthen, Carmarthenshire

*c.*1785

The plain two-storey, three-bay house called Green Gardens was reputedly built by Nash for his own use. It suffered many vicissitudes after he left, including being used as part of a school lavatory. The house, now restored as living accommodation, bears a plaque recording Nash's association with it.

W. Spurrell, *Carmarthen and its Neighbourhood*, 1879

Green Gardens

Downton Castle: the octagonal corner tower was probably capped by Nash

6

BRICKYARD LANE COTTAGE

Carmarthen, Carmarthenshire

*c.*1785

Spurrell records a cottage by Nash as having been built in Brickyard Lane in the town. It was demolished in 1858, and no record of its appearance appears to have survived.

W. Spurrell, *Carmarthen and its Neighbourhood*, 1879

7

LLANFECHAN
Llanwnen, Cardiganshire
1786

Llanfechan was built for Admiral Thomas ten years before Nash designed Llanaeron (No. 28), which so much resembles it. Farington records in his *Diary* that Nash told him in 1787 that 'he had employment which produced him £500'. The fee for designing Llanfechan could have been part of that. Alternatively, Nash might have seen the house and liked the composition of recessed centre with projecting porch and round-headed windows, and appropriated the design, which he used from time to time throughout his career. The house was demolished around 1900.

T. Lloyd, *The Lost Houses of Wales*, 1986

Llanfechan, by an unknown artist (Collection T. Lloyd)

BELOW LEFT Six Bells Inn: the much altered public house shortly before its demolition (Collection I. Wyn Jones)
RIGHT Jeremy's Hotel: staircase window

8

SIX BELLS INN
Carmarthen, Carmarthenshire
c.1786

The Six Bells Inn was situated at 7 St Peter's Street, close to Jeremy's Hotel (also built by Nash), and similarly facing the church. It was a simple, one-bay elevation of four storeys, with a canted oriel window at first-floor level, presumably with the entrance door under. The Inn was popular with the clergy visiting St Peter's. It was recently demolished to make way for the town car-park.

W. Spurrell, *Carmarthen and its Neighbourhood*, 1879

9

JEREMY'S HOTEL
Carmarthen, Carmarthenshire
c.1786

The narrow, bow-fronted building still exists in St Peter's Street, facing the church. At the side overlooking the car park is Nash's tall, narrow, Gothic staircase window, possibly the only original feature remaining, the front having been coarsened over the years. All the interior details have gone, and it is now used as offices by the Registrar's Department.

Arch. Cambrensis, 1948

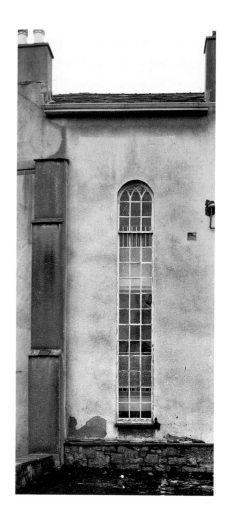

10

ST DAVID'S CATHEDRAL

St David's, Pembrokeshire
1789 and 1791

When Nash was called in, the west front of St David's Cathedral, built on poor soil and with the thrust of the arcade behind, was bowed out twelve inches at the cill level of the great window. After erecting shores, he had the wall taken down to cill level, thickened the lower part by eighteen inches at the base and rebuilt the upper part on it. Structurally the design was impressive, with flying buttresses and massive piers carried on firwood piles; aesthetically it was not considered to be so successful and was replaced in 1862 by Sir George Gilbert Scott. Two years after the work on the

LEFT Jeremy's Hotel: the fenestration is probably original

ABOVE St David's Cathedral: west front by Nash. Photograph before 1862
BELOW Nash's Chapter House is the white building with four upper windows, in front of the tower. Artist unknown (NMR Wales)

west wall was completed, Nash was given the job of improvising a Chapter House out of the old Grammar School built over an earlier workroom; a new dining-room was provided alongside. They remained in use for forty-five years before being demolished.

W. B. Jones and E. A. Freeman, *History and Antiquities of St David's*, 1856

ABOVE The entrance wing of Carmarthen Gaol as originally designed by Nash. Undated photograph

BELOW Aerial view of Carmarthen Gaol: the main entrance is from the street at the top of the picture. Undated photograph

11

GOLDEN GROVE
Carmarthenshire
*c.*1787

Farington records that Nash inserted a bathroom in the house at Golden Grove for John Vaughan – an unusual thing to do at this time in Wales, where baths were still built as outhouses away from the house. Vaughan was delighted, and his unsolicited payment of an honorarium was later claimed by Nash to have been his first professional earning.

The Diary of Joseph Farington, 1793–1821 (unpublished manuscript in the British Library)

12

CARMARTHEN GAOL
Carmarthen, Carmarthenshire
1789–1792

Carmarthen Gaol was the first of Nash's three prisons. It was built after the visit to the town of the prison reformer, John Howard. Nash's design was based, presumably, on Howard's recommendations and replaced two squalid lock-ups. The gaol was built in the castle grounds, with a suitably forbidding front; it was divided horizontally into a rusticated ground floor, pierced only by the entrance door, and a first floor with three semicircular windows. Records are few, but Nash's building was apparently quite small, with the cells contained in short wings on either side of the central hall. The prison complex was much enlarged over the years. In 1938 it was demolished to make way for council offices.

E. Vincent Jones, 'Twelve months in a Victorian Gaol', *The Carmarthen Historian*, 1980

The north elevation of
Clytha Castle, facing
Clytha Court

Entrance arch and
gatehouse to Clytha
Court (later extension
on right)

13

CLYTHA COURT
Near Abergavenny, Monmouthshire
1790

Clytha Castle, a Gothic folly built by
William Jones on his estate, Clytha Court,
as a memorial to his wife, Elizabeth, is set
in a clearing on the wooded hilltop facing
north to the house, from which it is in
constant view. It has an L-shaped plan, the
hollow eastern tower being linked by a
scalloped curtain wall to the habitable
western wing. It has recently been restored

by its present owners, the Landmark Trust. Nash also designed the Gothic entrance arch and gatehouse at the entrance to the estate.

William Coxe, *A Historical Tour through Monmouthshire*, 1904

14

MILTON PARK
Near Peterborough, Northamptonshire
1791

Humphry Repton's proposals for improving Earl Fitzwilliam's estate near Peterborough included building a cottage at a fork of the drive; his *Red Book*, written shortly after he had been introduced to Nash, when they had been 'charmed with each other' (Repton), shows a plain Gothic building. The version as built has a gable, a rose-window and a porch, and a chimney designed as a turret; to stress the verticality, Repton's side wings were moved to the back. Ferry Cottage, a lodge at the western entrance, was also 'Gothicized' at the same time. Both buildings could have been designed either by Nash or by William Wilkins sen., who had been Repton's usual collaborator before his meeting with Nash.

C. Hussey, 'Milton, Northants', *Country Life*, iii, 1 June 1961

Milton Park: (ABOVE) Gothic lodge; (BELOW) Ferry Cottage

15

NEWPORT BRIDGE

Monmouthshire

1791

Nash submitted a design to the Bridge Committee for a single-arch bridge over the River Usk. The masonry bridge was to span 285 feet, making it the largest span in the world for a bridge of this type. Work was started and after £700 had been spent was suddenly stopped. The reason is not known.

T. Ruddock, *Arch Bridges and their Builders* (1735–1835), 1979

16

SION HOUSE

Tenby, Pembrokeshire

1792

This impressive town house was built in Tenby for William Routh, a printer from Bristol. Full-height, canted bays dominated both stuccoed elevations, three storeys high to the front and four to the back, where the steeply sloping site enabled the kitchens and offices on the lower ground floor to enjoy natural light. The unusual plan of the ground floor was to the owner's special requirements and is unlike any other by Nash. In both the drawing-room and the dining-room the interiors of the bay windows were finished as segmented curves. Sion House was more than doubled in size and given a ponderous cornice in the late nineteenth century. It was completely destroyed by fire in 1938.

T. Lloyd, *The Lost Houses of Wales*, 1986

1 Drawing-room
2 Dining-room
3 Gallery
4 Hall

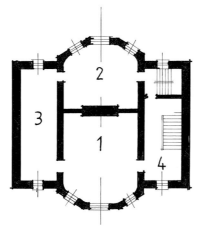

GROUND-FLOOR PLAN OF SION HOUSE

The street elevation of Sion House. Artist unknown, *c.*1850

17

DOLAUCOTHI

Pumpsaint, Carmarthenshire

1792

John Johnes, whose sister Jane married their cousin Thomas Johnes of Hafod (No. 26), asked Nash to improve his eighteenth-century farmhouse as cheaply as possible. Nash refaced the old house and added an entrance porch and possibly the third floor; plain, two-storeyed wings were built at each end with lean-to roofs behind – all for £436, not including chimney pieces and glazing for a new greenhouse. George Borrow visited the estate at Pumpsaint in 1854 and commented 'with what satisfaction I could live in that house' (*West Wales*). Later the wings were raised, and balustrades and bay windows added. After

the house had been empty for ten years the National Trust took over the estate in 1955 and demolished what remained of the derelict house.

F. Jones, 'The Hand of Nash in West Wales', *The Transactions of the Carmarthen Antiquary Society*, 1939

18

RHEIDOL BRIDGE
Aberystwyth, Cardiganshire
1792

The Magistrates of Cardiganshire commissioned Nash to design a new bridge over the River Rheidol. He produced a traditional structure of five arches built in masonry. It stood until 1886, when it was swept away by floods. The temporary bridge in timber erected immediately after the flood was probably to Nash's design.

Summerson 1980

ABOVE Dolaucothi. Photograph before 1876
BELOW View of Aberystwyth, showing Rheidol bridge. H. Gastineau, 1828 (NLW)

19

FFYNONE
Boncath, Pembrokeshire
1792–1796

Built at Boncath for Captain John Colby, the classical house stands at the head of a wooded valley. It originally had three similar elevations in stucco, each five bays wide, the centre three projecting, with the wide eaves taken up to form pedimented gables. The front had three arcaded arches, which disappeared when the Doric porch was built across the front in 1828, possibly by Nash. The plan is a variation on Nash's usual square one, this time with a service staircase rather awkwardly inserted. Inside, a nice stone cantilevered stair rose out of a hall decorated with vaulted ceilings and circular fanlights. In 1904 the house was dressed up by Inigo Thomas with heavy

Ffynone: (RIGHT) entrance front, with later addition on right; (BELOW) later Doric porch, possibly by Nash, on left; later addition on right

keystones and quoins; the façades were coarsely rendered and extensions stuck on apparently at random. The house is still a private residence.

Davis 1966

20

SUNDERLAND BRIDGE
County Durham
c.1793

The credit for the design of the Wear bridge went to Rowland Burdon, MP. Nash later claimed that Burdon had stolen the

45

design from him. What is known is that Nash submitted a design for an iron bridge which was not accepted. A version of Nash's story was published nearly fifty years after the event in the *Mechanics' Magazine* (xxiv, 1836).

T. Ruddock, *Arch Bridges and their Builders (1735–1835)*, 1979

21

TRE-CEFEL BRIDGE

Near Tregaron, Cardiganshire

1793

Nash designed for the Magistrates of Cardiganshire a conventional stone bridge over the River Teifi to carry the Tregaron–Lampeter road. It was demolished in the late nineteenth century.

Summerson 1980

22

CARDIGAN GAOL

Cardigan, Cardiganshire

1793

After the prison reformer, John Howard, had condemned the old gaol, the Town Council commissioned Nash to build a new one on the outskirts of Cardigan. It was the second and smallest of his three prisons, designed as the common gaol and house of correction, with twenty-two cells in two wings; it also had six day-rooms and six exercise-yards, one of which contained a treadmill. It was planned in the form of a cross, with the cell wings on either side of the centre core and the chapel at the rear.

S. Lewis, *Topographical Dictionary of Wales*, 1849

23

SHARDELOES

Amersham, Buckinghamshire

1793

The Sale Catalogue (1835) of Nash's library, sold after his death, contained a drawing of a bridge at Shardeloes for William Drake, MP. Humphry Repton's *Red Book* (1793) proposed building a

Cardigan Gaol. Undated photographs

bridge, a grotto and a Tuscan temple to embellish the grounds; possibly Nash designed all three for Repton.

Summerson 1935

24

FOLEY HOUSE

Haverfordwest, Pembrokeshire

1794

Foley House was built for a local solicitor, Richard Foley. The Palladian town house

stood on one of Haverfordwest's hills, partly surrounded by plantations and enjoying extensive views; it is now used as local government offices and has been engulfed by the town. The end canted bay, taken across the entire front, was also used at Sion House (No. 16) and the Priory, Cardiganshire (No. 44). Internally, the bay at Foley House is incorporated in a serpentine curve, and the stair still has Nash's favourite S-shaped balusters and mahogany handrail. On the first floor were five bedrooms and a nursery suite. The estate was well equipped with offices, stables and two coach-houses.

F. Jones, 'The Hand of Nash in West Wales', *Transactions of the Carmarthen Antiquary Society*, 1939

Foley House: (ABOVE) entrance front; (RIGHT) garden elevation

25

COUNTY HALL
Stafford, Staffordshire
1794

Several architects, including Nash, submitted designs for a new County Hall. Included in Nash's presentation was a striking perspective showing a busy market-place, with Nash's imposing domed and pedimented building filling one side of it. The chosen design was by John Harvey, later architect to the Office of Woods and Forests, where he was succeeded by Nash.

Summerson 1980

ABOVE Hafod: the bridge, corner pavilions, octagonal library and long conservatory were by Nash. Artist unknown

BELOW Stafford County Hall: the busy market scene was possibly added by Thomas Rowlandson to the architectural drawing

26

HAFOD
Devil's Bridge, Cardiganshire
1794

Thomas Johnes's first house was designed by Thomas Baldwin of Bath. In 1793 Nash was called in, and built the octagonal galleried library, thirty feet in diameter, which stood outside the house and was linked to it by a rotunda; opening off the library was his new conservatory, some 150 feet long. Nash is also credited with refacing the front elevation in the Gothic style and adding the corner pavilions. The bridge crossing the River Ystwyth was also his design. John Piper attributes the arched gate of the Adam and Eve garden to him,

too. The painting by J. M. W. Turner presumably shows a proposal for rebuilding the house that was not carried out. In 1807 the house was destroyed by fire; it was rebuilt by Baldwin, and in 1845 Salvin, a former pupil of Nash's, engulfed it in a huge Italian mansion. After years of neglect the remains were demolished in 1956.

J. E. Smith, *A Tour to Hafod*, 1810 (unpublished; Linnean Society, Burlington House, London)
Summerson 1980

Abergavenny market, by an unknown artist

27

ABERGAVENNY

Monmouthshire
*c.*1794–1795

In 1793 Nash was asked to design a new complex to cover all the market activities of a country town; he was also to advise on paving and lighting the streets, and supplying the town with new drainage and water services. The works were completed in 1795.

Summerson 1980

28

LLANAERON

Cardiganshire
*c.*1794

The estate of Llanaeron once belonged to the Parry family, descendants of the thirteenth-century Prince of Wales, Llewellyn the Great. At the end of the eighteenth century, the land was acquired by Major Lewis, who built a small, compact villa in the valley of the Afon Aeron; once finished in stucco, the house is now rendered and colour-washed. The plan is Nash's usual one of this period: the staircase-hall is at right angles to the main axis, with four main rooms grouped around it. A simple exterior is made up of pavilions projecting either side of the

Llanaeron: the modest main entrance

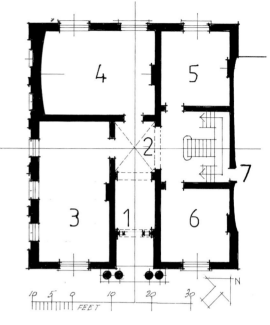

1 Hall   5 Library
2 Inner hall   6 Breakfast-room
3 Drawing-room 7 Offices
4 Dining-room

The kitchen courtyard at Llanaeron

Llanaeron: this building was possibly built as the billiard-room

Llanaeron: the entrance, with recessed centre and projecting porch; the bay window and window above are later alterations

recessed centre and Doric porch; ground-floor windows are set in relieving arches. The front and rear elevations have Palladian windows with radial fluted heads; the canted bay with dropped window over is an unfortunate later alteration.

Davis 1966

29
ABERMYDYR
Llanaeron, Cardiganshire
*c.*1794

The cottage known as Abermydyr was in
the north-west corner of Major Lewis's
Llanaeron estate (No. 28), at the meeting
of the Aeron and Mydyr rivers. The
cottage was built at the same time as
Llanaeron house, and Nash was responsible
for the splay-ended western half of the
cottage, with the grouped door and two
windows below the dormer.

BELOW
Abermydyr: the left-
hand end is probably
by Nash
RIGHT
St Non's Church:
Llanaeron is behind
the trees

30
ST NON'S CHURCH
Llanaeron, Cardiganshire
*c.*1795

The church of St Non is within a quarter of
a mile of Llanaeron House (No. 28), and
within its desmesne. W. J. Lewis remarks
that Major Lewis, for whom Nash was
building Llanaeron, was responsible for
rebuilding the church at about the same
time. On examination it can be seen that
the plinth of the nave does not align with
that of the tower, making it likely that
Lewis added the domed tower and
refurbished the body of the church, both
probably to Nash's designs. The dome has
recently been replaced by one made of
fibreglass.

W. J. Lewis, *Aberaeron* (guidebook), n.d.

Hermon Hill: Nash's three-storey extension is at the back

Llysnewydd: entrance front and side elevation showing the round-headed staircase window, before 1890 (Collection T. Lloyd)

31
HERMON HILL HOUSE
Haverfordwest, Pembrokeshire
*c.*1794

Llysnewydd: the five-bay rear elevation (left), before 1872 (Collection T. Lloyd)

32
LLYSNEWYDD
Henllan, Carmarthenshire
1795

Behind the two-storey house built in the middle of the eighteenth century, there is a taller rectangular block of a later date attributed to Nash. The full-height, canted bay window, the eaves with paired brackets, and the half-round basement windows are all typical details used by Nash during this period. The extension was probably built at the same time as the nearby Foley House.

Preseli (Pembrokeshire) District Council, *Schedule of Listed Buildings*, 1951

Llysnewydd was built for Colonel Lewes at Henllan Bridge as a square Palladian house with different elevations to each of the three exposed sides; the fourth side was the service wing. The entrance front of three bays, faced with a Tuscan porch, had an attic with an oval window, the first instance of a feature that Nash was to use many times. The back elevation, five bays wide, had three oval attic windows, while on the third side the eaves were carried up to form a pediment containing an ocular window. The plan is a variation on Nash's usual square one of this period. After drastic alterations in 1890 and again in 1910, the house was demolished in 1970.

T. Lloyd, *The Lost Houses of Wales*, 1986

ABOVE Kentchurch: the south front, with pitched roof marking the remains of the old house; the porch range on the right is later, possibly by Nash; the corner buildings and towers behind are by Nash

RIGHT The gatehouse, probably adapted by Nash

33
KENTCHURCH COURT
Pontrilas, Herefordshire
*c.*1795

The Scudamores came to Kentchurch over 600 years ago. In 1795 Colonel John Scudamore instructed Nash to rebuild the medieval and eighteenth-century house. It was his first commission outside Wales and his first use of the gallery plan, here possibly developed from the earlier great hall. The house is entered at one end of the gallery, and at the other a short flight of steps rises up to the traceried 'chapel' window. The death of the Colonel brought Nash's work to a stop after he had completed the eastern end and raised the medieval tower and turret by another storey. Work was resumed in 1825 under the direction of the agent, Mr Tudor, who presumably followed Nash's master plan but with simplified detailing. Nash also partly rebuilt the stables and outbuildings, adding Y-traceried windows and oriels as eye-catching details. The estate was originally entered through the fourteenth-century gatehouse, which is now severed from the house by a public road. It appears to have been later embattled and given a turret, possibly by Nash.

J. Cornforth, 'Kentchurch Court', *Country Life*, 15 December 1966

ABOVE The tower raised by Nash, and his hall window
BELOW Nash's east wing, from the oriel window to the raised square tower

RIGHT
Whitson Court was
almost certainly by
Antony Keck,
probably finished by
Nash
BELOW
Whitson Lodge,
designed by Nash

34
WHITSON COURT
Near Newport, Monmouthshire
1795

Whitson Court was built for William
Phillips in the moorlands south-east of
Newport as a three-storey symmetrical
block, linked to pavilions. The plan has
rooms of equal size in each corner. Both
the elevations and the plan are unlike
anything else by Nash, but they do
resemble at least two other houses in South
Wales, one of which is attributed to
Antony Keck (1726/7–1796/7). The
attribution to Nash comes from James
Baker: 'Witston [*sic*] . . . it is finishing by
Nash' (*Guide Through Wales*, 1795). As
Lloyd points out, if taken literally this
would suggest that somebody else had

started it; as Keck was at the end of his career it could be that Nash completed only the interior. The slightly later Lodge is most probably by Nash; its lattice casements in cast iron are early examples of a material Nash used in an original manner throughout his life. The front of the house is completely walled off from the rear, except for one communicating door.

T. Lloyd, *The Lost Houses of Wales*, 1986

35
BRIDGE AT BEWDLEY
Worcestershire
1795

Nash sent the Trustees of the Highways an unsolicited design and estimate for a new

LEFT Whitson Court: an early example by Nash of a cast-iron window

ABOVE Glanwysc today

road bridge over the River Severn at Bewdley. As this was the same year as the collapse of Nash's first Stanford on Teme bridge, the offer was not accepted.

T. Ruddock, *Arch Bridges and their Builders (1735–1835)*, 1979

36
GLANWYSC
Llangattock, Breconshire
c.1795

The design of the villa, Glanwysc, built for Admiral Gell at Llangattock, near Crickhowell, is attributed to Nash. It appears to have had a cruciform plan with a porticoed entrance, and was much admired. It was completely remodelled in 1850; none of Nash's work seems to have survived. No illustration of Nash's house has yet been found.

R. Haslam, *Buildings of Wales: Powys*, 1979

The entrance front of Temple Druid, probably as Nash designed it except for the right-hand lower window

37
TEMPLE DRUID
Maenclochog, Pembrokeshire
1795

A sale was advertised in the *Cambrian* (1821) for an estate called Temple Druid in the parish of Maenclochog, described as 'an excellant Mansion-house (built by Nash)'. Built for Henry Bulkeley as Bwlch-y-Clawdd, it was renamed when a cromlech was found on the estate. It was described in the sales particulars as having six servants' rooms in the attic; six bedchambers and three dressing-rooms on the first floor; and a nursery, drawing-room, dining-room and breakfast parlour on the ground floor. When viewed from the side it is apparent that the back half of Nash's house has been demolished, leaving only the front part of his original square plan intact. It still has a front doorcase with Tuscan columns and entablature. Inside, the end wall of one room is built in an arc, with doors and fitted cupboards following the curve.

F. Jones, 'The Hand of Nash in West Wales', *Transactions of the Carmarthen Antiquary Society*, 1939

CASTLE HOUSE
Aberystwyth, Cardiganshire
c.1795

In 1788 Sir Uvedale Price, who with Richard Payne Knight led the Picturesque movement in England, was made a Burgess of Aberystwyth and was presented with a piece of land by the shore. His first thoughts were for a conventional house, echoed by Nash when he was called in. Price then realized the picturesque possibilities of the site and explained them to Nash, and between them they produced an unusual house. The original plans, unfortunately lost, were for a stuccoed triangular building with an octagonal tower

Castle House c.1870, during its period as a hotel

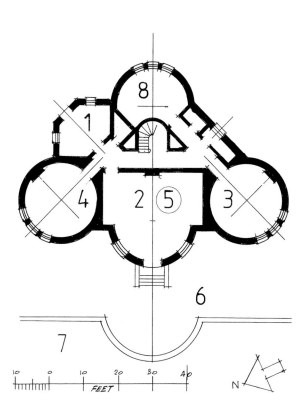

RECONSTRUCTED PLAN OF CASTLE HOUSE, WITH CONJECTURED NAMES OF ROOMS

at each corner; the drawing-room was on the first floor, facing the sea, and opened on to the canopied balcony. After Price's death, Lady Price lived in the house until her death in 1826. It became a hotel in 1865, and from 1874 until its destruction by fire in 1895, it was occupied by the University College of Wales.

E. Inglis-Jones, 'Castle House', *Country Life*, 4 July 1952

1 Hall
2 Saloon
3 ?Dining-room
4 ?Library
5 Drawing-room (above)
6 Terrace
7 Sea
8 Kitchen

RIGHT
Engraving of Castle House, after J. P. Neale, 1818–1829 (Collection T. Lloyd)

39

NEW PARK

Near Lyndhurst, Hampshire

*c.*1795

For Peacock's 1795 Annual, Humphry Repton depicted New Park, J. Sutton's estate in the New Forest. According to local lore the thatched lodge was designed by Nash, possibly as part of Repton's proposed improvements.

W. Peacock, *The Polite Repository*, 1795

RIGHT New Park: the *cottage orné* lodge
BELOW RIGHT Stanford on Teme: the eye-catching cottage

40

STANFORD ON TEME BRIDGES

Worcestershire

1795 and 1797

While staying with Sir Edward Winnington at Stanford Court, Nash was asked to replace the unsafe village bridge. He designed a slender, cast-iron structure spanning nearly 100 feet; immediately prior to completion it collapsed. Two years later Nash designed another bridge, using a system of cast-iron, voussoir-shaped boxes bolted together to form a shallow arch (a design later patented by him). This bridge stood until dismantled in 1905. The brick abutments still stand and a section of the iron railings is at the local inn. On the east bank, facing the remains of the bridge, is a cottage of some rural sophistication:

ABOVE LEFT
Stanford on Teme:
Nash's first bridge,
which collapsed.
Artist unknown
ABOVE RIGHT
Nash's second bridge,
which stood for over
100 years; his
patented boxes form
the lower arch. Artist
unknown

ABOVE
One of Nash's
abutments to the
bridge at Stanford on
Teme
RIGHT
A section of the bridge
balustrade

perhaps it was placed here by Nash as an
eye-catcher.

T. Ruddock, *Arch Bridges and their Builders (1735–
1835)*, 1979

41

SARSDEN HOUSE
Sarsden, Oxfordshire
1795–1796

The improvements proposed by Humphry
Repton to Sarsden House, John Langston's
newly inherited estate, contained several
architectural features: a triple-arched
bridge, which was built with a single arch;
a boathouse under an Ionic temple, which
was built as a rustic portico; an unbuilt
arched gateway and lodges, for which a
rustic cottage was substituted, since
demolished; and a keeper's cottage, the
prototype of Circular Cottage at Blaise
Hamlet (No. 133), also demolished. For
the house Repton recommended covering
the open quadrangle with a domed roof,
and building within it an Ionic rotunda.
Repton's usual practice was to decide on

LEFT Sarsden: the rotunda
ABOVE The unbuilt classical temple and
boathouse (RIBA)
OPPOSITE LEFT The gamekeeper's cottage at
Sarsden (RIBA)

BELOW LEFT The simplified bridge at Sarsden
still exists
BELOW The proposed classical temple was built
as a rustic one

the site and style of his estate buildings, and then have them designed and constructed by an architect. In 1795–6, if not already in partnership with Nash, he was actively considering such a move, making it most likely that the final designs for the architectural work were by Nash. The buildings built on or around the estates at Sarsden Glebe, Sarsgrove and Churchill in 1818 and 1825 were almost certainly by George Repton after he had left Nash's office.

N. Temple, 'Sarsden, Oxfordshire', *The Journal of Garden History*, 6, 1988

42

FLAMBARDS (THE PARK)
Harrow-on-the-Hill, Middlesex
1795–*c*.1798

In 1795, when Richard Page acquired the medieval Flambards estate, it extended down the eastern side of Harrow Hill. Page at once began building a new house, almost certainly designed by Nash. Correspondence between Page, Nash and a firm of decorators (Trollope & Sons of Sloane Street, London) shows that the house was ready to be decorated in early

Flambards: the entrance front, looking down from Harrow Hill, with (LEFT) detail. Painting by John Glover (1767–1849). Collection Harrow School

1798. In 1803 the estate was bought by the second Baron Northwich, who, among further building work, added the bas-relief lion – part of his coat of arms – over the entrance-porch. The house was renamed The Park in 1831, when it became a boarding-house for Harrow School. Nothing of the Regency house shown in the painting by Glover exists, except for the Northwich lion, now on the opposite side of the house.

E. D. Laborde, *Harrow School*, 1948
Trollope & Sons, *Letterbook*, GLC Record Office, London (unpublished)

LEFT
The garden elevation
BELOW
The conservatory,
built to a gentle curve

43
BLAISE CASTLE
HOUSE

Henbury, Gloucestershire
1795–*c*.1806

John Scandrell Harford commissioned
Blaise Castle House from William Patey,

who received '. . . the assistance of Mr Nash' (J. Brewer, *Delineations of Gloucestershire*, 1824). This referred perhaps to some general advice, as nothing about the house points to Nash. The Main Lodge and Woodman's Cottage were both shown in Humphry Repton's *Red Book* of 1796, the year of the Nash–Repton partnership (until then Repton had engaged other architects to design his buildings). In this case the authorship is not known, but as Repton makes no direct claim to the buildings, they were probably by Nash. Nash's dairy (*c.*1805), sitting at the bottom of a wooded dell, makes a delightful eye-catcher from the house terrace. The conservatory (*c.*1806), almost certainly by

ABOVE Woodman's Cottage

BELOW LEFT The gatehouse
BELOW RIGHT The dairy

ABOVE RIGHT
Design for a Druid's temple, by George Repton (RIBA)

Nash, was built for Harford's aquatic plants. It is sited on the rim of the dell, looking down on the pond and dairy. The Druid's temple and a cattleshed, not yet dated, are in George Repton's Sketchbook (RIBA and Brighton respectively). The temple was not built, and the cattleshed, in timber and thatch if built, has not survived.

N. Temple, *John Nash and the Village Picturesque,* 1979

44
THE PRIORY
Cardigan, Cardiganshire
1795 (or possibly 1808)

The Priory: (LEFT) the bay-fronted house, with the service wing behind (undated photograph: Collection T. Lloyd); (BELOW) the left-hand bay is all that remains of Nash's work

The Priory estate was once owned by Colonel Thomas Johnes of the Hafod family (see No. 26), and he was considered to have been the builder of Cardigan Priory in 1795. The house is sited at a right angle to the remains of the fourteenth-century Benedictine church, now St Mary's. It consisted of two storeys over a semi-basement, with a canted bay window facing the River Teifi. The plan is considered by Thomas Lloyd to have been similar to that of Foley House, Haverfordwest (No. 24), with drawing-room, dining-room and breakfast-room on the ground floor. The house, now part of the Memorial Hospital complex, has been much altered; the hipped roof has been replaced by an extra storey, and the house doubled in width. Thomas Lloyd has recently pointed out to the writer that in Pritchard's book, Mr Bowen is credited with building the house in 1808; this is based on the memory of an old man recalling something his father told him. The book does confirm that Colonel Johnes was a previous owner of the estate and that Nash was the architect.

E. M. Pritchard, *Cardigan Priory,* 1904

45
NEWTON PARK
Newton St Loe, Somersetshire
1796

Humphry Repton worked at Newton Park for William Gore-Langton, MP, producing

Newton Park: (RIGHT) the restored medieval gatehouse; (BELOW) the summer-house

his *Red Book* in 1797. The associated building works, most likely by Nash, included an arcaded temple (later the orangery, now demolished) and a design for a Palladian bridge to cross Repton's proposed new lakes. Neither the lakes nor the bridge were constructed. The remains of St Loe's Castle still stand in the grounds. Nash repaired the medieval gatehouse and added buttresses and crenellations for use as the entrance to Repton's Italian garden. The summer-house recessed in the garden wall is probably also by Nash.

N. Pevsner, *Buildings of England: Somerset*, 1958

46

ST MARY'S ISLE
Kirkcudbright, Kirkcudbrightshire
1796

George Repton's RIBA Sketchbook shows
a retainer's cottage marked 'Lord Selkirk'.

This was presumably on Selkirk's Scottish
estate, as Nash, in a letter dated December
1796, refers to 'ye cursedest journey to
Scotland'. Terence Davis also refers to a
mausoleum. Nothing is to be found of
either, but a small walled enclosure
containing family graves is hidden away in
the surrounding hills.

Davis 1966

47

HILTON PARK
Near Essington, Staffordshire
1796

Some time before 1796, Humphry Repton
visited Henry Vernon at Hilton Park; there
is no record of a *Red Book* being produced.
The cottage shown in George Repton's
RIBA Sketchbook is similar in appearance
to Oak Cottage at Blaise Hamlet (No. 133)
and was possibly Nash's contribution to
Humphry Repton's landscape
improvements.

G. Carter, P. Goode, K. Laurie, *Humphry Repton,
Landscape Gardener*, 1982

St Mary's Isle: (LEFT) the existing graveyard,
which probably replaced the proposed
mausoleum; (BELOW) ground-floor plan and
elevation of proposed farmhouse, from George
Repton's RIBA Sketchbook

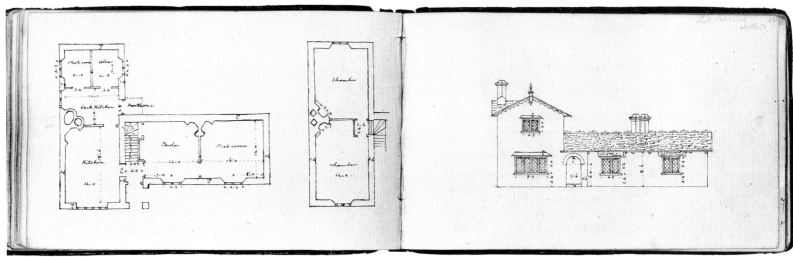

48

POINT PLEASANT

Kingston upon Thames, Surrey

*c.*1796–1797

Point Pleasant, or Bank Farm, was a small villa built for Major-General St John. It was sited to enjoy several views of the River Thames, according to the Picturesque precepts of Uvedale Price as taught to Nash at Castle House, Aberystwyth. Little is known of the house. Only one view and the sale particulars of 1888 seem to have survived. The plan, reconstructed from these sources by the writer, is basically that of Nash's earlier Welsh houses. The single-storey corner room, with a canopied balcony over, recalls Castle House (No. 38). Humphry Repton, Nash's partner at the time, referred to it as a 'new and unexampled plan by my ingenious friend'. In 1884 the grounds were sold for building; the house became the Albany Club and was destroyed by fire in 1907.

H. Repton, *Red Book for Point Pleasant*, 1796
J. Prosser, *Select Illustrations of Surrey*, 1826

1 Porch
2 Hall
3 Drawing-rooms
4 Dining-room
5 Conservatory
6 Offices
7 Study

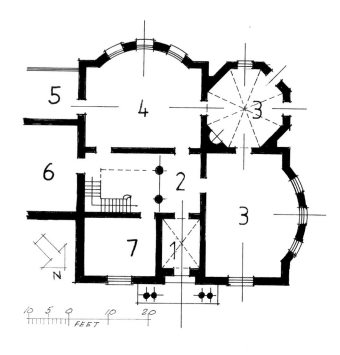

RECONSTRUCTED
GROUND-FLOOR
PLAN OF POINT
PLEASANT

49

CASINA

Dulwich, Kent

1797

Built for Warren Hastings' solicitor, Richard Shawe, Casina was a classical house of some originality. The house at Dulwich stood on high ground overlooking Humphry Repton's canal. The garden front had two single-storey wings with full-height windows between Ionic columns set *in antis*; in the centre a two-storeyed,

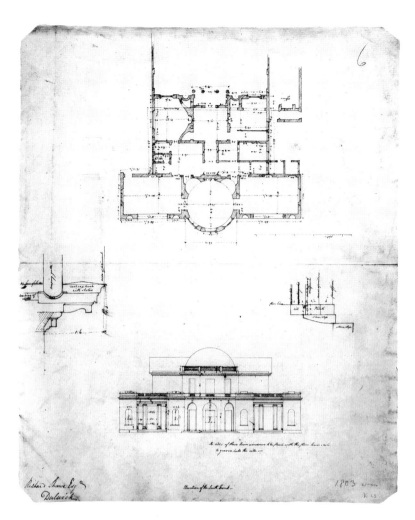

Casina: ground-floor plan and perspective drawing, produced in Nash's office, possibly by George Repton as part of his training

semicircular bow carried a plain dome. Behind this façade rose the two-storeyed, windowless wall of the main house. The house was demolished in 1906. The only surviving illustrations appear to be a rather poor perspective and George Repton's drawing (RIBA).

J. Hassell, *Views of Noblemen and Gentlemen's Seats in the Counties adjoining London*, 1804

Hereford Gaol: (ABOVE RIGHT) the cell wings radiated from the central hall; (RIGHT) the interior shows Nash's use of cast iron for the brackets and balustrades. Undated photographs

HEREFORD GAOL

Hereford, Herefordshire
1796

Hereford Gaol was the third of Nash's gaols and the most impressive, with its cruciform plan based on that of Cardigan Gaol (No. 22). Three wings of cells, built in stone with a heavily rusticated ground floor, opened off the great hall, above which was the chapel. The fourth wing contained the reception suite and the main entrance. Demolished in 1928, Hereford Gaol is the best documented of Nash's prisons. The Governor's house, built outside the prison walls, still exists. It is built in the same, massive style as the prison and gives a good idea of what the prison must have looked like.

J. Price, *Historical Account of the City of Hereford*, 1796

The Governor's house, now the bus station

LEFT
Nash's tough prison architecture

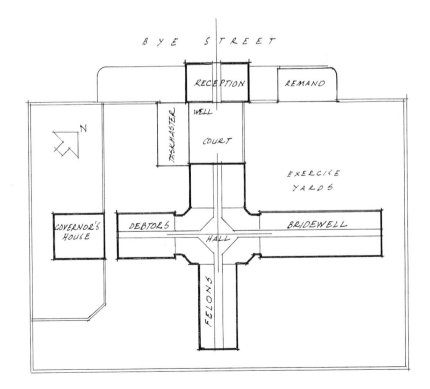

DIAGRAMMATIC
PLAN OF
HEREFORD GAOL

SOUTHGATE GROVE
Old Southgate, Middlesex
1797

Designed for Walker Gray, the house and park were the work of the Repton–Nash partnership. Nash used an enlarged version of his earlier Welsh plans for the house, the main rooms having views in enfilade to enjoy Repton's park. The neo-classical elevations are in stucco with stone Ionic columns; the shell-and-fan window decorations are unique to Nash. The view exhibited at the Royal Academy in 1797 shows the porches topped with sphinxes and urns. The newly restored house is now Grovelands Priory, a private hospital; Repton's grounds and lake form a public park. The gatehouse is probably by Nash, as is the octagonal game-larder.

G. Richardson, *New Vitruvius Britannicus*, 1802

RIGHT
Detail of south front

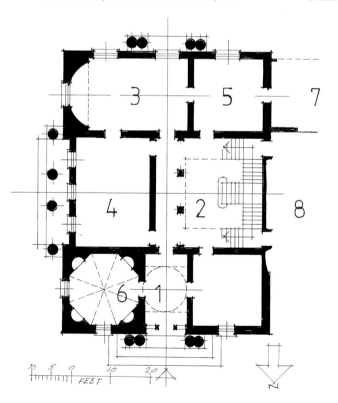

RIGHT
The octagonal
game-larder

1 Hall
2 Inner hall
3 Drawing-room
4 Dining-room
5 Library
6 Breakfast-room
7 Conservatory
8 Offices

GROUND-FLOOR
PLAN OF
SOUTHGATE
GROVE

ABOVE LEFT
The main staircase
ABOVE RIGHT
The east front
LEFT
Small octagonal room
painted to resemble
the inside of a
birdcage

The gatehouse

Atcham: row of cottages with the eye-catching bay window

BELOW General view of Atcham. Artist unknown
BELOW RIGHT A block similar to this was built. Artist unknown

52

ATCHAM

Shropshire

1797

Atcham village was once on both sides of the London to Shrewsbury road. In 1802 Lord Berwick had the public roads crossing the grounds of Attingham Park (No. 55) re-routed and the village buildings on his side removed. Nash designed for him a village of picturesque cottages surrounding a green in front of a new inn and facing the entrance to Attingham Hall. One of a series of seven painted panels now on view in the Hall bears a label: 'J Nash, 28 Dover Street, Piccadilly'. Several cottages were built, including the row of four with the eye-catching Gothic bay window; the thatched one next door was probably remodelled by Nash. The Old Rectory, once with a canted Gothic bay, still has internal details similar to those at Longner Hall (No. 77).

N. Temple, *John Nash and the Village Picturesque*, 1979

ABOVE The Old Rectory, with Nash-like porch and chimneys

RIGHT
A pair of cottages

53
ST JOHN'S
Ryde, Isle of Wight
1797–1799

Edward Simeon purchased the estate of St John's in 1796 and engaged Humphry Repton to create a park for him. Repton laid out a new drive, with a pair of matching stone-built and thatched cottages, each with an unusually large round-headed window facing the public road. One was lived in by the gatekeeper; the other, a *cottage orné*, was for occasional visits by Simeon and his friends. As they were built in the middle years of the Repton–Nash partnership, it is most likely that Nash designed them and that George Repton, then eleven years old, later redrew them as part of his training. By the sea, on the far

St John's: (ABOVE) the entrance lodges; (RIGHT) the marina. From W. Cooke, *A New Picture of the Isle of Wight*, 1808

side of the estate, Simeon had a towered and embattled marina built, from which to enjoy the sea views; it also formed a bandstand for concerts to entertain the promenading public on Sunday afternoons. It is not known whether Nash or Repton was involved with the design.

W. Cooke, *A New Picture of the Isle of Wight*, 1808

Corsham: Nash's north front, from *The Beauties of England and Wales*, 1814, after a drawing by Thompson

54
CORSHAM COURT
Wiltshire
1796–1813

The first major work of the Repton–Nash partnership was for Paul Cobb Methuen at Corsham, where Nash, possibly at Repton's instigation, took over from James Wyatt. Nash replaced the interior of the Elizabethan centre by a long gallery, with staircases opening out of it. The octagonal Gothic saloon was between the classical dining-room and music-room on the garden front. The music-room, also a picture-gallery, was one of the earliest to be top-lit. Nash's Gothic Tudor elevation, symmetrical at a time when asymmetry was the fashion, logically followed the plan. The ornate centre recalls Henry VII's chapel at Westminster Abbey and was linked to the corner towers by plain ranges. Nash's pioneering use of cast iron made it structurally possible, whilst his lack of knowledge of the material's properties caused future problems. The main building works were completed in 1803. The construction was a calamity: poor workmanship, careless detailing and lack of supervision led to dry rot. The remedial works lasted another ten years, when Nash was paid off. Wholesale demolition of Nash's work was carried out in 1846, with only his east and west façades being retained in Thomas Bellamy's rebuilding. Internally, Nash's library (a refurbishment of the Elizabethan parlour) and his breakfast-room survive.

During the time Nash was working on the house, he also designed several ancillary buildings in the grounds, where Repton was carrying out his improvements.

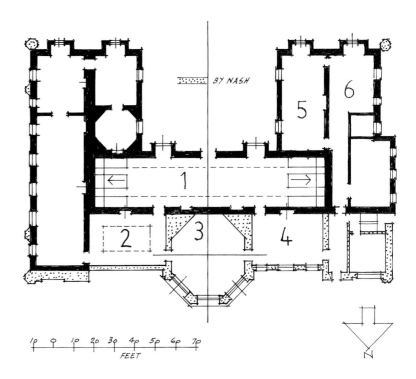

GROUND-FLOOR PLAN OF CORSHAM. Nash's work is indicated by dots

1 Gallery
2 Music-room
3 Saloon
4 Dining-room
5 Library
6 Breakfast-room

LEFT
Corsham: the east elevation

Corsham: converted Elizabethan stables

BELOW Lake Cottage

ABOVE The folly wall

The Gothic dairy and cloisters were built on the north-west corner of the house. The Elizabethan stables were refurbished with new windows, pinnacled buttresses and false gables. A new coach-house was built, and folly ruins rose up with debris from the demolitions. Nash also partially refaced Capability Brown's bath-house by inserting the front arches and their colonnettes; he also rebuilt the roof and added battlements. The interior was renovated and a radial vaulted ceiling installed over the bath. At the eastern end of Repton's lake, Nash built the boathouse to form a *point de vue*. All these buildings are extant.

J. Britton, *An Historical Account of Corsham*, 1806
F. J. Ladd, *Architects of Corsham Court*, 1978

Corsham: the coach-house

The dairy and cloister, with remains of the east elevation behind

ABOVE The bath in the bath-house
RIGHT The bath-house

The main entrance
screen

55

ATTINGHAM PARK

Atcham, Shropshire
*c.*1797–1808

The gallery, which
Nash originally
proposed lighting by
oval lights in cast-iron
frames

Built in 1782 by George Stewart,
Attingham Park was altered by Nash to
house Lord Berwick's picture collection
between 1805 and 1807. Nash removed the
main staircase and took half the hall to
form the centre of his new gallery, with
each end screened off by Corinthian
columns. Opening out of the gallery he
built a new circular staircase with fluted
walls. The new entrance-hall was given
marbled walls and grisaille panels. The

The bee house,
possibly by Nash or
Humphry Repton

built by Nash when John Adey Repton was his assistant. Humphry Repton proposed that one should be built on each side of the road to give the impression of entering an estate. It has been assumed that the matching one to Tern Lodge, if built, has been demolished. On Repton's new minor road from Atcham, built in 1801, is Attingham Back Lodge, with a battlemented tower. Almost opposite, but belonging to Longner Hall, is another towered lodge, its battlements missing. Together they give the impression proposed by Repton more convincingly than the Tern lodges on the London trunk road would have done. The weather-boarded bee house is possibly by Nash or Repton. The house and grounds are now owned by the National Trust.

N. Temple, *John Nash and the Village Picturesque*, 1979
J. Cornforth, *Attingham Park* (The National Trust), 1981
I. C. Bristow, 'Mixing the colours at Soane's Dulwich', *The London Architect*, May 1981

gallery was top-lit and is almost certainly the earliest example of curved cast-iron ribs supporting continuous glazing. To set off the paintings and their gilded frames, the walls were painted a shade of Venetian red, predating Soane's use of the same colour at the Dulwich Picture Gallery in London.

The main entrance screen and gates are set back from the road. On emerging, one is attracted by the Gothic bay window on the Atcham Terrace on the opposite side of the road. Behind the screen walls are a pair of gatekeepers' lodges. By Tern Bridge to the east is a hexagonal lodge, probably

Tern Lodge, the secondary entrance to Attingham Park

West Lodge, reading as one of a pair with Longner East Lodge (see p.107)

56

HIGH LEGH HALL

High Legh, Cheshire
1797–1818

George John Legh inherited High Legh Hall
in 1791 and engaged Humphry Repton to
improve the estate. Nash was called in when
Legh considered building a new village.
Nash's design philosophy is expressed in his
letter to Legh (January 1798): '. . . the
Cottages should be scattered and intercepted
by plantations . . . they should be set back
in the manner of a green . . . the clumps
should screen the gardens and yards – at the
same time that the view of the Cottages are
not intercepted but are seen through the
glades . . . to make the lodge of High Legh

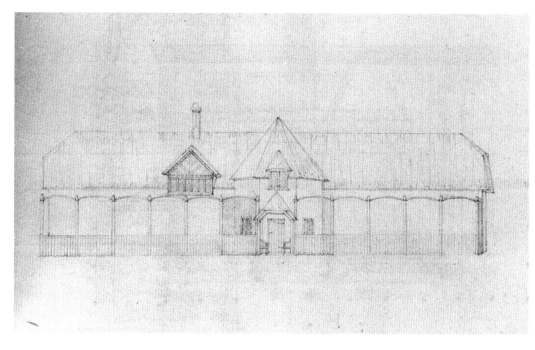

BELOW A farm building, from George Repton's
Brighton Sketchbook

ABOVE A *cottage orné*, from George Repton's
RIBA Sketchbook

BELOW A *cottage orné*, from George Repton's
RIBA Sketchbook

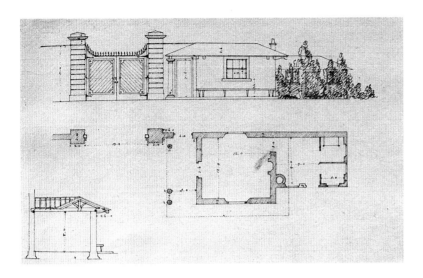

The entrance gates and lodge, from George Repton's Brighton Sketchbook

Blacksmith's shop and cottage, from George Repton's Brighton Sketchbook

The existing schoolhouse; the right-hand gable is a later extension

the termination of the picture . . . In coming out of the lodge, the Inn, cottages and blacksmith's shop should burst together on the sight . . . the smith's shop should look up the road so that the fire may illuminate the road and give a cheerfulness at night to the whole village . . . a cupola should be placed on the Chapel to be seen among the trees.' It seems unlikely that the village or any part of it was built. Nash was still working for Legh in 1810, when he designed the schoolhouse for Legh's daughters, and a smithy. George Repton's RIBA Sketchbook contains designs for three *cottages ornés*, an inn and a bookcase for the Hall. The Sketchbook in Brighton has a farm building, entrance gates and lodge, a blacksmith's shop and the schoolhouse; only the last has survived.

N. Temple, *John Nash and the Village Picturesque*, 1979

1 Drawing-room
2 Library
3 Study

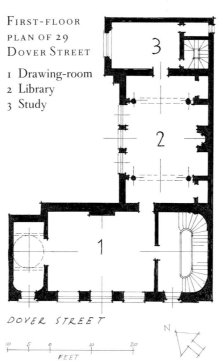

DOVER STREET

FEET

58
SUNDRIDGE PARK
Bromley, Kent
1799

In 1799 Nash exhibited at the Royal
Academy two views of the house he had
designed for the corn-merchant and banker
Claude Scott. Sited by Humphry Repton on
a hillside, the house was planned by Nash
as a triangle, with the apex *tempietto* facing
across the valley, and the canted sides
looking down its length. Repton and Nash,
still partners, were beginning to disagree.
Repton claimed the credit for the plan,
whereas the philosophy – of taking
advantage of all the natural attributes of the
site – can be traced through Nash's designs
from Castle House (No. 38), where he

57
29 DOVER STREET
Mayfair, London
1798

In 1796 Nash bought No. 28 Dover Street,
where he lived while building a new house
next door. In December 1798 he married
his second wife, Mary Anne Bradley, and
moved into No. 29. It faced down Hay Hill
to the gardens of Lansdowne House. The
drawing-room and library were on the first
floor; the second floor of drawing offices
was extended by adding an attic storey in
1814. The building was a striking
advertisement for both the architect and his
architecture. The house was slightly altered
in the 1930s, damaged during the Second
World War, and finally demolished in
1941.

Summerson 1980

ABOVE LEFT
29 Dover Street
before 1941

1 Hall
2 Inner hall
3 Drawing-room
4 Dining-room
5 Library
6 Ante-room
7 Offices

GROUND-FLOOR
PLAN OF
SUNDRIDGE
PARK

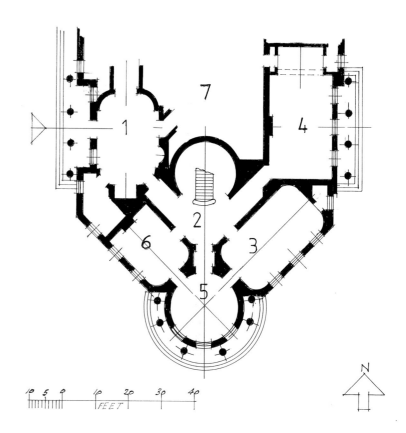

FEET

received his schooling in the Picturesque
from Uvedale Price, to Point Pleasant (No.
48). The interior was the work of Samuel
Wyatt. The house, now a management
centre, stands overlooking the golf course
that today fills the valley.

W. Angus, *Seats of Nobility and Gentry*, 1804

59
EAST COWES CASTLE
Isle of Wight
1798–1835

East Cowes Castle, built on a hilltop
overlooking the Medina Valley and the
Solent, was a composition of towers and

turrets, round, square and octagonal; embattled walls built in coursed rubble; and arcaded loggias with two conservatories bordering the lawn. In 1798 Nash had bought a property in East Cowes, enlarging the small house by stages throughout his life until finally in 1834, the year before his death, he moved the gallery from his house in Regent Street and re-erected it in the long conservatory. The plan shows a comparatively small house built around a circular staircase-hall, which, according to local lore, was the remains of a windmill and which gave on to the suite of reception rooms. A second centre of circulation was the octagon room, giving access to the library, long conservatory and lawn. The Nashes entertained on a large scale; their guests ranged from the Prince Regent and his circle to local people and junior members of Nash's London drawing office. J. M. W. Turner stayed in the house

East Cowes Castle: the entrance front. Watercolour by John Buckler (1770–1851). British Museum, London

1 Hall
2 Inner hall
3 Octagon room
4 Library
5 Drawing-room
6 Ante-room
7 Dining-room
8 Conservatory
9 Conservatory
10 Gallery
11 Regent's room
12 Garden room

GROUND-FLOOR
PLAN OF EAST
COWES CASTLE

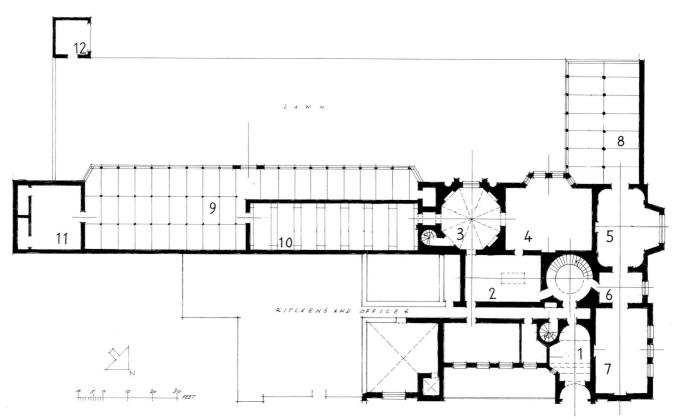

and was commissioned to paint two pictures; Joseph Farington left detailed descriptions of a visit in his *Diary;* and Charles Vereker liked the castle so much that he ordered a similar building, Lough Cutra in County Galway (No. 132). Shortly after Nash's death the castle was sold to the Earl of Shannon, whose heir had married the youngest daughter of Sir George Seymour of the adjoining Norris Castle. After various vicissitudes the final demolitions took place in 1950. Only South Lodge (recalling Diamond Cottage, Blaise Hamlet, No. 133) and a street in a new housing development, John Nash Avenue, remain.

J. Greig (ed.), *The Farington Diary*, 1928
Summerson 1980

East Cowes Castle
from the south-east,
1949

South Lodge: all that remains of East Cowes Castle

BELOW The Castle and the view over the Medina to the West Solent. Artist and date unknown. Private collection

60

HOLWOOD HOUSE

Keston, Kent

1799

Nigel Temple's investigations into the works of Nash reveal a letter, apparently in Nash's writing, found in the Cornwall–

Legh papers and headed 'Pitt's Cottage'. William Pitt, MP, had consulted Humphry Repton about his estate, Holwood House, in 1791. There was a circular, rustic cottage which was possibly part of Repton's improvements to the estate in 1798 and designed by his then partner, Nash. It no longer exists.

N. Temple, *John Nash and the Village Picturesque*, 1979

61

BALLINDOON
County Sligo
Early nineteenth century

Ballindoon, once Kingsborough House, was built for the King Harmons of Rockingham and is locally attributed to Nash. Bence-Jones also comments that it is Nash-like. The house is situated north-west of Rockingham, at the head of Lough Arrow. The plan is similar to Nash's square houses, but the detailing of the entrance elevation, with its giant portico, and of the garden elevation, with the half-round bow

The stable block at Ballindoon

ABOVE The garden front of Ballindoon

BELOW The entrance front of Ballindoon

and flat dome, gives the impression that the architect made a hurried sketch and left the local builder to get on with it. At a right angle to the house is an interestingly designed stable block, presumably built at the same time.

M. Bence-Jones, *Burke's Guide to Country Houses, Volume I: Ireland*, 1978

62

CHALFONT HOUSE

Chalfont St Peter, Buckinghamshire
1799–1800

On purchasing the estate in 1794, Thomas Hibbert employed Humphry Repton to improve the grounds, originally laid out by Capability Brown. The house '. . . was given a new contour and façade by Nash' (Main). This possibly refers to the entrance front, as the only drawings that have been found are of the east elevation and show that only the pinnacled bay was added; however they do show that the service wing was substantially altered and given a curtain wall, behind which can be seen a tall tower and lantern. The house was

ABOVE Chalfont House: the projecting entrance pavilion is probably by Salvin; the ranges on each side, including the conservatory, are by Nash, with ornamentation by Salvin
BELOW LEFT Chalfont Lodge, lived in by Thomas Hibbert's son Robert, was almost certainly designed by Nash when the estate was extended to the north-west in 1799
BELOW RIGHT Engraving of Chalfont House by Busby for the *European Magazine*, 1812

again remodelled in 1836 by a former pupil of Nash, Anthony Salvin (1799–1881). On the entrance front the awkward junction of Salvin's centrepiece, with the smaller-scale conservatory, could indicate that the conservatory has survived from Nash's works.

J. Main, review of *The Planter's Guide* in *Loudon's Gardeners Magazine*, iv, 1828

63

HOTHFIELD PLACE
Hothfield, Kent
*c.*1800

George Repton's RIBA Sketchbook shows a model farm layout for Lord Thanet. The farm, consisting of three linked yards enclosed by cattle stalls and barns with the farmhouse at the top, cannot now be found. However, three estate cottages of about 1800 do exist. The smallest is a gatehouse with the roof swept over the attic window; the other two are small houses for senior estate staff. All have in common wide eaves and a wide centre pier, and the larger two also have wide corner piers. They were obviously designed by the same hand, at a time when Nash could have been working here.

Ashford Borough Council, *Schedule of Listed Buildings*, 1967

One of the estate cottages at Hothfield

Gatehouse, now called Outer Gate Lodge

Another of the estate cottages at Hothfield

LEFT
Hothfield Place:
sketch and ground-
plan of an estate
cottage, from George
Repton's RIBA
Sketchbook

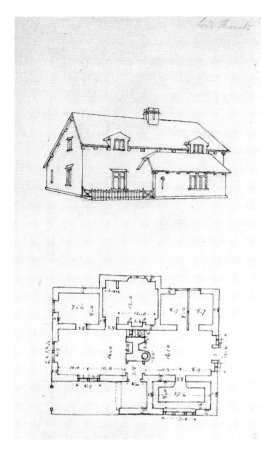

64

HOUGHTON LODGE
Houghton, Hampshire
*c.*1800

BELOW Houghton: the garden elevation,
looking down the Test Valley

Houghton Lodge is sometimes attributed to Nash. If one imagines the tall chimneys over roofs softened with thatch, and the glazed veranda replaced by a thatched pent roof, it could well be; but the picturesque exterior is decidedly at odds with the unpicturesque plan. Nash had been indoctrinated by Uvedale Price to make the most of the natural features of a site, as he did at Castle House (No. 38) and Point Pleasant (No. 48), built during the previous five years. At Houghton, the dining-room and drawing-room were given the most uninteresting outlooks, straight up the short drive into the adjoining hillside. Only the music-room had a view of the Test Valley. The designer was most probably John Plaw (1745–1820), who had built other *cottages ornés*, including another fishing lodge, in the New Forest area.

C. Hussey, 'Houghton Lodge, Hampshire', *Country Life*, 2 September 1954

65

THE WARRENS

Bramshaw, Hampshire

1800–1802

The Warrens was built for George Eyre, Verderer of the New Forest, on the forest's northern boundary. The entrance front is symmetrical, with a recessed centre and projecting porch, an arrangement Nash used many times, from Llanaeron in 1794 (No. 28) to Cambridge Terrace in 1824 (No. 222). The garden elevation is asymmetrical. Wide eaves are supported on

RIGHT The Warrens from the south-east: in the distance can be seen the later addition, which is a copy, in reverse, of the original house
BELOW The south front of the Warrens: the single storey beneath the balustrade was the site of Nash's conservatory

paired brackets, another favourite device of Nash's. In 1804 the house was doubled in size by Eyre himself; he took Nash's elevation, reversed it and built it in facsimile at the other end of the service wing. George Repton's notebooks show designs for a greenhouse. They also show a brewhouse furnished with a cupola, which still exists.

N. Temple, *Hants Society*, 1988

66

HELMINGHAM HALL

Helmingham, Suffolk

1800–1803

The sixth Earl of Dysart engaged Nash to modernize the old manor house, built in 1511. On the entrance front the porch was

The Warrens: the entrance front, with Nash's favourite recessed centre and projecting porch

LEFT Helmingham Hall: the entrance front

given a large oriel window and pinnacled stepped gable. On all fronts battlements replaced the parapets; mullions and labels were added to the windows. The kitchen block was rebuilt in the north-east corner. An octagonal bay window, capped with an ogee dome, was added to the west elevation but was demolished in 1841, when the house was enlarged and Nash's rendering stripped from the walls. Nash replaced both brick bridges with cast-iron ones that included drawbridge sections.

A. Oswald, 'Helmingham Hall', *Country Life*, 23 August 1956

ABOVE
Helmingham Hall:
detail of the main
entrance; Nash added
the gables,
battlements and oriel
window and replaced
the old drawbridge
with a cast-iron one

ABOVE RIGHT
Nash's kitchen block

RIGHT
Nash's second bridge,
to the service
entrance; his stucco
to all the walls has
been removed

Luscombe Castle: the
entrance front

67

LUSCOMBE CASTLE
Dawlish, Devonshire
1800–1804

From Nash's simple gatehouse the drive
winds up Humphry Repton's landscaped
valley to the castle built for the banker,
Charles Hoare. Nash exhibited two views
of Luscombe at the Royal Academy in
1800. The plan is similar to Nash's Welsh
houses, with the drawing-room occupying
the base of the octagonal tower and the
porte-cochère the base of the square one. The

Engraving of
Luscombe by I. Smith
for T. H. Williams,
*Picturesque Excursions
into Devonshire*, 1815.
A *cottage orné* can be
seen on the right

ABOVE LEFT
Luscombe: the stable
yard and brewhouse
ABOVE
The dairy
LEFT
The garden front,
with Sir George
Gilbert Scott's chapel

Luscombe: the valley, landscaped by Humphry Repton

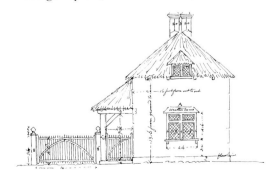

interiors are simply decorated in the classical style; at the head of the staircase, a pretty oval lobby gives access to the bedrooms. The large bay window to the drawing-room and the oriel window over the dining-room were added by Nash after the house was completed. At the end of the Victorian service wing Nash's stable yard and brewhouse still exist, as does the Gothic dairy, hidden away in its own grove. Nash's gatehouse appears to have been replaced, and the hilltop *cottage orné* (not shown in Humphry Repton's *Red Book*) was probably added by Nash when he made the later alterations to the house.

C. Hussey, *English Country Houses: Late Georgian*, 1958

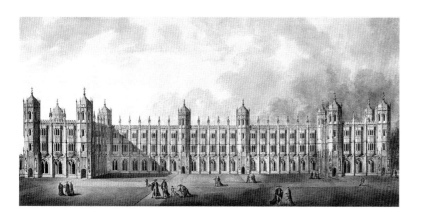

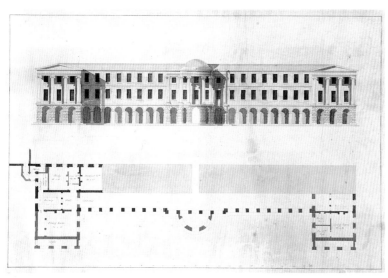

68

MAGDALEN COLLEGE
Oxford
1801

Nash and Repton appear to have been independently invited to submit designs for an extension to the College. Neither scheme was built. Nash's plan was for a quadrangle incorporating the existing New Building. Gothic buildings lined three sides, the fourth being left open to the park and the River Cherwell. A drawing, possibly by Auguste Charles Pugin (1762–1832), was exhibited at the Royal Academy in 1801 and is probably one of those in the College library. Also in the College collection is an anonymous design showing the addition of a dome and a half-round portico to the New Building, similar to Nash's Rockingham House in Ireland (No. 127).

T. S. R. Boase, 'An Oxford College and the Gothic Revival', *Journal of the Warburg and Courtauld Institutes*, xviii, 1955

69

BARR HALL
Great Barr, Staffordshire
*c.*1801

Great Barr Park, the seat of Joseph Scott, had been in his family's possession for two hundred years. He had refronted the house in the Gothic style in 1777. In 1790 Humphry Repton was working on the estate of Edward Foley, kinsman and friend of Scott, at nearby Prestwood, where it is possible that Repton, Scott and Nash met. In about 1800 Nash is recorded as having built a Gothic arched gateway to the adjacent chapel. Prior to this a flurry of building had taken place: an icehouse in 1797, three lodges built between 1797 and 1800 to close vistas from newly made drives, and a new steeple added in 1800 to Barr Chapel. All these works were probably by Nash and Repton. The three lodges were demolished and rebuilt between 1854 and 1856, the chapel gateway has gone and the chapel has been altered. The house was converted into a hospital in 1913 and is now empty.

S. Shaw, *History of Staffordshire*, ii, 1801
De Bois Group, *Landscape Survey of Great Barr*, 1985 (unpublished)

NORTHWOOD HOUSE
West Cowes, Isle of Wight
Before 1801 to 1829

George Ward, later to become a close friend of Nash, was in 1771 the owner of the Belle Vue estate, shortly to be renamed Northwood House. Unsigned plans dated 1811 show an extension to the house containing a study for Ward and domestic offices with three bedrooms above, reached by a new oval staircase. Further alterations described in a specification of 1822 converted a stable block into additional bedrooms. Both were most probably the work of Nash. In 1837 Charles Lee, who had trained in Nash's office, was the architect for the domed annexe. The demesne was embellished with several buildings by Nash, including, in 1816, the tower to St Mary's Church and Ward's mausoleum. The square tower of the church is finished with *antefixae* at each corner; the belfry openings have Doric columns *in antis*. At the base of the tower is the mausoleum, with more *antefixae* between stylized pediments over a Gothic

LEFT The tower and mausoleum of St Mary's
BELOW Debourne Lodge

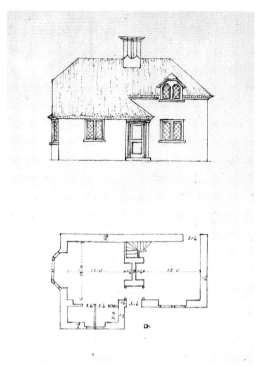

arch. Inside are monuments to the Ward family.

One of Nash's two classical lodges still stands beside the church, but the other, at the north entrance, has been demolished. In George Repton's sketchbooks are drawings of a gazebo that has not been found and a thatched lodge similar to Oak Cottage at Blaise Hamlet (No. 133), now known as

Debourne Lodge. Facing it is a companion-piece, the Round House. This has so far only been attributed to Nash, as the round house shown in the RIBA Sketchbook does not tally with it. The four attached triangular cottages, also shown in this notebook, have been identified by Nigel Temple as probably having been built at nearby Egypt Point as the core of the

ABOVE LEFT Northwood: the Round House
ABOVE Elevation and plan of a farm cottage, from George Repton's RIBA Sketchbook

present Egypt Cottages. The covered seat and another cottage, also shown, have not been found. The Round House is shown on a map of 1801.

British Museum MS 18157–8 (unpublished)
N. Temple, *IOW Society*, 1987

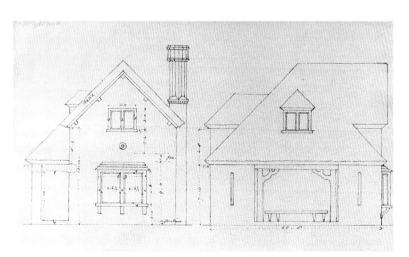

LEFT
Northwood: estate cottage, from George Repton's Brighton Sketchbook
RIGHT
Gazebo and store, from George Repton's Brighton Sketchbook

ABOVE Northwood: the classical south lodge
(the matching north one has been demolished)

72

CRONKHILL
Atcham, Shropshire
1802

Built for Francis Walford, Lord Berwick's
agent at Attingham, Cronkhill was the
earliest of Nash's 'Campagna' villas. The
house, beautifully situated high on a
hillside overlooking the River Severn, was
almost certainly inspired by Claude's
painting of a farmhouse near the Ponte
Molle, owned by the second Earl
Ashburnham and now in the Birmingham
City Art Gallery. Cronkhill has a simple
plan, with the round-tower axis crossing

BELOW Cronkhill: the entrance front (the blank
window to the tower was originally glazed)

71

BONLONDEB
Conwy, Caernarvonshire
1802

Humphry Repton illustrated the 1800
edition of Peacock's Annual with a drawing
of Bonlondeb, near Conwy. Nash exhibited
a design for a 'House near Conway' at the
Royal Academy in 1802; Summerson
(1935) suggested that it was for Mrs
Holland Roberts at Bonlondeb. The house
was not built, and the Nash picture cannot
be found.

W. Peacock, *The Polite Repository*, 1800

Cronkhill: Italian vernacular in a Shropshire
landscape

the main one at right angles; the drawing-
room in the angle is enclosed by the loggia
linking both towers. It is externally finished
in crisp white stucco, with sandstone
columns and balustrade. The design for
Cronkhill was exhibited at the Royal
Academy in 1802.

Summerson 1980

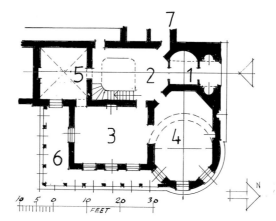

1 Porch
2 Hall
3 Drawing-room
4 Dining-room
5 Study
6 Veranda
7 Offices

GROUND-FLOOR PLAN OF CRONKHILL

73
BULSTRODE HOUSE
Near Fulmer,
Buckinghamshire
1801–1802

Humphry Repton visited the third Duke of
Portland's estate in 1789, later removing
the formal gardens and extending the drive.
In 1801 Nash made a design for rebuilding
the house: a seventeen-bay colonnade of
paired columns standing on a rustic arcaded
base was stretched across the entire garden
front and flanked by orangeries and
conservatories, and the roof was finished
with dome and drum. The design was
exhibited at the Royal Academy in 1801.
Nothing of any significance appears to have
been built, as James Wyatt was
commissioned to make another design some
time between 1805 and the Duke's death in
1809.

J. Harris, 'Bulstrode', *The Architectural Review*,
November 1958

Cronkhill: the service wing, on the left, originally
had one storey, with a two-storey tower at the
end, acting as a stop

The staircase-hall at
Cronkhill

ABOVE Bulstrode: design for the garden front,
produced in Nash's office, *c.*1801

KILLYMOON CASTLE
Cookstown, County Tyrone
1802

Killymoon Castle, built for Colonel James Stewart, was Nash's first castle in Ireland. This brought him further commissions, as Lord Lorton of Rockingham (No. 127) was Stewart's cousin, and the Reverend John Staples of Lissan Rectory (No. 106) a nephew. The castle replaced an earlier house, which was destroyed by fire around 1800 and whose surviving parts were incorporated in Nash's design. It was a two-storeyed, embattled house with machicolated towers and turrets built in cut stone, overlooking the Balinderry River. On the south side Nash placed a Saxon doorway next to a Norman arcaded

BELOW The south front, overlooking the Ballinderry River

ABOVE The Gothic chapel on the left was the library and formed part of the earlier house

BELOW The east or entrance front, with the prominent *porte-cochère*

window, possibly salvaged from, or inspired by, the earlier house. In its heyday the estate had four entrance lodges, two gardeners' houses and a conservatory. None has survived.

B. de Breffny, *Castles of Ireland*, 1977

75
DEENE PARK
Deene, Northamptonshire
*c.*1800–1810

The sixth Earl of Cardigan (1769–1837) decided in about 1800 to add a new wing to the old Tudor house. It is not known how long it took to carry out the works. The Earl's bank-books show that payments were made to a Mr John Nash during 1816–19, but whether they referred to Deene Park or to the Earl's London house, or even whether they relate to John Nash the architect is not known. The Regency wing, which is divided into three parts by stepped buttresses, lies between a Tudor tower (raised to master the new storey heights) and a new matching tower at the far end. Inside are three reception rooms in enfilade, the first with a bowed end wall and built-in bookcases. A small courtyard was enclosed and a staircase inserted to serve the new first-floor bedrooms.

J. Cornforth, 'Deene Park, Northamptonshire', *Country Life*, 1 April 1976

76
NONSUCH PARK
Sutton, Surrey
1802

Nash's design for rebuilding the house was exhibited at the Royal Academy in 1802. Nothing came of it, as the owner, S. Farmer, Esq, eventually preferred Wyatville's design.

Summerson 1935

Deene Park: the garden façade, showing the Regency extension to the left of the central tower

LONGNER HALL

Atcham, Shropshire

1803

The estate of Longner Hall adjoins Attingham Park (No. 55) to the west and was the last on which Nash and Humphry Repton were employed at the same time. The Tudor Gothic house, in red and grey sandstone, was built for Robert Burton on the site of the old house and looked down from an escarpment on to the Severn Valley. Repton, in a diatribe against his former partner (*Red Book*), objected to the site but was overruled by the client. The house has an L-shaped plan, with the conservatory, originally an open veranda, in the angle; the matching conservatory on the other side of the house was not built. The entrance, on the north side, opens off the courtyard formed by the service wing. The interior, also in the Gothic style, contains a fine staircase-hall with a fan-vaulted ceiling, which is repeated in the library.

The estate is entered at Nash's Tudor Gothic gatehouse off the Berwick Road. Further along the road a towered cottage belonging to Longner opposes a similar one at Attingham, both by Nash. At the back of the house is a rambling complex of courtyards formed by the stables, offices and farm buildings, including a dovecote and kennels. These were added to by Nash. Abutting the service wing is the kitchen court, surrounded by battlemented walls; it contains the icehouse, with the game-larder standing on it.

Davis 1960
Shropshire County Council, *Listed Buildings' Descriptions*, 1986 (unpublished)

The north-facing entrance front: the large pointed window lights the staircase

The main entrance lodge

ABOVE The main staircase and the upper and lower halls
RIGHT The dining-room

RIGHT The south and east fronts
BELOW The towered cottage, East Lodge, designed to be read with a similar one at Attingham Park (see p.81)

Pyrton Lodge: once the main entrance to Shirburn Park, now a private house; the pointed roof has been removed

SHIRBURN PARK
Watlington, Oxfordshire
1803

Shirburn Castle, at Shirburn Park, was built in 1377 and remodelled in about 1716, with subsequent early nineteenth-century minor alterations and additions, probably by Nash. George Repton's RIBA Sketchbook shows a cottage for Lord Macclesfield, which has not been traced. Other estate buildings of about the same time are probably by Nash and were built in expectation of a Royal visit in 1808. Pyrton Lodge, once the main entrance to the estate, is a hexagonal lodge with a rear wing; it once had a pyramidal slate roof. It features plain, tough gateposts, as favoured by Nash; it dates from the early nineteenth century. The orangery, also dating from this period, is a single storey with nine bays and has windows with cast-iron

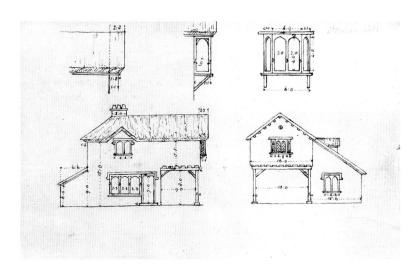

LEFT
Design for a cottage, from George Repton's RIBA Sketchbook
RIGHT
The stables: the battlemented gable and the three-gabled group are original

glazing bars. Shirburn Park Lodge, on the Watlington Road, was built in limestone in the early nineteenth century and has been attributed to Nash. It is now deliberately being allowed to rot. The north gatehouse was built in limestone; it opens into a U-shaped stable courtyard, with a gatehouse across one corner and a matching tower at the end of a stuccoed range of six pointed, arched openings. The parapet has two central gablettes, similar to Corsham coach-house (No. 54); the brick north range still has the original battlemented gable end wall. All were built in the early nineteenth century, probably by Nash.

Permission to inspect the buildings is strictly forbidden. Details have been compiled from the sources given below and from observation of the buildings from the public roads.

Victoria County History: Oxfordshire, viii, 1964
Historical Buildings & Monuments Commission, *Register of Gardens at Grade II*
Oxfordshire Statutary Listed Buildings Register

ABOVE The entrance to the stable yard (the building on the left was built later)
BELOW The arched entrance and lodge are being allowed to decay

79
ORCHARD COTTAGE
Niton, Isle of Wight
Before 1805

George Repton's RIBA Sketchbook shows a house marked 'James Mackenzie Esq, near Niton, I.O.W.' It has been located and identified by Nigel Temple as Orchard Cottage. It had a simple plan of eating room, 'Parlor' and kitchen opening off a small staircase-hall with two main and three small bedrooms above. Mackenzie's main island house was in West Cowes, so presumably Orchard Cottage was built to be enjoyed on visits to the south of the Island.

N. Temple, *IOW Society*, 1988

Orchard Cottage: elevations of cottage, from George Repton's Brighton Sketchbook

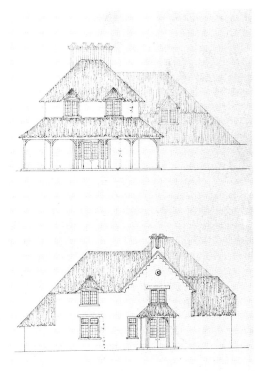

The entrance to Antony

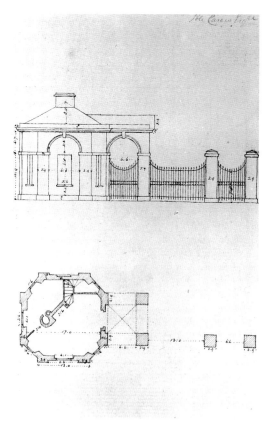

The unbuilt entrance and lodge, from George Repton's RIBA Sketchbook

80

ANTONY HOUSE
Torpoint, Cornwall
1803

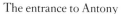

George Repton's RIBA Sketchbook shows two designs for gate lodges at Antony, made for Reginald Pole-Carew. Humphry Repton had produced a *Red Book* for the estate in 1792, two years after being introduced to Nash, who probably designed the lodges for him. The present lodge, built around 1803, could be a more modest third version. It was built in limestone, with one main room in the first block and the kitchen in the second; the third block is a recent addition.

Repton, RIBA Sketchbook

St Mildred's Rectory: in the much rebuilt elevations, Nash's great bay window is still recognizable

81

ST MILDRED'S RECTORY
Whippingham, Isle of Wight
1804

A sketch plan of the extension to the old St Mildred's Rectory at Whippingham is given in George Repton's Brighton Sketchbook. On the ground floor were dining- and drawing-rooms and a study, all entered from the hall, in a corner of which a narrow secondary stair gave access to the bedrooms above. The date of building is uncertain. The Reverend James Hook, who is credited as the owner, was in residence between 1817 and 1825, and was succeeded by his son Walter. The rectory was always noted for its outlook, and the view over the Medina River is still superb.

N. Temple, *IOW Society*, 1988

82

EMLYN COTTAGE
Newcastle Emlyn, Cardiganshire
? c.1803

Emlyn Cottage, built on a hillside overlooking Newcastle Emlyn, had a curved ornamental pediment on the porch, recalling Nash's entrance front to Hafod (No. 26). The house was demolished in the 1880s. There is no firm evidence of any involvement by Nash.

T. Lloyd, *The Lost Houses of Wales*, 1986

BELOW The entrance front of Emlyn Cottage. Drawing by Peter Richard Hoare, 1818 (Collection T. Lloyd)
BELOW RIGHT Ground-plan and elevation of the *cottage orné* at Osborne, from George Repton's RIBA Sketchbook

83

OSBORNE COTTAGE
East Cowes, Isle of Wight
Before 1805

Osborne Cottage was a large thatched *cottage orné* that stood near Nash's own East Cowes Castle. Unusually for a Nash building, part of the front was half-timbered. George Repton's RIBA Sketchbook has two versions of the plan, differing only in detail; both have a drawing-room, library and kitchen (the stairs to the upper floor are not shown on the plan). Queen Victoria bought the cottage to house the Clerk of Works while Osborne House was being built; when the house was completed, she had the cottage demolished in 1856.

N. Temple, *IOW Society*, 1988

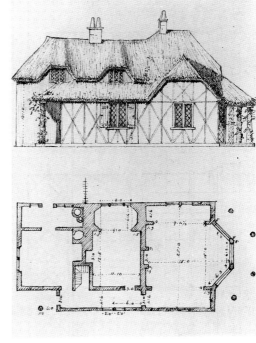

ABOVE Bridge Cottage: the porch is a recent addition

BELOW Daw Cottage

MOCCAS COURT
Moccas, Herefordshire
1804

Nash built two lodges for Sir George Cornewall in what was almost Nash's own corner of the county, containing Foxley, Belmont, Stoke Edith and Garnstone. Both the stone-built Daw Cottage, with its arched porch, and the brick-built Bridge Cottage have projecting bay windows with pent roofs, dormer windows and diagonally set chimney stacks. Except for the glazing and Bridge Cottage's porch, both are almost as Nash left them. George Repton's sketchbooks contain designs for another cottage and a barn, but neither can now be found.

Repton, RIBA Sketchbook
Repton, Brighton Sketchbook

The entrance to Daw Cottage

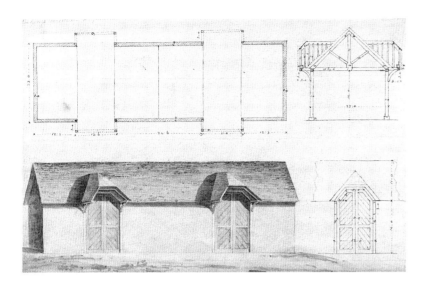

85

MERLEY HOUSE
Canford Magna, Dorsetshire
1805

The stable ranges of Merley House, built for Ralph Willet, form three sides of the stable courtyard, which is entered through the archway set in the curved screen wall. The two-storeyed coach-house has a tiled roof carrying an octagonal cupola and

ABOVE
Moccas: design for a barn, from George Repton's Brighton Sketchbook

RIGHT
Merley: the archway and coach-house, now being restored as a dwelling, with later additions removed

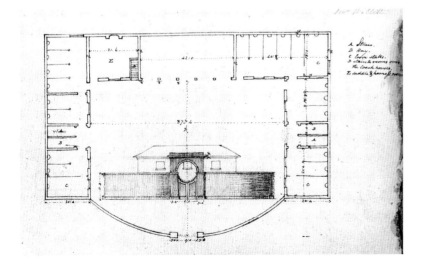

LEFT
A preliminary design for the stables at Merley, from George Repton's RIBA Sketchbook

weather-vane. The low wings on either side once housed loose boxes and stalls. George Repton shows an early scheme in his RIBA Sketchbook. The buildings and yard are being restored by their new owner, Mr B. Hammick.

J. Hutchins, *Vitruvius Dorsettiensis*, 1816
Royal Commission of Historical Monuments, *Dorset*, ii, SE, 1970

WITLEY COURT
Great Witley, Worcestershire
1805–c.1806

After conversion from a Jacobean house into a Georgian mansion, Witley Court was again altered, this time by Nash for the third Baron Foley in 1805. Nash gave the house an Italian vernacular look with a stucco finish and wide eaves. He dressed the two towers as *campanili*, and between them he added the Ionic entrance porch; a similar porch, two bays wider and doubled in depth, was built on the garden front, with an arcaded orangery at the end of the new terrace. The interior was replanned around Nash's usual central gallery, and the east wing was rebuilt. All of Nash's work, except the porches, was swept away in Victorian times. The house was gutted by fire in 1937, and the shell is now under the guardianship of the Department of the Environment.

Against the west side of Witley Court Nash built, in about 1806, two courtyards of service buildings, including stables to replace the Georgian ones that stood in the park; they were altered and extended in about 1860. Further west is a long range of Italianate buildings, formerly gardeners' accommodation, entered through Regency wrought-iron gates set between open-work piers, suggesting that the original cottages possibly date from Nash's time. Away from the house were the kennels, made up of interlocking octagonal pavilions and exercise yards, with the kennelman's quarters on the first floor of the two-storey blocks. The yards have gone and the

ABOVE The great south portico, recently restored
LEFT Only the portico is by Nash

Witley Court: (ABOVE) the entrance front (ABOVE RIGHT) the garden front; (RIGHT) the north front. Watercolours, possibly by George Repton

buildings have been converted into two houses. George Repton's drawing of the stables shows an octagonal layout, but not as built. The paper is watermarked 1828.

George Repton, Plans in the RIBA Drawings Collection
W. Pardoe, *Witley Court*, 1986

The kennels at Witley, now two houses

87

CAERLEON BRIDGE
Monmouthshire
1805

From London in 1805 Nash submitted three designs for a new bridge over the River Usk at Caerleon. None was accepted and the bridge was built by David Edwards, a local bridge-builder. Nash's drawings have not been found.

The Cambrian, 2 February 1805

88

HOLLYCOMBE

Sussex
1805

Designed by Nash for Sir Charles Taylor in
the style of a *cottage orné*, Hollycombe was
in fact a substantial villa and a link in the
line leading to Nash's vast 'thatched
cottage' at Windsor for the Prince Regent.
George Repton's plan shows the house
entered by a projecting porch into a wide
corridor running the width of the house;

The gatehouse at
Hollycombe, from
George Repton's
RIBA Sketchbook

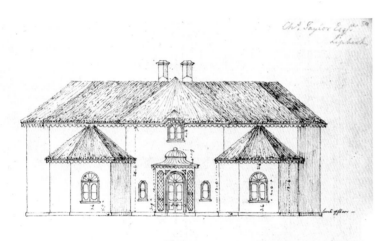

The entrance front of
Hollycombe, from
George Repton's
RIBA Sketchbook

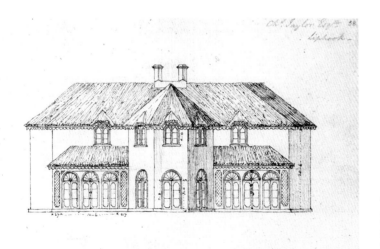

The garden front of
Hollycombe, from
George Repton's
RIBA Sketchbook

opposite was a square ante-room between
the drawing-room and dining-room, and
straight ahead was a small hexagonal
sitting-room with a veranda on either side.
In the front right-hand bay Repton shows
the stair, but this does not agree with the
elevation, which has only a single-storey
bay. To the north of the house, at the end
of a long drive, was a thatched gatehouse,
of which only a gatepost survives. The
house was rebuilt in the 1890s, but some of
Nash's work in one bedroom still exists and
the staircase has been reused.

Repton, RIBA Sketchbook

89

NUNWELL HOUSE

Brading, Isle of Wight
1805–1807

Sir William Oglander employed Nash in
1805 to design a new house to replace his
sixteenth-century manor. A drawing now in
the Isle of Wight Record Office is marked
'Mr Nash's plan for a house at Nunwell'. It
is similar to the plan of Aqualate Hall (No.
92), with the main rooms arranged round a

RIGHT
Nunwell: Nash's
stable block, now the
main residence
BELOW
Ground-plan of the
proposed new house
at Nunwell. Drawing
from Nash's office

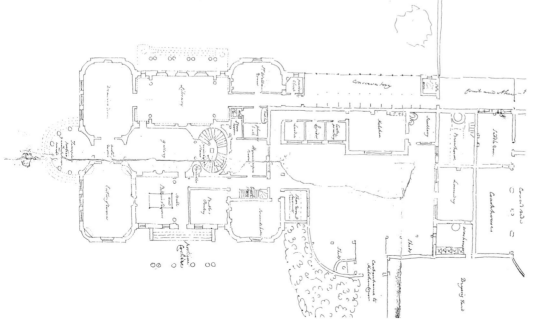

top-lit gallery. Externally Nash appears to
have proposed classical elevations with
columned porticoes and porches, possibly
English Baroque, with the rounded corners
recalling the bow window at Barnsley Park
(No. 101). Nunwell was not rebuilt,
probably because in 1807 Sir William
inherited Parnham House (No. 109) and
employed Nash to modernize it. In 1807
Nash carried out repairs to Nunwell; these
included the removal of the panelling from
the room occupied by Charles I on his last
night of freedom before imprisonment in
Carisbrooke Castle. The stable block,
rebuilt by Nash at the same time, is now
used as the main residence. The manor
house is open to the public.

N. Temple, *IOW Society*, 1987

LEFT
The south front

90

SANDRIDGE PARK
Stoke Gabriel, Devonshire
1805

Sandridge Park was the second house in
the Cronkhill series (see No. 72) and was
similarly built on a wooded hillside. It is
dominated by the square tower, on one
side of which the canted bay window was
once balanced by a conservatory on the
other; both sides were faced with wreathed
columns. The plan is unusual in that the
entrance front is also the garden one, and

Engraving after a
drawing by
T. H. Shepherd

118

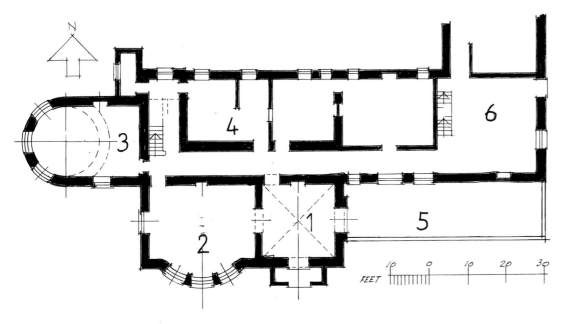

the stable block is placed in front of the house, acting as an eye-catcher from the main drive and garden terrace. Built for Lady Ashburton, widow of a banker, the house was exhibited as a design at the Royal Academy in 1805. The conservatory, porch and loggia, all demolished some time ago, have been replaced to show Nash's intentions but are not to his detailing.

Summerson 1980

GROUND-FLOOR PLAN OF SANDRIDGE

Sandridge: the stable block, as seen from the house

91

WARWICK HOUSE
St James's, London
1805–1817

Built in the seventeenth century, Warwick House adjoined Carlton House to the east. The house was rented by the Prince of Wales, then purchased by him in 1792; from 1805 to 1817 it was the London home of his daughter, Princess Charlotte. Nash surveyed the building and reported that, while structurally sound, it would need general repairs costing £1,200. There is no record of these having been carried out. In 1827 the site was cleared for the erection of Carlton House Terrace and Mews.

Survey of London, xxix, 1960

Nunwell on the Isle of Wight (No. 89).
The building was destroyed by fire in 1910
and was replaced by the present house.
Two picturesque lodges, with huge
moulded chimney stacks, survive. Away
from the house there is a round,
battlemented tower rising above crow-
stepped gables and punctuating the
landscape. It was possibly an earlier
building adapted by Nash as a folly.

Boughey Papers in the William Salt Library, Stafford
Summerson 1980

Aqualate Hall: the south front. Watercolour,
possibly by Joseph Nash. Collection Mrs C. Juhre

92

AQUALATE HALL

Forton, Staffordshire
1805–1809

John Fenton Fletcher (of the Betley Court
Fletchers) took the name Boughey when he
inherited Aqualate. He commissioned Nash
to rebuild the Hall, whilst retaining the
service wing of the existing house. It was
one of Nash's largest castles, with
battlemented towers topped by vast Tudor
domes. The plan is of Nash's usual central
gallery type, with the grand rooms entered
from either side, and is remarkably similar
to the proposed plan for rebuilding

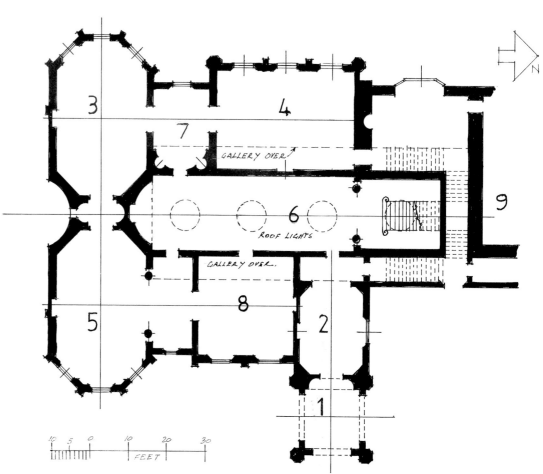

GROUND-FLOOR PLAN OF AQUALATE HALL

1 *Porte-cochère*   6 Gallery
2 Hall   7 Ante-room
3 Drawing-room   8 Study
4 Dining-room   9 Offices
5 Library

ABOVE Aqualate Hall: the north front. Artist unknown. Collection Mrs C. Juhre

The second lodge, now badly decaying

ABOVE The folly, or eye-catcher. Photograph 1961
RIGHT The main entrance and lodge

93
HARPTON COURT
Radnorshire
1805–1812

Frankland Lewis engaged Nash to design new interiors for Harpton Court, which had been in the family since the sixteenth century. Nash probably designed the classical south elevation, with its unusual grouping of windows in each wing. He also built a brewery and wash-house among the service buildings to the west. The battlements, machicolations and diagonally set chimney stacks are in his usual style. He also designed an entrance gateway opening into the broad avenue of trees that leads to the house, but it was never built. The house was demolished in 1956, and the service buildings were converted into dwellings.

Repton, RIBA Sketchbook
T. Lloyd, *The Lost Houses of Wales*, 1986

ABOVE Harpton: the service buildings, now divided into flats; the block containing the door was once a tall tower

Harpton: Nash's refacing of the old house. Undated photograph

94
WOOLBEDING
Near Midhurst, Sussex
Before 1806

George Repton's RIBA Sketchbook contains a design for a rustic cowshed marked 'for Lord Robert Spencer', almost certainly intended for the Woolbeding estate, near Midhurst. As could be expected, no trace of the wooden building has been found.

Summerson 1980

OPPOSITE LEFT Woolbeding: design for a cowshed, from George Repton's RIBA Sketchbook

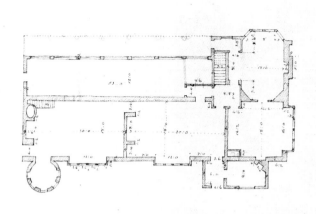

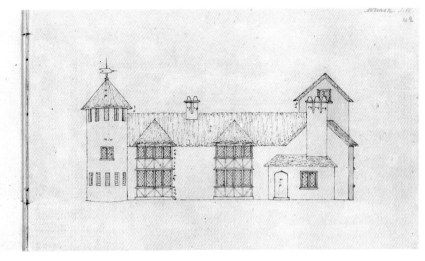

95
HAMSTEAD
Isle of Wight
*c.*1806

Nash purchased the manor of Ningwood in about 1806. It included the old towered farmhouse of Hamstead, which stood on a ridge overlooking the West Solent and the marshes and creeks of Newtown River. He began altering the house at once and was still making improvements in 1832. George Repton's RIBA Sketchbook shows an early plan and elevation of the thatched house; the round tower bears a date of 1410, which possibly confirms its rumoured monastic beginnings. Nash's early alterations are not readily apparent in Repton's drawings but may have included the addition of both bay windows and the entrance porch. The view dated 1834 shows the tower doubled in height and a new projecting gable end. Nash kept and enjoyed Hamstead all his life, and Mrs Nash retired to it after his death in 1835. Later it became the Isle of Wight home of the Pennethorne family, who eventually destroyed all of Nash's work.

Summerson 1980
Victoria County History: Hampshire

ABOVE Ground-plan and elevation of Hamstead, probably after first alterations had been carried out, from George Repton's RIBA Sketchbook

ABOVE AND BELOW Drawings of Hamstead, from the Lee-Duesbury Album (RIBA)

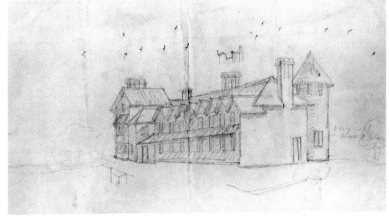

96

HALE HALL
Hale, Lancashire
1806

Nash rebuilt the south front of Hale Hall for John Blackburne in the Jacobean style of the old house, whose towered north front, shown in Neale's book, was in red brickwork, with quoins and mullions in stone. The ground floor of Nash's wing contained a museum for Blackburne's collection of medals and natural-history specimens. It also held a drawing-room and a dining-room, each measuring 36 by 22 feet. The Hall has been demolished.

J. P. Neale, *Views of Seats*, ii, 1825

Hale Hall: the original Jacobean entrance front, the style of which Nash had to follow. Drawing by C. and G. Pyne, *c.*1829

Hale Hall: Nash's elevation to his new wing consisted of the two canted bays and the three bays between them. Photograph by S. A. Harris, 1937

97

HYDE PARK
London
1806 and 1824

John Harvey (active 1785–1810), the winner of the Stafford Town Hall (No. 25) competition in which Nash was unplaced, was appointed Architect to the Office of Woods and Forests in 1805. One of his first jobs was to repair a bridge in Hyde Park's Rotten Row. His work was so unsatisfactory that Nash was brought in as an independent adviser. Nash solved the problem and was given Harvey's job. The introduction to an official department, together with his earlier introduction to the Prince of Wales, probably by Humphry Repton, set in motion Nash's Metropolitan Improvements that altered London from Marylebone to St James's.

Hyde Park was allocated to Nash by the Board of Works as one of his 'districts' in 1814. George Repton's Sketchbook at the RIBA contains an undated view of a cottage noted as being in Hyde Park. A watercolour dated 1835 by William Evans of Bristol (1809–58) shows what is almost certainly the same cottage, described as the Keeper's Lodge, Hyde Park. Summerson (1935) cites a memorandum in the Office of Works, dated 1824, which refers to a design by Nash for an ornamental pleasure garden between Hyde Park Corner and Stanhope Gate. Such a garden is shown on a map of London of 1827 as occupying a triangular site behind a group of houses on the corner of Park Lane and stretching up to Stanhope Gate.

Summerson 1935
Summerson 1980
M. Gregory, *William Evans of Bristol* (Catalogue 49), 1987

Design for the Keeper's Cottage, in Hyde Park. Watercolour by William Evans of Bristol, 1835. Collection Martyn Gregory

end facing the study, with the library and drawing-room on the south side. The dining-room was at the east end, in the keep, next to the service wing. The castle was demolished in 1949 and the estate swallowed up by the outskirts of Liverpool.

J. P. Neale, *Views of Seats*, ii, 1825

99
GARNSTONE CASTLE
Weobley, Herefordshire
c. 1806

Garnstone Castle was commissioned by Samuel Peploe, son-in-law of Sir George Cornewall, through whom Nash presumably obtained the introduction. The plan was of two parallel wings separated along their length by Nash's usual gallery, this time with the stair in the vast central tower lit by high-level traceried windows; the main rooms ran along the garden wing. The castle was built in green sandstone in a Tudor Gothic style. The embattled walls

98
CHILDWALL HALL
Childwall, Lancashire
1806

Childwall Hall, the Gothic castle belonging to Bamber Gascoyne, MP for Liverpool, was built in red sandstone. The main block was between the diagonally placed octagonal tower, containing the study, and the square keep. The two-storey bay window on the west side lit the library. The Hall was compactly planned around Nash's usual castle gallery; the stair was at the east

Childwall: (BELOW LEFT) the garden front. Engraving after J. P. Neale, 1824–9; (BELOW RIGHT) entrance front. Undated photograph

and towers were pierced with mullioned windows and decorated with turrets and buttresses. Garnstone Castle was generally considered to have been one of Nash's least inspired compositions. After much alteration it was finally demolished in 1959.

J. P. Neale, *Views of Seats*, iv, 1828

100

BRAMPTON PARK
Brampton, Huntingdonshire
1806–1810

After the death in 1805 of her husband, Brigadier-General Sparrow, Lady Olivia Sparrow decided to modernize the old house. In 1806 Nash was instructed to replace the service wing with new kitchens and servants' quarters; he also built a dairy, brewhouse and hot-house. Nash went on to

Garnstone Castle: (ABOVE) the garden front; (LEFT) the entrance front; (RIGHT) the main staircase and clerestory windows. Photographs dated 1959

make substantial alterations to the main house: bay windows were added and the whole house was reroofed. Internally rooms were replanned and refurbished. After a long and tedious argument as to who should have paid the Clerk of Works's wages, an arbitration found in Nash's favour, and as a result he was paid off in 1810. The house was destroyed by fire in 1907. It would seem that part of Nash's service wing survived and now, much repaired and rebuilt, forms the Officers' Mess at RAF Brampton.

N. Temple, *Records of Huntingdonshire*, 1986

RIGHT
Brampton Park immediately after the fire of 1907; Nash's bow window is on the right

BELOW
The gabled elevation of Nash's service wing, rebuilt as the Officers' Mess

Barnsley Park: Nash's garden elevation and orangery

RIGHT
Barnsley House, with the gabled dormers, wing and loggia probably added by Nash when used as the Dower House

101

BARNSLEY PARK

Barnsley, Gloucestershire
1806–c.1810

Built on the site of a Saxon manor, the present Barnsley Park dates from the late seventeenth century. Nash built the orangery and the octagonal Bibury Lodge for Sir John Musgrave. As well as decorating the library he almost certainly designed the whole east wing, which is not coaxial with the older house. The Wykeham–Musgrave papers contain a priced schedule for stonework, from the mason John Mills, dated 1806; it begins,

ABOVE Barnsley Park: the wing on the right is by Nash

'commenced 22 May 1806'. Later Nash arranged for Norwegian oak flooring for the library, breakfast-room and drawing-room to be sent from London, as well as deal flooring for the bedrooms and attics. He also sent four iron girders for the floor over the library, the accommodation of which would account for the difference in the first-floor level. As with other old houses he extended, Nash produced a sympathetic and harmonious design.

In the village of Barnsley stands Barnsley House, a late seventeenth-century building owned in Nash's time by the Musgraves. It is reputed to have been used as the Dower House after Sir John's death in 1814 before becoming the rectory in 1820. Around this time the south-west front was refaced and given three gables in the sympathetic manner that Nash usually showed to old buildings. The diagonal chimney shafts are almost a trademark of his and the castellated veranda, also added at this time, could stylistically be given to him. No documentary proof of Nash's involvement has yet been found.

Wykeham–Musgrave MSS, 1806–9 (Bodleian Library, Oxford)
C. Hussey, 'Barnsley Park, Gloucestershire', *Country Life*, 2 and 9 September 1954

'Wished me to Build the additions to your house at Barnsley Park', and ends, 'Sir, I understand there is to be a bow to the front.' He then asks to see the plan of it before pricing. The stonework descriptions agree with the built elevation. The schedule is marked in another hand (Musgrave's?):

LEFT
Nash's orangery, with his almost standard cast-iron trusses
RIGHT
Bibury Lodge, an octagonal gatehouse with classical loggia

REGENT STREET

London

1809–1826

The Planning

The successful development of Marylebone Park depended on the provision of a direct link with Whitehall and Westminster. Leverton and Chawner, the Land Revenue Surveyors, had proposed a route through Golden Square and Soho to Great Portland Street. Nash, in his plan of 1814, swung his street to the west on its way north from Piccadilly, 'hugging' the West End. At the same time he bought properties in the run-down area of Soho. There were many difficulties. One was the existence of Foley House, blocking the south end of Portland Place, which Nash was to incorporate as a link with the Park. The Duke of Portland proposed to buy Foley House to stop Nash's scheme but Nash stepped in at the last moment and bought it himself. Another difficulty was to bring the new street in line with Portland Place while avoiding the demolition of part of the properties on the east side of Cavendish Square. Nash solved this problem by curving the street to the east as it came down from Portland Place, thus creating Langham Place. A second bend, after Oxford Street, regained the original line. When the commissioners objected to Nash's square before Piccadilly, he replaced it with the Quadrant. This revised scheme of 1813, together with the provision of a new sewer, was accepted by the Treasury with Nash's estimated cost of nearly £400,000. The New Street Act received the Royal Assent in July 1813. Nash, at his best when making a virtue of necessity, had produced a typical English winding road out of his original, almost alien, formal street.

a

b

a Waterloo Place, looking north, with the County Fire Office in the distance. Engraving by W. Tombleson after T. H. Shepherd for Elmes, *Metropolitan Improvements*, 1827. See also *d*

b St Philip's Chapel, attributed to George Repton. Engraving by J. Tingle after T. H. Shepherd for Elmes, q.v.

Waterloo Place to Piccadilly

Waterloo Place, in front of Henry Holland's Ionic screen to Carlton House, was to be the *Grand Place*. Nash repeated its Ionic order as pilasters and columns on the terraces of formal town houses. Building began in 1815, with the great speculative builder James Burton taking up the whole of the Place. The formal character was dropped after Charles Street. A club, a bank, a hotel and a church were now intermingled with the houses, which included the double mansion of Nash and his cousin John Edwards. These new works caused the removal of the old market of St James's. Nash, with a humanitarian gesture, insisted on its being replaced 'as essential to the poor, who cannot pay high rents'. The new market and houses were built by James Burton between Haymarket and the New Street. When George IV decided to have Carlton House demolished, Waterloo Place was doubled in length. The southern corners of Pall Mall were given to the United Service Club and the Athenaeum Club, and a gap between the new Carlton House Terraces allowed a glimpse of St James's Park.

c Regent Street, looking south from Piccadilly to Waterloo Place and Carlton House. The tower of St Philip's Chapel is seen on the right. Engraving by J. Bluck after T. H. Shepherd for Ackermann's *Repository of Arts*, 1824

The buildings along Waterloo Place and the southern end of Regent Street, from Pall Mall on the left to St Philip's Chapel (see opposite) and Carlton Street on the right. From John Tallis, *Street Views of London*, 1838–40

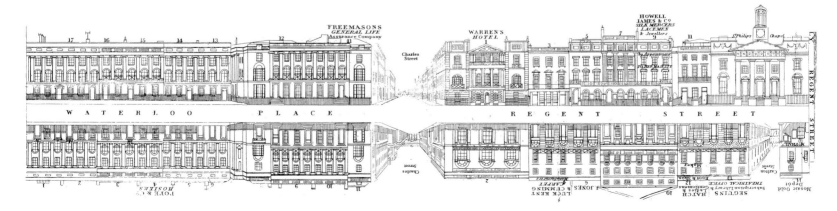

d The Quadrant, looking west, with, on the right, the County Fire Office, which closed the vista from Carlton House. Engraving by J. Bluck after T. H. Shepherd for Ackermann's *Repository of Arts*, 1824

e The Quadrant, looking north-west. Engraving by W. Wallis after T. H. Shepherd for Elmes, q.v.

Piccadilly to Oxford Street

The New Street crossed Piccadilly at a circus with four segments. To the north, Nash placed the County Fire Office, to close the vista from Carlton House. To the west – but not entering the circus – began the sweep of the Quadrant, with its Doric colonnade. No speculators could be found to take on this section, so Nash leased, built and financed the whole Quadrant himself. After this formality, buildings in a variety of styles and by several architects (among them Soane and C. R. Cockerell) took over. The shop fronts continued to Oxford Street, interrupted by two churches sited by Nash to close vistas. The north corners of Vigo Street and Little Argyll Street were given domes to form *points de vue*, and the skyline was further broken with towers, pediments and attics. After the last gentle bend before Oxford Street, All Souls Church, with its spire and chaplet of Corinthian columns, came into view.

The buildings of Piccadilly Circus, looking east (top) and west (bottom). From John Tallis, *Street Views of London*, 1838–40

OPPOSITE PAGE Regent Street:
f The west side (115–227), with Vigo Street on the left. The domed corner building formed a *point de vue* from the Quadrant, just visible on the right. Engraving by W. Tombleson after T. H. Shepherd for Elmes, q.v. See also e
g The west side (121–131). Detail of f. Engraving by M. Barrenger after T. H. Shepherd for Elmes, q.v.
h The west side (171–195), with New Burlington Street on the left and Conduit Street on the right. Engraving by W. Watkins after T. H. Shepherd for Elmes, q.v.

i The east side (106–130, numbering from right), with Glasshouse Street and the Quadrant on the right. The main block, 106–128, was designed by Nash. Engraving by W. Wallis after T. H. Shepherd for Elmes, q.v.
j The east side (132–154, numbering from right), possibly designed by Nash. 132 is incorrectly numbered as 123. Engraving by W. Wallis after T. H. Shepherd for Elmes, q.v.
k The east side (224–240, numbering from right), with the Harmonic Institution (with dome) on the corner of Little Argyll Street, where Regent Street bends, and All Souls on the left. Engraving by W. Wallis after T. H. Shepherd for Elmes, q.v.

f

i

g

j

h

k

133

Oxford Street to Portland Place

The Completion

On both sides of the New Street, long formal blocks of shops led into and out of the four segments of Oxford Circus with short returns to Oxford Street. Next came facing residential terraces (the first since Waterloo Place), then a mixture of shops and houses broken in the centre of the west side by low arcaded stables, opposite the London Carriage Repository, which was also low. The street ended with All Souls closing the vista from the south. On the other side of the road from All Souls, the gardens of Langham House made a welcome break before the magnificence of Adam's Portland Place.

By 1819 the New Street had been named Regent Street, the sewer had been laid and gas lighting installed. Although some building work was still outstanding, the account was closed in 1826 at a cost of £1,500,000. Nash must be given all the credit, not only for deciding the line of the New Street, but also for designing, or approving, all the building and engineering works, dealing with valuations and lettings, and giving financial advice. All of this was carried out from his own private office for a total remuneration of some £30,000 – not, as Nash himself declared, 'an overpayment'. Throughout this period

Nash was also engaged in building Regent's Park, overseeing the Regent's Canal, designing Brighton Pavilion and Buckingham Palace, building at least four churches and designing another ten, carrying out private commissions in England, Wales and Ireland, and still finding time to build two homes for himself. It is hard now to appreciate the spaciousness of nineteenth-century Regent Street, with its low, four-storeyed buildings on either side, glistening with stucco freshly painted every four years.

H. Hobhouse, *History of Regent Street*, 1975
Summerson 1980

The buildings in the northern end of Regent Street, running north from present-day Oxford Circus (top left), past Great Castle Street, Margaret Street and Mortimer Street, to Langham Place and the gardens of Langham House (bottom right). From John Tallis, *Street Views of London*, 1838–40

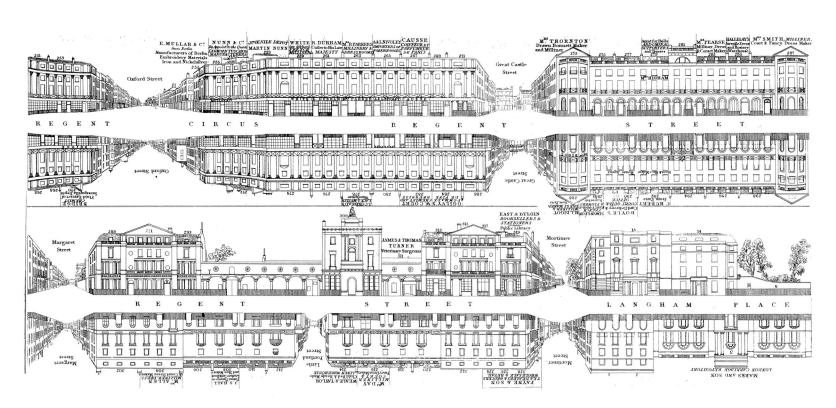

THE QUEEN'S HOUSE
Lyndhurst, Hampshire
1807

In a letter dated September 1807 to George Eyre, a New Forest verderer and owner of the Warrens (No. 65), Nash refers to his having been consulted about possible improvements to the Queen's House and the Verderer's Court at Lyndhurst (N. Temple). A specification, dated 1818, lists repairs to the windows, brickwork and lead gutters amounting to £2,742, which was possibly part of the advice given by Nash, as Fowler considers that at least some of the work in the specification was carried out.

D. J. Fowler, *The Queen's House, Lyndhurst*
N. Temple, *Hants Society*, 1988

The Market House: the top storey was added later   PLAN OF THE SINGLE-STOREY MARKET

103

THE MARKET HOUSE
Chichester, Sussex
1807

The single-storey market house built for the city council was ten bays deep, with the back three bays divided off to form the Fish Market. Behind the Doric screen, the single-storey market had seven open-fronted stalls on each side. The set-back upper storey of 1900 replaced Nash's hipped roof, which he had masked from the street by the balustrade bearing the city coat of arms.

Repton, RIBA Sketchbook II
T. W. Horsfield, *History of Sussex*, ii, 1835

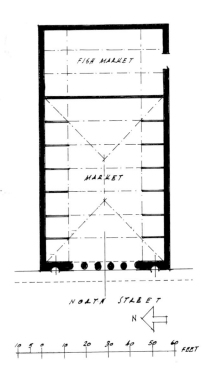

FISH MARKET

MARKET

NORTH STREET

N

10 5 0   10   20   30   40   50   60 FEET

105

HAWARDEN CASTLE
Hawarden, Flintshire
1807

In 1807 Sir Stephen Richard Glynne, the eighth baronet, commissioned Nash to castellate his recently acquired house, Broadlane, and to harmonize it with the ruins of the medieval castle on the nearby hill. Nash's proposals, contained in a written description and shown in a watercolour painting, probably by A. C. Pugin, closely resemble the house as built. The construction was supervised by Thomas Cundy, then a little-known architect; whether he was the executant or

LISSAN RECTORY
Near Cookstown, County Tyrone
1807

Lissan Rectory was built for the Reverend John Staples, nephew of Colonel James Stewart of Killymoon Castle (No. 74), who probably introduced Nash to his relative. It was a picturesque villa in the Claudean Cronkhill series (see No. 72), built in local sandstone with the outside covered with harling, the Irish–Scottish version of roughcast. The square entrance tower dominated the two-storey house, with the round one used as a stop for the lower service wing. On the garden front the covered balcony over the loggia is a later addition; recently the service wing and its tower were demolished and the pitched roof of the square tower removed, making a travesty of Nash's charming villa.

E. M. Jope, 'Lissan Rectory and the Buildings in the North of Ireland designed by John Nash', *Ulster Journal of Archaeology*, xix, 1956

Hawarden: Nash's proposed front elevation; the old castle can be seen on the left. Watercolour, 1807. Collection Sir William Gladstone, Bt.

replacement architect, with or without Nash's consent, is not known. The finished house showed some comparatively minor alterations: the conservatory and great tower were omitted, and the bay window and service wing were simplified. Further small alterations were made by W. E. Gladstone when he became the owner in 1884. The house is still in his family's ownership.

J. Cornforth, 'Hawarden Castle', *Country Life*, 15, 22 and 29 June 1967

Hawarden: Nash's proposed elevation. Drawing by Charles Lee, from the Lee-Duesbury Album (RIBA)

Ground-floor plan of Lissan Rectory, produced in Nash's office. Watercolour. Private collection

Lissan Rectory: the north, or entrance, elevation. Watercolour, possibly by George Repton. Private collection

The south, or garden, elevation. Watercolour, possibly by George Repton. Private collection

The entrance elevation, showing the demolished service wing, and (BELOW) the garden elevation, from George Repton's RIBA Sketchbook

The covered balcony on the first floor is a recent addition

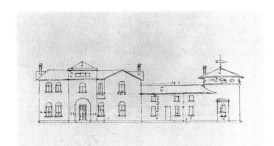

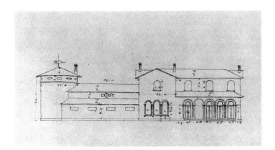

Bushey House: Nash was only concerned with reports and repairs on Bushey House

107

BUSHEY HOUSE
Hampton, Middlesex
1807

Whilst at the Office of Works, Nash carried out minor alterations and repairs for the Duke of Clarence (later William IV) when he became Ranger of Bushey Park.

King's Works, vi, 1973

108

KILWAUGHTER CASTLE
Near Larne, County Antrim
1807

To the one remaining room of the seventeenth-century castle of Kilwaughter, Nash added, for Edward Agnew, the castellated Gothic house built in basalt with

Kilwaughter Castle: the three-window range survives from the earlier house

Kilwaughter Castle. Photograph before 1951

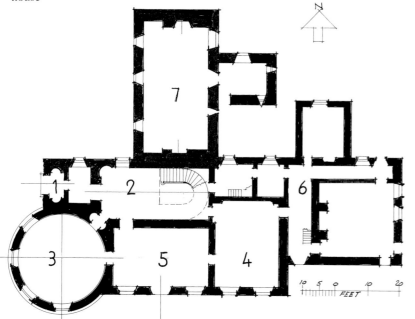

1 Porch
2 Hall
3 Drawing-room
4 Dining-room
5 Library
6 Offices
7 17th-century castle

GROUND-FLOOR PLAN OF KILWAUGHTER CASTLE

109

PARNHAM HOUSE
Beaminster, Dorsetshire
1807

The fifteenth-century Great Hall, with wings added in Elizabethan times to make the almost obligatory E-plan, was inherited by Sir William Oglander of Nunwell, Isle of Wight. Nash was already working at Nunwell but was switched to modernize Parnham. He added the dining-room along the back wall of the hall, moved the fireplace and replaced it with a window to make up for the loss of light; the new bedroom over the dining-room was panelled and given the Royal coat of arms. Externally, buttresses and pinnacles were added to the elevations, and the drawing-room bay window was built to match the original Tudor one at the front of the house. Behind the offices Nash built a detached brewhouse and a similar laundry; in the grounds an icehouse was dug. The

sandstone dressings. The round tower contained the circular drawing-room, then came the library and the dining-room, all opening off the staircase-hall to form a compact plan. The kitchen quarters were at the far end of the building, behind the dining-room. Externally, the Gothic tracery to the windows was in wood, added in front of the sashes. Unusual for Nash were the *tourelles*, or cantilevered turrets, built on the corners of the main block. The house was stripped of its fittings in 1951 and left to decay.

E. M. Jope, 'Lissan Rectory and the Buildings in the North of Ireland designed by John Nash', *Ulster Journal of Archaeology*, xix, 1956

Parnham House: the garden front (the terrace is later)

house is now occupied by Mr and Mrs John Makepeace, with the Nash buildings forming part of the School for Craftsmen in Wood.

T., 'Parnham House, Dorsetshire', *Country Life*, 24, 29 August & 5 September 1908

The entrance front

The kitchen wing, on the left, was given a gable and bay window

ABERAERON

Cardiganshire

*c.*1807

Aberaeron was a small fishing hamlet until, under the Harbour Act of 1807, the Reverend Alban T. J. Gwynne of Monachty turned it into one of the few examples of a comprehensively planned Georgian town. It was laid out on a grid pattern based on the harbour quays, with a large square off the main Aberystwyth-Cardigan road, which, with Regency insouciance, closes the east end at an angle. Terraced houses surround the square, and streets are lined with three-storey houses marking the centres and ends, with two-storey houses between. The street vistas are all closed by more prominent buildings. Local tradition has it that Nash made the master plan and supplied rough sketches for the various house types, but no documentary proof has yet been found.

W. J. Lewis, *Aberaeron* (guidebook), n.d.

Alban Square, Aberaeron: the centre and ends of each side are marked by bigger houses

Market Street, leading to the harbour, was one of the first streets to be built

1	Town Hall and Gaol	5 Chapel
2	Harbour Master	6 Inn
3	School	7 Workhouse
4	Church	8 Shipyard
		9 Tabernacle

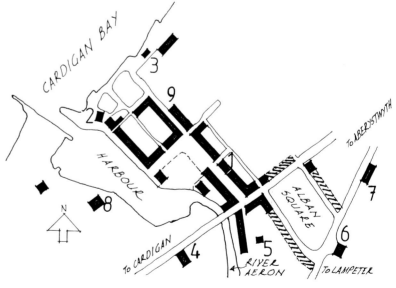

STREET PLAN OF ABERAERON, BASED ON A MAP OF ABOUT 1845

LEFT
Ravensworth Castle:
the entrance front.
Photograph 1934
BELOW
The view from across
the lake. Undated
photograph

III

RAVENSWORTH CASTLE

Near Gateshead, County Durham
Begun 1807

Ravensworth Castle was one of Nash's largest castles, built for Sir Thomas Liddell, Bt, later Lord Ravensworth. After building work had begun, Liddell's eldest son, Thomas Henry, took over the direction of the work; the design, still by Nash, was greatly altered and continued to be altered up to and after Nash's death. It was eventually finished in 1846. Nash's early plans show his unique top-lit gallery, which, with detailed variations, was to remain the core of the house. The

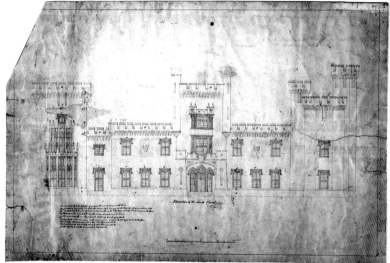

The stable entrance at Ravensworth; the wall between the towers over the archway is a later addition

ABOVE Proposed south front of Ravensworth, *c.*1824. Drawing produced in Nash's office (RIBA)
BELOW Castellated gate and lodge at Ravensworth

elevations at the beginning were more compact and had fewer towers than the completed house, which was demolished in 1953. Some of Nash's castle and stables were left standing. Together with the remains of the thirteenth-century castle, they now form picturesque ruins. A castellated gatehouse and lodge also survive.

N. Pevsner, *Buildings of England: Durham*, 1953
Gateshead Metropolitan Borough, *Schedule of Listed Buildings*, 1961, 1966, 1967

ST JOHN'S CHURCH
Caledon, County Tyrone
1808

Nash added a timber spire to the church of St John, in the village of Caledon. It was replaced, in stone facsimile, in 1830.

A. Rowan, *Buildings of Ireland: North West Ulster*, 1976

BELOW St John's: stone facsimile of Nash's needle spire; the pinnacles are probably also by Nash

ABOVE
Goodwood: estate lodgings, possibly by Nash

GOODWOOD HOUSE
Near Chichester, Sussex
*c.*1807

That Nash worked at Goodwood is borne out by a letter, dated 4 February 1807, from him to James Musgrave of Barnsley Park recommending the employment of one Edwards, Clerk of Works at Goodwood until the death in 1806 of the third Duke of Richmond. Previously James Wyatt had succeeded Sir William Chambers and had built most of the estate buildings. The only one that does not appear to be by him or Chambers is the L-shaped Gothic range. Summerson considers that some of the interior details appear to be by Nash. The fourth Duke was appointed Lord-Lieutenant of Ireland from 1807 until 1813, and the villa for him referred to in the Sale Catalogue of Nash's drawings was probably intended for Ireland. It was not built.

Wykeham–Musgrave MS, 1806–9 (Bodleian Library, Oxford)
Nash Sale Catalogue, 1835

Monachty: the entrance front

The main gatehouse

The secondary gatehouse

MONACHTY
Near Aberaeron, Cardiganshire
*c.*1808

Monachty, or Mynachdy (Welsh for Monk's House), was once part of the Abbey lands of Strata Florida. The house was built for the Reverend Alban T. J. Gwynne on the high ground inland from Aberaeron (No. 110). It is a plain, neo-classical house with stripped pilasters and frieze. The conservatory, entrance porch and canted bay window are dressed with minimal mouldings. As with the town of Aberaeron, local tradition attributes the design to Nash, who would not have been bothered by the central duality of two windows, a feature which he later repeated at Park Village West (No. 221). The main gatehouse matches the house in style and detail, whilst the secondary one has barge-boarded gables, a canted bay window with pent roof, and diagonal chimney stacks – all features used by Nash for buildings on other estates.

Davis 1966

115

HOUSE FOR THE COUNTESS OF SHANNON

County Cork
1807–1827

Entrance Front.

The Drawings Collection of the RIBA has a comprehensive set of drawings with the heading 'house to be built in Ireland for the Countess of Shannon'. The house has not been identified, but two possible candidates are Moss House at Castlemartyr, known locally as the Dower House and now in ruins, and the Hexagon at Courtmacsherry. If it was built, it would have been during the Countess's widowhood (1807–27). The Countess was the widow of the second Earl

of Shannon; the fourth Earl bought East Cowes Castle from Nash's widow.

J. Lever (ed.), *Catalogue of the Drawings Collection of the Royal Institute of British Architects*, 1973

ABOVE Proposed entrance front of Lady Shannon's house and (BELOW) ground-floor plan. Drawings produced in Nash's office (RIBA)

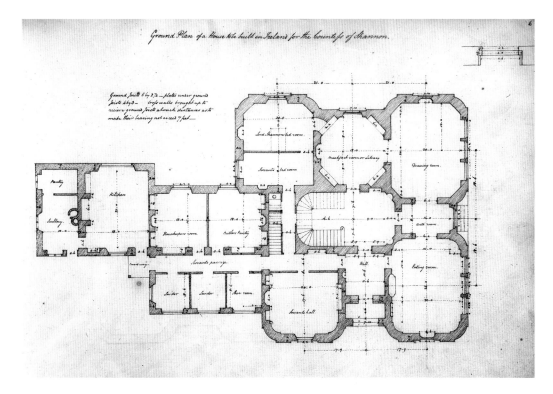

Ground Plan of a House to be built in Ireland for the Countess of Shannon.

116

CALEDON HOUSE

Caledon, County Tyrone
1808–1820

Caledon was built for the second Earl of Caledon by Thomas Cooley in 1779. Nash added to it by building the screen of paired Ionic columns between two domed pavilions: the west one housed the library, and the other a gunroom. On the ends of the pavilions are window heads decorated with Nash's unique shell-and-fan motif. The interior of the library is almost engulfed by the dome, decorated with paterae. Bookcases are recessed into the walls, and one end is screened off by Corinthian columns. Nash's proposed design also included the addition of a pedimented second storey, which was not

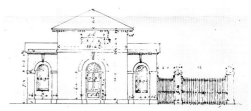

built until 1825 but was probably to his design, as he was working for Lord Caledon on Carlton House Terrace until about 1830. The main entrance – with a pair of matching lodges, piers surmounted with sphinxes and wrought-iron gates – was built in about 1820, for which Nash's original sketches are in Caledon library. The other lodge, of 1815, with a simplified Doric portico similar to the Park Square lodges in Regent's Park, was built to house a gatekeeper and was later used as a schoolroom. This was possibly by Nash. It is known that Nash visited Caledon at least twice, in 1808 and 1810.

A. Rowan, *Buildings of Ireland: North West Ulster*, 1976

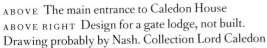

ABOVE The main entrance to Caledon House
ABOVE RIGHT Design for a gate lodge, not built. Drawing probably by Nash. Collection Lord Caledon

Caledon House as originally enlarged by Nash. Painting possibly by A. Pugin. Collection Lord Caledon

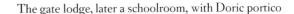

The gate lodge, later a schoolroom, with Doric portico

The high ground
between Caerhays
Castle and the
seaward boundary
was removed in
Victorian times

117

CAERHAYS CASTLE

St Michael Caerhays, Cornwall
1808

Caerhays is the only remaining example of Nash's four great castles – Aqualate (No. 92) was destroyed by fire and Ravensworth (No. 111) and Shanbally (No. 181) were demolished. The house, built for John Trevanion, MP, is entered through a *porte-cochère* into the top-lit long gallery, with main rooms opening off the south side and the staircase rising at one end. Externally, it is a tough, picturesque composition, reflecting the Cornish stone rubble and granite dressings in which it is built. The domestic gardens and house are enclosed by embattled walls with various corner towers and arched gateways. At the western end are the two service courtyards. Each of Nash's two main entrances to the estate has an arched gateway, battlemented tower and screen walls.

Summerson 1980

Southborough Place: the garden front

SOUTHBOROUGH PLACE
Surbiton, Surrey
1808

Southborough House, as it is now known, originally stood in a hilltop plantation, Thomas Langley, the owner, happily commenting that the only building visible was Hampton Court Palace. Nash finished the elegant neo-classical house with wide Italian eaves in his Cronkhill style (see No. 72) and decorated the entrance with a domed octagonal porch. The single-storeyed service wing, two-storeyed summer-house and detached coach-house have all been converted into dwellings. Two gatehouses have been demolished. A drawing in George Repton's Brighton Sketchbook shows a farmhouse and buildings marked 'Langley Esq'. They do not appear to have been built.

Repton, Brighton Sketchbook
Summerson 1980

Ground-plan of the farmyard, from George Repton's Brighton Sketchbook (no trace has been found of the farm having been built)

1 Porch
2 Hall
3 Drawing-room
4 Dining-room
5 Library
6 Breakfast-room
7 Offices

GROUND-FLOOR PLAN OF
SOUTHBOROUGH PLACE

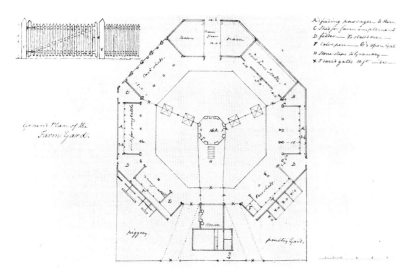

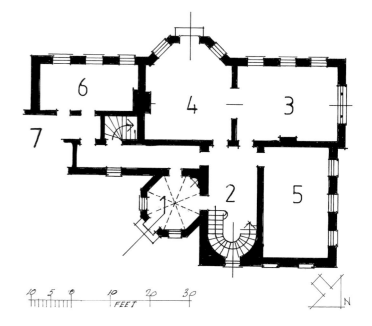

RIGHT
Southborough Place:
the garden front

BELOW
The domed entrance
porch

BELOW RIGHT
The service buildings
and summer-house
have been converted
into dwellings

Ombersley Court:
Nash's proposed
rebuilding of the
entrance front.
Watercolour produced
in Nash's office, 1808.
Collection Lord
Sandys

Ombersley Court: the entrance and lodge were
possibly built by Nash before he was replaced by
Webb

119

OMBERSLEY COURT
Ombersley, Worcestershire
1808

The Marchioness of Downshire
commissioned Nash to modernize the three-
storey brick house which had been built in
the early eighteenth century for the first
Lord Sandys. Three watercolours have
survived, marked 'made by Mr Nash in
1808 for the proposed improvement of
Ombersley, not adopted or acted on'.
Nash's proposed entrance front shows new
two-storey pavilions projecting from each
end of the old house, linked by a seven-bay
screen of giant Ionic columns. The decision
not to carry out Nash's proposed plans was
presumably taken on grounds of expense,
as the later refaced house by J. Webb
(1812–14) was much plainer and apparently
not as large.

A. Oswald, 'Ombersley Court, Worcestershire',
Country Life, 2, 9 and 16 January 1953

120

INGESTRE HALL
Ingestre, Staffordshire
1808–1813

Nash was employed by the second Earl
Talbot to replace the nondescript north and
west fronts of Ingestre Hall. He did this
with great sympathy, using details from the
south front, where he replaced the straight-
sided gables with shaped ones and added
the pepper pots. The porch tower was
given an open lantern resembling that of
Hatfield House. After the fire of 1882 the
damaged parts of the house were carefully
restored, using salvaged materials. At the
same time, the end bays of Nash's north

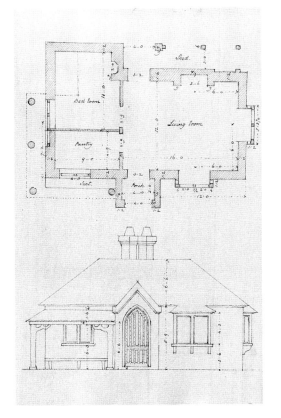

LEFT A gardener's cottage, probably at Ingestre,
from George Repton's Brighton Sketchbook

elevation appear to have been enlarged and
his porch lantern was replaced by a dome.
The house is now a Residential Arts
Centre.

J. P. Neale, *Views of Seats*, 1821
G. Nares, 'Ingestre', *Country Life*, 24 October 1957

121

WEST GRINSTEAD PARK

West Grinstead, Sussex
1809

The crenellated Gothic house was
commissioned from Nash by Walter

Burrell, younger brother of the owner of
Knepp Castle. Splendidly situated on high
ground in the Sussex Weald, the house,
built of local stone, was a compact example
of Nash's gallery plan. At one end was a
towered *porte-cochère*, at the other an
octagonal tower. The main rooms were
along the south side, the dining-room in a
round tower and the library in a square
one, on either side of the drawing-room,
which had a round-arched loggia. The
house was ill-treated during the Second
World War, neglected afterwards and then
demolished. The pair of classical entrance
lodges was broken up to make way for
road widening. All that remains is a
fragment of the stables and a cottage.

Repton's Sketchbook contains designs for
three lodges. As the drawings follow after

those for the house and match in style of draughtsmanship, they are probably alternative designs for the Park entrance and were never built.

D. G. C. Elwes and C. J. Robinson, *Castles and Mansions of West Sussex*, 1867

West Grinstead Park: the dining-room, 1953

West Grinstead Park: the west front, showing the *porte-cochère*, from George Repton's Brighton Sketchbook

The 'tea-caddy' entrance lodges at West Grinstead Park, from the south-west, 1965

Probably a design for a lodge at West Grinstead Park that was not built, from George Repton's Brighton Sketchbook

West Grinstead Park: the south front, from
George Repton's Brighton Sketchbook

KNEPP CASTLE
West Grinstead, Sussex
*c.*1809

Nash was commissioned by Walter Burrell
to build West Grinstead Park in 1809. He
was then asked by Burrell's elder brother,
Sir Charles Merrick Burrell, Bt, to design a
new house on the adjoining estate of
Knepp. The house, to the west of the old
hammer pond, faces the South Downs and
overlooks the ruined eleventh-century
Norman keep of the Lords of Bamber. All
the buildings are in brickwork, now
rendered but originally in stucco and lined
out to simulate stonework. Of the materials
used, the bricks were fired on the site, the

The only surviving estate building by Nash at
West Grinstead Park

GROUND-FLOOR
PLAN OF WEST
GRINSTEAD PARK

1 *Porte-cochère*
2 Hall
3 Drawing-room
4 Dining-room
5 Library
6 Gallery
7 Veranda
8 Billiard-room
9 Offices

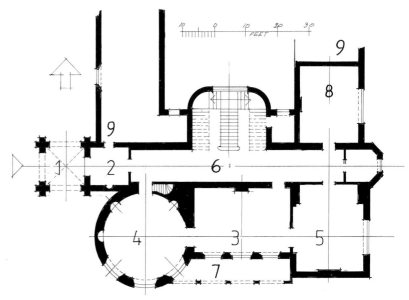

Knepp Castle:
the entrance front
and farm complex

RIGHT Knepp Castle: the entrance court

timber was cut from the estate woods, and the local Horsham stone was used for the main porch. After a fire in 1904 Knepp Castle was rebuilt to Nash's original design. As Ian Nairn commented, it was 'a remarkable thing to do at that time'. A perspective drawing dated 1808 is in the collection of Mr and Mrs Paul Mellon in America.

D. G. C. Elwes and C. J. Robinson, *Castles and Mansions of West Sussex*, 1867
I. Nairn and N. Pevsner, *The Buildings of England: Sussex*, 1965

156

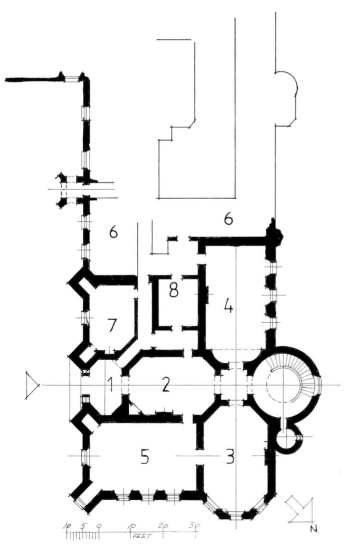

ABOVE LEFT Knepp Castle: the round staircase tower
ABOVE RIGHT The south front looks down on the old hammer pond

BELOW The gatekeeper's cottage at Knepp Castle

GROUND-FLOOR PLAN OF KNEPP CASTLE

1 Hall   5 Library
2 Inner hall   6 Offices
3 Drawing-room 6 Smoking room
4 Dining-room   8 Gunroom

REGENT'S PARK

London

1809–1832

In 1793, when John Fordyce was appointed Surveyor-General to the Department of Land Revenue, Henry VIII's hunting park at Marylebone consisted of 550 acres of open farmland, with the leases about to expire. In view of the profitable developments of the ducal estates to the south, it was decided that the Crown should also profit. In order to ensure success, a new street connecting the park with Whitehall was essential. This farsightedness resulted in Regent's Park, Regent Street and Trafalgar Square, the most comprehensive piece of planning ever carried out in London. Between 1820 and 1830 most of Regent's Park was built by the big speculative builders, such as James

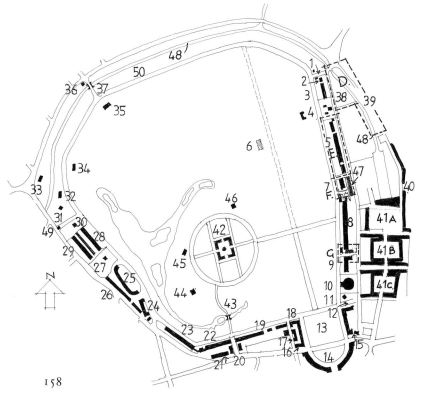

1	Gloucester Gate	20	York Gate	39	Park Village East
2	Gloucester (or Strathirne) Lodge	21	Nottingham Terrace	40	Augustus Street
3	Gloucester Terrace	22	York Terrace West	41A	Cumberland Market
4	St Katharine's Lodge	23	Cornwall Terrace	41B	Clarence Market
5	Cumberland Terrace	24	Clarence Terrace	41C	York Market
6	*Guinguette*	25	Sussex Place	42	King's College
7	Cumberland Place	26	Park Terrace	43	York Bridge
8	Chester Terrace	27	Sussex Villa	44	South Villa
9	Cambridge Terrace	28	Hanover Terrace	45	The Holme
10	Colosseum	29	Kent Terrace	46	St John's Lodge
11	Someries House	30	Abbey Lodge	47	Albany Street
12	St Andrew's Place	31	Albany Lodge	48	Regent's Canal
13	Park Square	32	Hanover Lodge	49	Hanover Gate
14	Park Crescent	33	Grove House	50	Carrick and Munster Terraces
15	Albany Terrace	34	Hertford Lodge	D	See plan on p. 257
16	Ulster Place	35	Holford House	E	See plan on p. 283
17	Brunswick Place	36	North Cottage	F	See plan on p. 280
18	Ulster Terrace	37	Macclesfield Bridge	G	See plan on p. 270
19	York Terrace East	38	Park Village West		

REGENT'S PARK ABOUT 1834, SHOWING THE BUILDINGS
PLANNED BY NASH

OPPOSITE
Ulster Terrace and
York Terrace

RIGHT
The scale of Nash's
buildings gives
spaciousness to the
Park (Sussex Terrace
is in the background)

Burton and William Nurse, and the remainder by small investors and tradesmen, with Nash himself taking up any unwanted sites. The overall plan was Nash's, as was the landscaping. He was also responsible for designing or approving every building and had the business acumen and drive to carry the whole project through to completion.

The Buildings

Nash's final design for Regent's Park left the northern boundary open, with unimpeded views to Hampstead. Ten grand terraces lined the other three sides, with six more forming the southern entrances. On the perimeter, facing outwards, he placed the five lesser terraces. Of the planned fifty-six villas only eight were built in the Park centre, though the addition of the two Park Villages more than made up for the loss in numbers. Nash's concern for the marketing facilities of the new suburb resulted in the provision of three open squares served by the Canal basin and decent houses for the poorer classes. Nash

gave the builders an outline block plan and elevational design, leaving the internal planning to the builder concerned and his own architect. Typical accommodation consisted of a ground-floor dining-room, two linked drawing-rooms over, then two floors of bedrooms, with the services in the basement. The leases contained Nash's instructions for the external painting: the stucco was to match Bath stone, the woodwork was to be painted to resemble oak, and the ironwork was to be painted a bronze colour.

Regent's Park: from the lake the ground slopes gently up to the Inner Circle

The Lake
1816

On the course of the Tyburn River Nash laid out the three-armed ornamental lake, with the intention of linking up with the new canal. This idea was abandoned, and the canal was moved to skirt Regent's Park. River water was not enough to cleanse the lake so it was arranged that 23,000 gallons a year would be taken from the Middlesex Water Company. Nash's only crossing of the lake was by York Bridge, which carried the access road to the Inner Circle. When Nash revived the idea of the King's *guinguette* in 1828, he extended the northern arm of the lake to embrace it; the *guinguette* was not built and this arm is now a bird sanctuary. Prince Puckler–Muskau compared the lake to a 'broad river flowing far into the distance between luxuriantly wooded banks and there dividing into several branches'.

The Royal Guinguette
1812–1828

Nash's plan accompanying the First Report of the Commissioners of Woods, Forests and Land Revenues (1912) shows a large mansion and a formal strip of water on the eastern side of Regent's Park. The *guinguette* is not mentioned in the Report; the first reference to its use is in John White's review of Nash's plan (published in 1815). The design had been changed by 1823, omitted by 1826 and reinstated in 1828. After this nothing was heard until Nash, after the death of George IV in 1830, wrote: 'The Plantation made for the express purpose of forming a site for a guingette [sic] which His late Majesty meant to build I have proposed to preserve.' The plantation still exists.

A. Saunders, *Regent's Park*, 1969
Summerson 1980

RIGHT
Regent's Park: herons
now nest on the island
BELOW LEFT
The Holme, sited to
be seen from across
the lake
BELOW RIGHT
York Bridge

BETLEY COURT

Betley, Staffordshire
1809

For Sir Thomas Fletcher of Betley Court, Nash added the central single-storey bow window as an extension to the drawing-room. Internally, on either side of the bow, he inserted a shallow-vaulted ceiling. Elsewhere Nash added a water-closet at a cost of £47 19s 8¾d. The present owner still has Nash's bills.

F. R. Twemlow, *The Twemlows, Their Wives and Their Homes*, 1910
Godfrey N. Brown, *This Old House*, 1987

NORTHERWOOD HOUSE

Lyndhurst, Hampshire
1810

Nash enlarged Northerwood house for Charles Mitchell by adding pavilions at the ends of the garden front and linking them with a single-storey range carrying the canopied veranda. The columns are of cast iron, with decorative open ironwork and

BELOW The preliminary design for Northerwood, from George Repton's RIBA Sketchbook

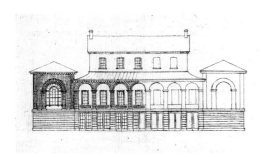

ABOVE Betley Court: the central bow window is Nash's extension; all the glazing bars are missing

BELOW Northerwood, with its Nash elevation recently restored; the wings outside the pedimented pavilions are modern

bulbous capitals. The balconied side ranges and the top storey are later additions. In 1975 the house was converted into flats.

G. F. Prosser, *Select Illustrations of Hampshire*, 1833
Repton, RIBA Sketchbook

CHARBOROUGH PARK
Almer, Dorsetshire
1810

Nash enlarged the Commonwealth house for Richard Erle-Drax-Grosvenor by filling in the eastern corner. This extended the main façade from seven bays to eleven. The central five were given giant Ionic pilasters and a pediment. New parapets and a cornice replaced the old eaves. The main

RIGHT
Charborough Park, c.1852, after Nash's reconstruction and before later additions. Engraving published by Stannard & Dixon

ABOVE
The Peacock Gate. Photograph 1957
LEFT
The circular *cottage orné*

entrance was moved to the north-west front, where the windows were regrouped below a new attic. The tower, porch and two small windows are later additions. The single-storey library wing was rebuilt and given a large, shallow bow window on each side, to form an oval centre. In the grounds are a circular *cottage orné*, similar to Nash's earlier Welsh ones, and a lodge with an arched gate surmounted by a stag. The lodge, known as Peacock Lodge, was built either at the beginning of the

ABOVE LEFT Rockingham: drawing of the garden elevation,
ABOVE RIGHT Drawing of the elevation facing the lake
BELOW Plan of Rockingham. Drawing from Nash's office

nineteenth century (and could therefore
have been designed by Nash) or possibly a
little earlier.

J. B. Burke, *A Visitation of Seats and Arms*, vii, 1853

127

ROCKINGHAM
Boyle, County Roscommon
1810

Rockingham, the seat of the first Viscount
Lorton of Boyle, was one of the most
beautiful estates in Ireland. Nash's classical
house was built in the woods and parkland
facing Lough Key. On the plan the library,
in the centre bow, was flanked by the
drawing-room and the parlour. Behind
them Nash's usual top-lit gallery had the
entrance-hall at the west end, with the
music-room at the east. Nash's dome was
removed when a third floor was added in
1822. After fire damage and subsequent
restoration in 1860, fire was again

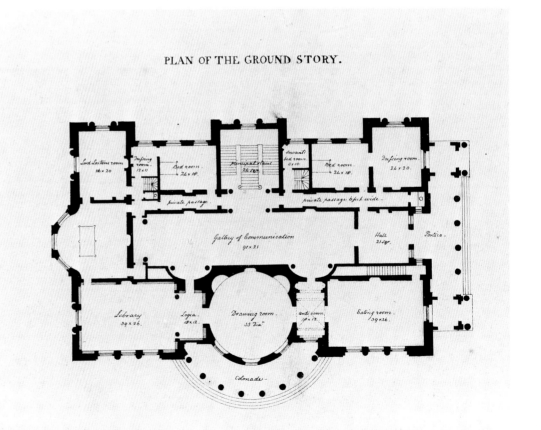

PLAN OF THE GROUND STORY.

The estate chapel at Rockingham

BELOW The inner gatehouse
BELOW RIGHT The Boyle Road arched gate
and lodge (demolished)

ABOVE RIGHT
The gabled and
barge-boarded
Adarn Lodge

responsible for the house's final destruction in 1937.

Many estate buildings survive. The Gothic chapel and lakeside gazebo are both locally attributed to Nash, as is the folly built out of the remains of medieval ruins on Castle Island; another island is reached by a high-arched stone bridge that could have been designed by him. The main drive leads past a Gothic lodge to a Tudor gatehouse, and another lodge (this time gabled and barge-boarded) stands at the south-west corner of the estate; all have features typical of Nash.

Summerson 1980

The tower of St Beadh

ABOVE Rockingham: Drummons Bridge
BELOW Rockingham: the lake gazebo

128

ST BEADH

Ardcarn, County Roscommon
*c.*1810

The village church of St Beadh, Church of
Ireland, was built on the site of an old
monastery in the hamlet of Ardcarn, which
abuts the south-eastern corner of the
Rockingham estate (No. 127). According to
local tradition Nash was involved in the
alterations to the church while building
Lord Lorton's country house. The single-
storey canted wings at the foot of the tower
were possibly added by Nash, and the
tower itself might have been raised by him
as an eye-catcher to be seen from
Rockingham.

LEFT
Preshaw House: the
entrance front of the
old house (the roof at
the back is a Victorian
extension)
BELOW LEFT
The garden elevation

129

PRESHAW HOUSE
Near Warnford, Hampshire
1810

Preshaw House, Walter Long's
seventeenth-century house, was
sympathetically enlarged by Nash with the
addition of a new wing across the whole
length of the garden elevation. The single-
storeyed extension, with a canted bay at
each end, was roofed with alternating wide
and narrow gables. In 1908 the house was
again enlarged; Nash's design was raised in
facsimile and the ends extended, with
another storey inserted underneath.

G. F. Prosser, *Select Illustrations of Hampshire*, 1833

130

YNYSLAS COTTAGE

Glyncorrwg, Glamorgan

c.1810

Ynyslas Cottage (c.1810) had wide eaves, diagonal chimney stacks and a curved end wall with brash duality in its fenestration – all features used by Nash, although there is no evidence to support such an attribution. The house was demolished in 1963.

T. Lloyd, *The Lost Houses of Wales*, 1986

131

GWERNANT

Trodeyraur, Cardiganshire

Before 1811

Gwernant resembles Harpton Court (No. 93). There is no firm evidence that Nash designed the house.

T. Lloyd, *The Lost Houses of Wales*, 1986

132

LOUGH CUTRA CASTLE

Gort, County Galway

1811

On seeing East Cowes Castle in 1811, Charles Vereker, MP, commissioned Nash to build him a castle like it. Superbly sited by the lough, Lough Cutra Castle stands on a terrace cut out of the hillside. The plan is of Nash's gallery type. The castle is entered on one side, with the dining-room and the octagonal drawing-room opposite,

Ynyslas Cottage, early 1900s (Collection T. Lloyd)

overlooking the lough; the stair occupies the round tower. On the east side the detached service wing and stables are built around open courts. Two gates and lodges still exist, Limerick with hexagonal towers and arched gateway, and Lismore with square tower and iron gates bearing the military ornaments of the later owner, Lord Gort. In Victorian times Crace and Son of London refurbished the interiors, and massive additions were made to the house: these have recently been removed.

B. de Breffny, *Castles of Ireland*, 1977

OPPOSITE BELOW
Lough Cutra: the
service courtyard and
gateway to the castle
front
RIGHT
The entrance front,
with the lough beyond
BELOW
Lismore Lodge
BELOW RIGHT
Limerick Lodge

133

BLAISE HAMLET
Henbury, Gloucestershire
1810–1811

The group of cottages was built by J. S. Harford, a Quaker banker, for his retired servants. Nash persuaded him to hide the cottages away in a wooded clearing, giving peace and privacy to its residents. In fact, the opposite effect was achieved, and Blaise Hamlet has been inundated by curious visitors ever since. The ten cottages are all different and are placed in a deceptively simple layout. The group is entered from one corner and fresh vistas are brought into view the further one advances. The seclusion and background forest have gone, but the charm of Nash's humane creation remains. Pevsner summed it up as 'the *ne plus ultra*' of the Picturesque movement.

N. Pevsner, *Buildings of England: North Somerset and Bristol*, 1958
Summerson 1980

Dial Cottage, with sundial and pump

Diamond Cottage, with Vine Cottage in the distance

PLAN OF BLAISE HAMLET

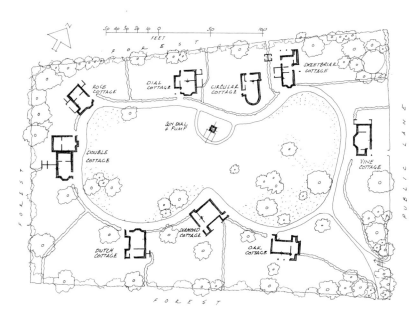

RIGHT
(left to right) Double
Cottage, Rose
Cottage, Dial Cottage
and Circular Cottage

BELOW
Double Cottage and
Rose Cottage; as one
of the focal points,
Double Cottage has a
white gable and the
tallest chimneys

BELOW RIGHT
Dutch Cottage

ABOVE Blaise Hamlet: Sweetbriar Cottage
ABOVE RIGHT Oak Cottage, with the entrance
to the hamlet behind

RIGHT Vine Cottage, in the distance, is the only
cottage visible from the road
BELOW Circular Cottage

134

HOPTON COURT

Hopton Wafers, Shropshire
1811

Hopton Court was originally a two-storey Georgian house in brick. Nash added an extra floor for Thomas Botfield and dressed the house with a pediment, two Ionic porches and canted bays. The walls, possibly stuccoed by Nash, are now rendered. Burke comments that the principal rooms, though small, were perfectly adapted to the requirements of

RIGHT Hopton Court: Nash added the top storey and the two porches
BELOW Nash's garden porch and canted bay window

their inmates. Loudon includes a plate showing the house castellated, and notes that this alternative treatment was not carried out.

J. C. Loudon (ed.), *The Landscape Gardening and Landscape Architecture of the late Humphry Repton, Esq*, 1840
J. B. Burke, *A Visitation of Seats and Arms*, i, 1852

135

HARFORDS BANK

Bristol
1811

The bank, at 35 Corn Street, was probably designed by Nash for J. S. Harford of Blaise Castle. It had a simple façade of three plain windows high above the pavement. Below them the wall was rusticated and pierced only by a single,

Harfords Bank: the door case, pediments and lower halves of the windows are later additions

plain door. The present elevational adornments were added in 1877. It is possible that the internal decorations to the Banking Hall and the glazed ceiling dome are original.

A. Gomme, M. Janner and B. Little, *Bristol*, 1979

ALBANY STREET
Regent's Park, London
1811

BELOW
Albany Street
(foreground) and
Chester Gate

Albany Street was laid out by Nash along the line of an earlier farm track. It divided the Park terraces from the service area surrounding the canal basin. Roadworks

RIGHT
206 Albany Street

began in 1811. The first two leases taken were both for replacement public houses: the Jew's Harp (now demolished) and the Queen's Head (extant). The new cavalry barracks and Nash's Ophthalmic Hospital faced the backs of the eastern Park terraces. Middle-class terraces occupied both ends of the street, with a shopping district in between. Nash's Park Village West filled in to the north.

A. Saunders, *Regent's Park*, 1969

The Royal Lodge: (BELOW RIGHT) 'Entrance Front of His Majesty's Cottage'; (BOTTOM RIGHT) 'His Majesty's Cottage as seen from the Lawn'. Engravings after Delamotte, from R. Ackermann's *Repository of Arts*, 1824

THE ROYAL LODGE
Windsor Great Park, Berkshire
1811–1820

The Treasury decided that the conversion of Cumberland Lodge to a temporary residence for the Prince Regent was uneconomical. Instead a nearby cottage,

31–33 Albany Street: the back elevation is also numbered 9 and 10 St Andrew's Place and carries the Corinthian portico

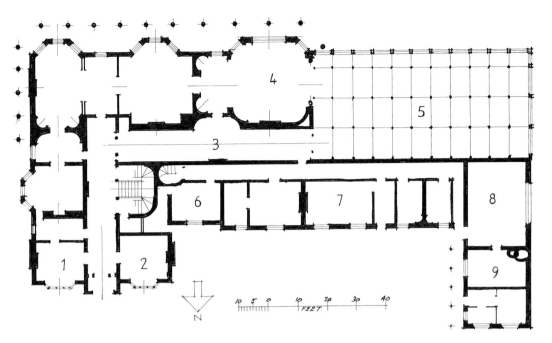

THE COUNTY CLUB
Newport, Isle of Wight
1811

Originally built as a museum and reading room, this later became the County Club. It was arcaded like the town hall but was more substantially built in Portland stone. It still stands on the corner of the main square in Newport. The shallow bow window in the end elevation is unusual for Nash.

Summerson 1980

GROUND-FLOOR PLAN OF THE ROYAL LODGE. Nash added the numbered rooms and decorated the others

1 Parlour	6 Housekeeper
2 Waiting-room	7 Servants' hall
3 Gallery	8 Kitchen
4 Eating-room	9 Scullery
5 Conservatory	

BELOW The County Club in Newport

Lower Lodge, was to be used. They made available £2,750 to cover the cost of the repairs and alterations. The final cost rose to £35,243, with a further £17,000 required for the furnishings. The Royal Lodge ended up as a very large building dressed as a *cottage orné*, with thatched roofs and verandas, dormer windows, a forest of tall chimneys, and a cast-iron conservatory. In the grounds a dairy and icehouse were built. Nash surrounded the whole with carefully placed groves and clumps of trees to reduce the apparent size. In 1823 Nash's building disappeared, when Wyatville enlarged and altered the Lodge.

O. Morshead, *George IV and the Royal Lodge*, 1965

139
THE REGENT'S CANAL
London
1811–1820

Between 1805 and 1810 the canal system reached London at Paddington, and the first docks were built on the Isle of Dogs. The need to connect the two systems was obvious, and, as the proposed route crossed Regent's Park, Nash was interested when approached by Thomas Homer, the promoter of the new linking canal. After

RIGHT Camden Lock and lock-keeper's cottage
BELOW Macclesfield Bridge over Regent's Canal

inspecting and amending the route, Nash took over the whole enterprise. He prepared a report, estimated the cost at £280,000 and set about raising the money. In 1811 the plans were laid before Parliament, receiving the Royal Assent in the same year; by 1820 the canal had been completed at a cost of over £500,000. This was Nash the entrepreneur – overcoming all obstacles, including shortage of money, and even, for a short time, financing the whole scheme himself.

H. Spencer, *London's Canals*, 1976

Nanteos: the proposed garden elevation

The front elevation and cross-section of the
gardener's house, also designed as a *point de vue*

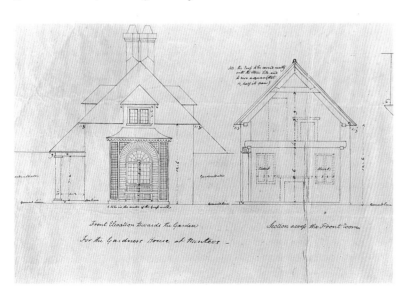

Front Elevation towards the Garden

Section across the Front Room

For the Gardeners House at Nanteos

140

NANTEOS
Near Aberystwyth, Cardiganshire
After 1811

Dr Nigel Temple recently discovered the
previously unsuspected association of Nash
and George Repton with Nanteos: designs
for five estate buildings are contained
amongst the Nanteos papers, now in the
National Library of Wales. The buildings,
which do not appear to have been built,
are: a gardener's house, a dairy and
icehouse, Keeper's Cottage, an entrance
lodge on the Aberystwyth Road, and an
entrance lodge on the Devil's Bridge Road.
Also among the papers are unsigned and
undated drawings for the enlargement of
the house itself. No documentary evidence

Nanteos: the lodge on the Devil's Bridge Road

The lodge on the Aberystwyth Road

The dairy and icehouse

Keeper's Cottage

has yet been found, but on stylistic grounds
they could be attributed to Nash and
George Repton. One drawing is
watermarked 1811.

N. Temple, *Society of Cymmrodorion*, 1985

SHANE'S CASTLE
Randalstown, County Antrim
*c.*1812–1816

Nash was probably involved with proposed alterations to the eighteenth-century castle for the second Viscount O'Neill as early as 1803. Building work to Nash's design began in about 1812 and had only risen to just above ground level when the disastrous fire of 1816 destroyed everything except for Nash's thirteen-bay camellia house and the towered and battlemented terrace. All work on Nash's extensions was abandoned.

Ulster Architectural Heritage Society, *West Antrim*, 1970

BELOW Shane's Castle: the sea walls and turrets were built by Nash

ABOVE The Highgate Archway from the south. Aquatint after A. Pugin

141

HIGHGATE ARCHWAY
Holloway, London
1812

To avoid the long drag up Highgate Hill it was proposed that the Great North Road be tunnelled through it. Work began in 1812, but after only 130 feet had been dug, the tunnel – possibly designed by Nash – collapsed. Nash then advised substituting a cutting for the tunnel, with a viaduct to carry Hornsey Lane across it. The design was based on a Roman aqueduct. The viaduct served its purpose and survived until the road was widened in 1897.

Summerson 1980

Shane's Castle: Nash's camellia house is on the left

Reconstruction of an early Nash design for Shane's Castle. Oil painting by Felix Kelly. Collection The Lord O'Neill

The Gothic dining-room in Carlton House, from W. H. Pyne, *The History of the Royal Residences*, 1819

143

CARLTON HOUSE
St James's, London
1812–1814

In 1802 Henry Holland withdrew from his commission to design Carlton House, and further new works were carried out by Thomas Hopper, who added the Gothic conservatory at the west end of the lower floor. James Wyatt was then instructed to convert the adjacent rooms. On his death Nash completed the conversion and decorated the Corinthian dining-room and drawing-room and the Gothic library. At the eastern end the new Gothic dining-room was built to his design. To celebrate Wellington's victories and 100 years of the Hanoverian succession in 1814, a grand fête was held in the grounds of Carlton House, for which Nash erected a complex of temporary buildings that included a polygonal ballroom with a tented roof (see No. 163), a design soon to be seen again at the Royal Pavilion in Brighton.

At one time the Prince Regent considered rebuilding Carlton House. Nash produced two designs, Gothic and Classical, but the Treasury refused to supply the finance.

King's Works, vi, 1973
W. H. Pyne, *The History of the Royal Residences*, 1819

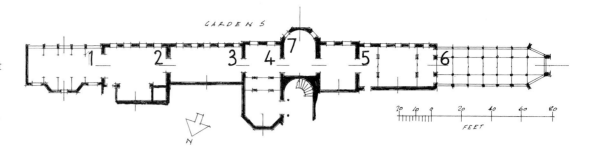

LOWER GROUND-FLOOR PLAN OF
CARLTON HOUSE

1 Gothic dining-room	4 Ante-room
2 Drawing-room	5 Dining-room
3 Library	6 Conservatory
	7 Bow room

Nash's proposed designs for Carlton House: (ABOVE) his Gothic design, seen from St James's Park, and (BELOW) his classical design, seen from Waterloo Place (Royal Collection, St James's Palace)

144
REGENT'S PARK MARKETS
London
1812–1826

Nash allocated the eastern area of Regent's Park to the three market squares of York, Cumberland and Clarence (Nos 145, 184 and 225). The linked squares reached down to the New (Marylebone) Road, enabling produce which had been carried on the Regent's Canal from the Midlands to be distributed by road in London. These markets were built mainly by small builders and were lined with working-class houses set in light, airy surroundings. Nash had a regard for the poorer classes, and provided them when he could with decent, affordable houses. In 1941 the whole area was badly damaged by bombing; the canal was filled in and the markets cleared. Their only memorial is the retention of the original Hanoverian street names.

A. Saunders, *Regent's Park*, 1969

York Market was never used as a market.
Photograph by J. Summerson, c.1936

Park Crescent, from Marylebone Road

146

PARK CRESCENT

Regent's Park, London
1812 and 1819–1821

Nash ended his grand route northwards from Carlton House with a short extension of Portland Place before opening into the Crescent. His elegant terraces, with Ionic colonnades set against the cool stuccoed façades, bring the Adam brothers' brick and stucco elevations of Portland Place to a satisfactory conclusion. Charles Mayor began building the Crescent in 1812, going bankrupt after six houses had been started. Six years passed before three builders (William Richardson, Samuel Baxter and Henry Peto) took over and completed the

145

YORK MARKET

Regent's Park, London
1812–1823

Originally allocated by Nash as the meat market, by the time York Market was completed its use had been changed to housing and its name to Munster Square. The stuccoed terraces were an unusual design, with a *piano nobile* and a frieze of square windows over. The architectural effect of this delightful square was summed up in a letter to Sir John Summerson by a Polish officer living locally during the Second World War: '. . . it gives the peculiar feeling of an immense room, with the skies as the roof: the same feeling you have in the evening on the Piazza San Marco in Venice: a ball room.' The market was demolished in 1951 and replaced by council housing.

Survey of London, xxi, 1949

ABOVE The sweep of Park Crescent, with Portland Place on the left
RIGHT Park Crescent, showing its Portland Place façade

twenty-nine houses. Park Crescent was badly damaged during the Second World War; it was then demolished and rebuilt with modern office buildings behind facsimile elevations. The redundant entrances and area bridges have been omitted.

Elmes, *Metropolitan Improvements*, 1827
A. Saunders, *Regent's Park*, 1969

147

LANGHAM HOUSE
Portland Place, London
1813–1815

In 1812, Foley House closed the southern end of Portland Place, an obstacle to Nash's New Street. Lord Foley, a client of Nash's at Witley Court (No. 86), in a complicated negotiation sold the house and grounds to Nash for £70,000. On the condition that he would be the architect for a new house, Nash then sold part of it to Sir John Langham, MP, in 1813, and began building Langham House. Shortly after it was finished the line of the New Street was moved, bringing it uncomfortably close to Langham's house; to protect his property Langham was forced to buy a further piece of land from Nash. The remaining land was sold to the Crown for the New Street. The south front of the stuccoed house carried an Ionic colonnade; on the eastern side a canted bay and pedimented pavilion faced the newly acquired garden, making almost a village scene of church, big house and cluster of smaller Nash houses set around with trees and lawns.

Summerson 1980

ABOVE The east front of Langham House and (BELOW) the south, or garden, front. Artist unknown

RHEOLA

Near Neath, Glamorgan

1812–1829

John Edwards sen. (1738–1818) bought the estate of Rheola in about 1800, and Nash was later asked to enlarge the existing cottage, while retaining its appearance. Nash did this by extending it southwards and building a wing to the east to house the new suite of drawing-room, ante-room and dining-room, behind which was the library. Another service wing, with an attached dairy, was added to enclose the kitchen court. The drawing in George Repton's Brighton Sketchbook is probably a survey of

ABOVE
The kitchen wing can be seen behind the cedar tree

LEFT
Rheola House from the garden

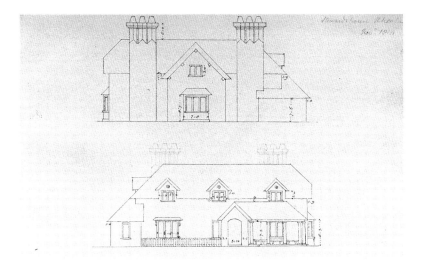

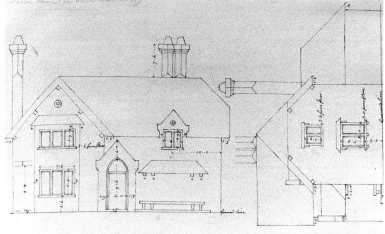

Rheola: Steward's House. Drawing by George Repton (Art Gallery and Museums, Brighton)

Farmhouse, now possibly incorporated in the lodge. Drawing by George Repton (Art Gallery and Museums, Brighton)

the earlier cottage. Other buildings for Edwards and his son – also John (1772–1833), who inherited on his father's death and changed his name to Vaughan – were:

Steward's House, now known as Brynawel, dated 1818 by Repton. Although many Nash features have been altered or removed it still strongly resembles Repton's sketches.

Bachelor's Hall, with false bridge in foreground, by Thomas Hornor, 1816–20. British Museum, London

Farmhouse, possibly incorporated in Rheola Lodge, which was partly reconstructed after the Neath to Merthyr Tydfil road was put in.

Bachelor's Hall, a decorative cottage built on the hillside to attract the eye both on entering the estate and from the house. Hornor described it as 'much too good for an anchorite and indeed rather more

comfortable than most bachelors deserve'. It has many of Nash's details, as the painting by Thomas Hornor of between 1816 and 1820 shows.

N. Temple, *Society of Cymmrodorion*, 1985

Rheola: the present lodge, possibly Nash's farmhouse much altered

St Mildred's after Nash's alterations, overlooking the Medina

149
ST MILDRED'S CHURCH
Whippingham, Isle of Wight
1813

The old church at Whippingham consisted of a chancel, nave and tower. Nash added two transepts, with galleries reached by external covered stairs, and a schoolroom at the foot of the tower. Externally he removed the tower's pitched roof and added a timber spire and pinnacled buttresses; he cut belfry openings and presumably installed bells. The church survived until 1824–5, when it was replaced by the present Victorian one. The church has two fonts: the earlier one, in limestone, has a plain head with a sunken bowl, supported by a fluted Doric column on a stone base. It can be attributed to Nash, as George Repton's RIBA Sketchbook shows three alternatives, one of which corresponds with the existing one. The Brighton Sketchbook shows the construction of the church spire, which is probably the one still standing.

N. Temple, *IOW Society*, 1988

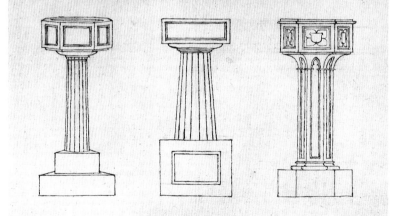

Alternative designs for the font in St Mildred's (the centre one was chosen), from George Repton's RIBA Sketchbook

150

TRAFALGAR SQUARE
London
1813–1830

In 1813 John Fordyce deemed it necessary to link the New (Regent) Street with Charing Cross; this meant demolishing the

Royal stables and their surroundings. Nash formed the irregular square with Smirke's new College of Physicians (now incorporated in Canada House) on the western side and Cockspur Street on the southern. Pall Mall was extended into the square, as was St Martin's Lane, with the church of St Martin-in-the-Fields exposed to view. The north side was allocated to the National Gallery. For the east, Nash

proposed erecting public buildings, but in fact speculative housing went up. The centre of the square was given to a new building for the Royal Academy of Arts, which was not built. The square was named Trafalgar Square in 1835.

See plan on p.287.

Summerson 1980

Trafalgar Square, with (from left) the corner of the College of Physicians, the National Gallery and the Church of St Martin-in-the-Fields

151

WESTOVER

Calbourne, Isle of Wight
1813–1815

When visited in 1984, the house contained a watercolour painting showing the original Georgian house built in brick. Neither bridge nor entrance lodge existed at that time, and the drive approached the southern corner of the house. For the owner, Sir Leonard Holmes (later Lord Holmes), Nash added the Doric entrance porch flanked by shallow bow windows (the two right-hand bays are a later extension). The south elevation was given a columned porch and canopied verandas. Both fronts were decorated with pediments and coated with stucco. At about the same time, the drive was moved to the northern corner, the stream was crossed by a new ornamental bridge, and an octagonal lodge was built in rubble and flints. Internally the plain decorations are classical. The house has a nice curved stair lit by an overhead lantern. Another lodge to the north-west is in the same style and has retained its thatched roof. Temple refers to a letter from Nash to Sir Leonard dated 9 December 1813 dealing with specifications and accounts for Westover.

N. Temple, *IOW Society*, 1988

The south front of Westover: the dome behind the pediment lights the staircase; the balustrade to the first-floor balcony is a recent replacement

OPPOSITE The entrance front of Westover (the two right-hand bays are later)

BELOW LEFT The west lodge at Westover
BELOW The main entrance and lodge at Westover

152

GREEN PARK

London
1814

Celebrations to mark a century of
Hanoverian rule took place in Hyde Park,
St James's Park and Green Park. All three
lay in Nash's 'district' at the Board of
Works, making him responsible for the
festival buildings. In Green Park, the
spectacle consisted of a Gothic castle
which, after a firework display and artillery
fire, disappeared behind a cloud of smoke
to re-emerge as the Temple of Concord.
The upper part of the temple, devised by
Sir William Congreve, revolved
mechanically to reveal paintings of the

ABOVE The Temple of Concord, in Green Park,
1814. Artist unknown

apotheosis of the Prince Regent and the
Triumph of England.

Summerson 1980
B. Weinreb and C. Hibbert (eds), *The London
Encyclopedia*, 1983

BELOW Hill Grove. Oil painting by Felix Kelly,
1979. Collection Lady West

153

HILL GROVE

Bembridge, Isle of Wight
1814

Hill Grove, built for the Earl of Ducie, had
fine views of the Solent and has been
described as the best early nineteenth-
century classical house on the island. It was
square in plan, with Doric pilasters at the
corners. The north front had a canted bay
with paired Ionic columns at each side,

surmounted by a dome; on the west side a shallow curved bow rose full height. The service wing to the east was separated from the house by a deep recess. Listed as a Grade II building, it had been stripped of all its features by 1967 and now survives as a mutilated shell.

Davis 1966

154
THE GUILDHALL
Newport, Isle of Wight
1814

The Guildhall was designed by Nash with the Council Chamber and Town Hall on the first floor and the town market at street level. It is a symmetrical building in stucco, with Ionic columns above the arcaded ground floor. The clock tower was added to commemorate Queen Victoria's Jubilee. Nash was elected a free burgess of Newport for his services.

Summerson 1980

155
CUMBERLAND LODGE
Windsor Great Park, Berkshire
1814

Nash carried out general repairs, costing £2,500, to Cumberland (or Great) Lodge. It was largely rebuilt in 1869 and again in 1912.

King's Works, vi, 1973

156
NEWMARKET PALACE
Newmarket, Suffolk
1814–1819

The Palace had been neglected during the second half of the eighteenth century until the Prince Regent, who loved horse-racing, had Nash prepare plans for general rebuilding. The plans were not carried out and the old buildings were eventually demolished. In a report to the Commissioners of Woods, Forests and Land Revenues on works carried out at Kensington Palace, dated April 1819, Nash applied for the plans of Newmarket Palace to be sent to him.

Works 19/16/1 and 2, Public Record Office, Kew
King's Works, vi, 1973

The Guildhall, Newport: the clock tower was rudely inserted to commemorate Queen Victoria's Jubilee

157
CRANBOURNE LODGE
Windsor Great Park, Berkshire
1814 and 1816

Cranbourne Lodge was one of the Royal houses in Windsor Great Park. Nash carried out repairs and lived there for a short while in 1814, when one of his guests was Benjamin West, President of the Royal Academy. In 1816 Nash was ordered by the Prince Regent to make plans for accommodating the Hunt. He appears to have done nothing about it and the idea was forgotten.

King's Works, vi, 1973

The White Lodge: the single-storey front, *porte-cochère* and curved wings were added by Wyatt and Nash

158

THE WHITE LODGE

Richmond Park, Surrey
1814

George III granted the Lodge to Lord Sidmouth in 1801. James Wyatt was instructed in 1806 by the Department of Woods and Forests to link the main house, built by Lord Pembroke and Robert Morris in about 1737, to the free-standing pavilions built by Stephen Wright in 1760–7. This he proposed to do by adding two quadrant corridors. Building began, and after Wyatt's death in 1813 it was completed by Nash.

King's Works, vi, 1973

White Hall: each of the three main elevations was given a different central feature

159

WHITE HALL
Winestead, Yorkshire
1814–1815

White Hall was built for Arthur Maister at the same time as nearby Wood Hall (No. 162) was built for his younger brother, and there are many similar internal details. The entrance front, with recessed centre, projecting porch and round-headed ground-floor windows, is like that at Llanaeron (No. 28), Southgate Grove (No. 51), and the Warrens (No. 65). The plan also resembles the one of Southgate. The house features Nash's favourite S-shaped balusters to the stairs, which are lit by an early example of a window with cast-iron sashes. The south elevation is dominated by a large bow window, and the eastern one by a pediment.

J. Cornforth, 'Winestead, Yorkshire', *Country Life*, 11 September 1980

160

LANGHAM PLACE
London
1814–1826

The 1814 alteration to the line of the new Regent Street to avoid Cavendish Square resulted in a double curve joining Portland Place to Regent Street. Foley House, at the southern end of Portland Place, was bought and demolished by Nash (see No. 147). On the west side he built a block of four houses; next to these were the gardens of Langham House and more stuccoed houses. The east side, after Portland Place, began with three Nash houses, next to which was All Souls Church, rising high above its

ABOVE White Hall: the recessed centre and projecting porch were often used by Nash

BELOW The west side of Langham Place, with All Souls Church on the right. Engraving by S. Owen after T. H. Shepherd for Elmes, *Metropolitan Improvements*, 1827

surroundings, and finally the London Carriage Repository. Except for All Souls, everything has been demolished.

Elmes, *Metropolitan Improvements*, 1827
J. Tallis, *Street Views of London*, 1838–40

OPPOSITE
ABOVE LEFT St James's Park before Nash's remodelling, looking towards Horse Guards (published by R. Harvell and Son, 1821)
ABOVE RIGHT The pagoda and bridge, built as part of the 1814 celebrations. Engraving by Rawle after J. P. Neale for *The Beauties of England and Wales*
BELOW The straight canal was replaced by Nash's picturesque lake

161

ST JAMES'S PARK
London
1814–1827

St James's is London's oldest royal park, remodelled under Charles II, when a canal was added on advice attributed to Le Nôtre. As part of the 1814 centenary celebrations of George I's accession, Nash built an eight-storeyed pagoda on an arched bridge across the canal. During the firework display the pagoda burnt down. In 1827 the Treasury ordered improvements to St James's Park. Nash, recalling an earlier suggestion of Capability Brown's, replaced the canal with a serpentine lake and planted groves and clumps of trees and shrubs. The Mall was widened with a carriageway centred on Buckingham House. Two of Nash's Carlton House Terraces were built; a third, together with his proposed buildings along Birdcage Walk, was abandoned.

Summerson 1980

ABOVE Some of the plane trees were planted by Nash's gardener
BELOW At the head of the lake is Buckingham Palace

162
WOOD HALL
Ellerby, Yorkshire
1814–1815

Wood Hall was built for Henry William Maister, the younger brother of Arthur Maister of nearby White Hall, also attributed to Nash. It is one of the Cronkhill series (see No. 72), with a similar Claudean tower, wide eaves with paired brackets, and oval frieze windows. The brickwork is here left exposed. Minor alterations made in around 1862 possibly account for the window hoods, which are out of keeping. The interiors are quite plain except for the Ionic-screened, rounded end to the dining-room. For financial

RIGHT Wood Hall, one of the Claudean series
BELOW The left-hand wing and the porch are later additions

reasons Henry Maister had to sell the house only five years after it was built, and it is from the advertisement of the sale that the attribution to Nash is made.

N. Pevsner, *The Buildings of England: Yorkshire, The East Riding*, 1978

163
THE ROTUNDA
Woolwich, Kent
1814 and 1820

After the celebrations at Carlton House in 1814 to mark the Treaty of Paris, the Prince Regent presented one of Nash's grand tented buildings to The Royal

JESUS COLLEGE
Oxford
1815

In 1815 Nash was asked to advise on the state of the College roofs. In the first quadrangle he reconstructed and reslated them, moved the upper windows to align with the lower ones and crenellated the walls. The inner quadrangle buildings were also reroofed and reslated, with the ogee pediments retained. The Principal's lodging was given a new decorative plaster ceiling at the same time, probably by Nash. The installation of the College clock was

The Rotunda: after the removal to Woolwich, Nash added the brick perimeter wall

BELOW The former ballroom of the Rotunda is now used as the Royal Artillery Museum

Regiment of Artillery for use as a museum. It was moved to Woolwich in May 1820. To make it a permanent building Nash reconstructed the 24-sided perimeter wall in brick, covered the outer layer of oiled cloth roofing with lead sheeting and added the central Doric column to take the additional weight. Except for the replacement of the lead roof in 1970, the Rotunda is as Nash left it.

King's Works, vi, 1973

ABOVE The inner quadrangle of Jesus College:
the canted bay window on the right was possibly
added by Nash

RIGHT The first quadrangle of Jesus College,
with the battlements and clock added by Nash

part of his work. Nash also gave advice
regarding College properties in London,
and in lieu of his fee the College
commissioned Sir Thomas Lawrence to
paint his portrait, which still hangs in the
Hall (see p.12).

J. Ingram, *Memorials of Oxford*, iii, 1837

RIGHT
The east front of the
Royal Pavilion
BELOW
The South Gate, in
Nash's time

165

THE ROYAL PAVILION

Brighton, Sussex
1815–1822

The Royal Pavilion was originally a
farmhouse; it was converted and enlarged
by Henry Holland in 1786 into a marine
pavilion for the Prince of Wales. It was
given Chinese interiors in 1802, and stables
in an Indian style were added in 1804 by

201

William Porden. Porden also made proposals for a Chinese pavilion, and Humphry Repton for an Indian one. Nash was given the task of enlarging and transforming Holland's Palladian villa into an Eastern pleasure pavilion. Work began in 1815, with the house being doubled in width and the typical Nash gallery inserted; 1816 saw the addition of new offices and the great kitchen, as well as the dining-room and music-room with their tented roofs. In 1818 Holland's dome was replaced by the large Indian one, and lesser domes and minarets were added. Between 1820 and 1822 the firm of John Crace and

The Royal Pavilion: (LEFT) the Prince Regent's apartments lay behind the north façade; (BELOW LEFT) the King's Library; (BELOW) the cast-iron frame supporting the dome and minarets

Son carried out the internal decorations to Nash's directive and under the auspices of the Prince Regent, now George IV. The conversion of the Castle Inn ballroom into the Royal Chapel completed the reconstruction in 1823. The grounds were landscaped by Nash and the South Lodge was built. After the King's death and Nash's retirement, William IV consulted Nash about the unbuilt North Gate. Joseph Good, who was now architect to the Pavilion, carried out the work, probably using an earlier Nash design.

The pavilion, besides being dressed in a light-hearted mixture of every Oriental, Gothic and classical style, also contained technical innovations. Nash's penchant for cast iron here pioneered early framed structures and made possible the construction of the complicated domes and minarets; his kitchen is a masterpiece of service engineering, and the King's bathroom was provided with five different means of bathing.

J. Dinkel, *The Royal Pavilion, Brighton*, 1983

BELOW The North Gate of the Royal Pavilion
BELOW RIGHT The entrance, with *porte-cochère*

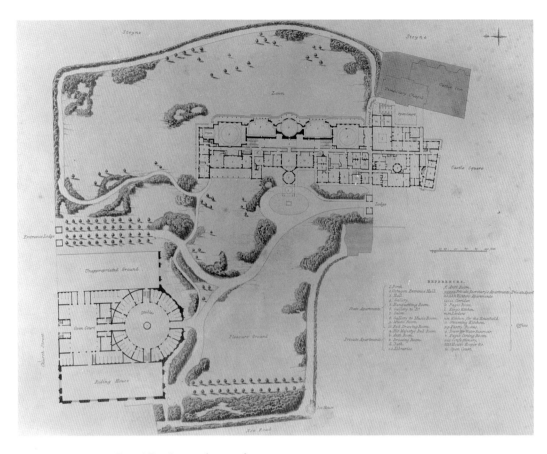

ABOVE Plan of the Royal Pavilion and grounds, from Nash's *Views of the Royal Pavilion*, 1826

Waterloo Place, looking north: the spaciousness is sadly missing from the later rebuilding

BELOW Nash's design for the fountain in Waterloo Place (Public Record Office)

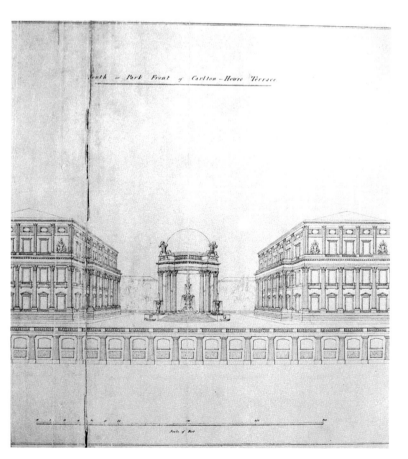

BELOW As an alternative, Nash designed a ramp from Waterloo Place to St James's Park (Public Record Office)

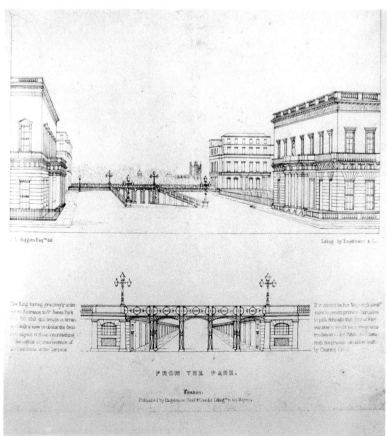

WATERLOO PLACE
St James's, London
1816–1828

When Carlton House, the terminal feature of Regent Street, was demolished in 1825, Nash replaced it with the two Carlton House Terraces. These were divided by the extension of Waterloo Place in order to give a prospect of St James's Park, with a circular domed temple containing a fountain in the foreground. The temple was unacceptable to the authorities and was replaced by the present flight of steps. The Duke of York's Column, designed by Benjamin Dean Wyatt, was erected in 1833. In 1816 Nash had proposed just such

Two proposed designs for the Wellington Column (Sir John Soane's Museum, London)

a column to commemorate the Duke of Wellington's victories. Two of the designs are in the Soane Museum. In the 1835 sale of Nash's drawings, one was described as 'a design for a fountain opposite Buckingham Palace'; this could actually have been the one for Waterloo Place, as the layout of St James's Park and the Palace at that time did not readily lend itself to such a feature.

Summerson 1980
Survey of London, xx, 1940

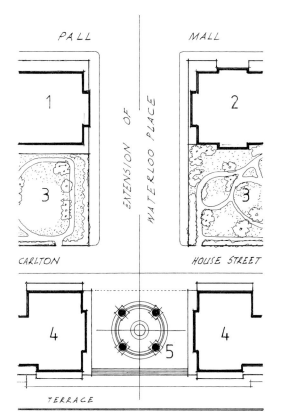

PLAN OF THE EXTENSION OF WATERLOO PLACE. Based on drawing from Nash's office, c.1828

1 Athenaeum Club
2 United Service Club
3 Public gardens
4 Carlton House Terraces
5 Temple and fountain

ABOVE The King's Opera House, Haymarket. Engraving by M. Fox after T. H. Shepherd for Elmes, *Metropolitan Improvements*, 1827

BELOW The Haymarket elevation and ground-plan. Drawing by A. Pugin for *Illustrations of the Public Buildings of London*, 1825 (RIBA)
BELOW RIGHT The northern entrance to the Royal Opera Arcade

THE KING'S OPERA HOUSE
Haymarket, London
1816–1818

Vanbrugh's original theatre (renamed the King's in 1714) burnt down and was rebuilt in 1789 by Novosielski, for an audience of 3,300; a concert hall was soon added. After Nash had widened Pall Mall and extended Charles Street, the Crown Lessee, Charles Holloway, commissioned him and George Repton to complete the street elevations, which had been left unfinished for lack of money. Pavements were arcaded, shops and houses were built on three sides, and the Royal Opera Arcade was built on the fourth, where it still stands. Under Queen Victoria, the King's was renamed Her Majesty's Royal Italian Opera House. It burnt down in 1867, was rebuilt in 1869 and was demolished in 1891. The present theatre, Her Majesty's, designed by C. J. Phipps, was opened in 1893.

D. Nalbach, *The King's Theatre*, 1972

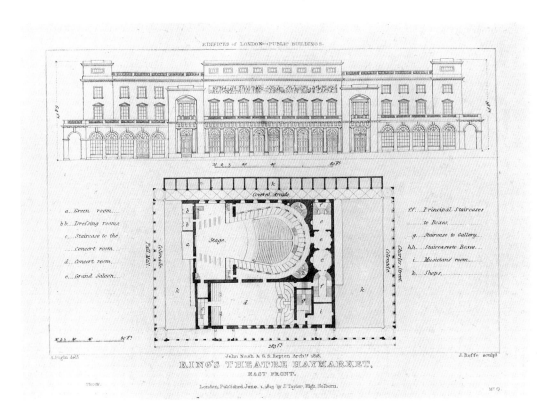

ABOVE The elevation to Pall Mall (the left-hand arch leads to
the Royal Opera Arcade), from George Repton's RIBA Sketchbook

BELOW LEFT The Arcade
BELOW A typical shop in the Arcade; all have some glazing bars missing

168

TYNAN ABBEY

County Armagh

*c.*1816

The Reverend James Stronge acquired the estate by marriage to the heiress Eleanor Manson in 1711. Tynan Abbey was built by him in 1750 on the site of an older house, and in about 1820 it was enlarged by Sir James Stronge, the second baronet.

Prior to this some work must have been carried out, as a Mrs Calvert, the mother-in-law of Sir James's son, recorded in 1816 that the house was 'devoid of doors and windows'. Three watercolour paintings, possibly dating from around 1812, show the elevations of an unexecuted design for a U-shaped house to be built around three sides of a courtyard. Mr J. A. K. Dean has pointed out that the design is in the style of Nash and is probably by him, as during this period Nash was working on, and visiting, nearby Caledon House (No. 116),

less than a mile away, and that after the abandonment of this scheme he was probably responsible for the work of about 1820, in a similar style. Internally the entrance-hall had Gothic fan-and-pendant vaulting like that at Longner (No. 77). Further alterations were made between 1850 and 1870.

J. B. Burke, *A Visitation of Seats and Arms*, 1855
M. Bence-Jones, *Burke's Guide to Country Houses, Volume I: Ireland*, 1978

ABOVE LEFT
Tynan Abbey:
the south front.
Watercolour by
an unknown artist,
*c.*1812
ABOVE RIGHT
The main entrance,
in the courtyard.
Watercolour by
an unknown artist,
*c.*1812

RIGHT
The battlemented
entrance and
screen wall

169

ST JAMES'S PALACE

London

1816–1829

Nash, in his official role of Attached Architect, was responsible for the upkeep of St James's Palace. He made his first report in 1816, advising that the building was fit only for demolition. This advice was repeated every year until 1821, when the Board of Works ordered him to refurbish the State rooms and make good the damage caused by the fire of 1809; this entailed rebuilding the south-east corner of the Palace and part of Priory Court. The work was completed in 1824 at a cost of over £60,000. The King had, as usual, constantly changed his mind and Nash had carried out his wishes without the formality of obtaining permission from the Board. In 1826 the King decided that Buckingham House should be rebuilt to form his residence and that St James's Palace should be demolished and replaced by a third block of Carlton House Terrace. The demolition of the Palace was firmly vetoed by the Prime Minister, Lord Liverpool. Between 1826 and 1829 Nash enlarged the apartments of the Duke of Cumberland, installed a new water supply to the Palace and carried out repairs to the Chapel Royal.

King's Works, vi, 1973

ABOVE St James's Palace: the tall building behind the chimney stacks is the rebuilt fire-damaged wing

BELOW The Great Stable, on the left, designed by William Kent, was retained in Nash's first proposals. Engraving by H. W. Bond after T. H. Shepherd for Elmes, *Metropolitan Improvements*, 1827

170

THE KING'S MEWS
Charing Cross, London
1816–1824

The King's Mews was surveyed by Nash in 1816. His report recommended demolition of all the Charing Cross buildings comprising the King's Mews except for William Kent's Great Stable of 1732. This building Nash considered could be converted into a new National Gallery. Nash's recommendations were carried out in 1824, the cleared area later becoming known as Trafalgar Square.

King's Works, vi, 1973

171

KENSINGTON PALACE

London
1816–1825

Nash took over the responsibility for the Palace after James Wyatt's death, and in 1816 he made his first survey. He reported general rot and decay, leaking roofs and defective drains. Three years afterwards he supervised some general repairs, including those to the chapel floor. He also recommended the replacement of the decayed portico with a more suitable *porte-cochère*. This was possibly done in 1823–5, although it is considered that the present porch is a twentieth-century replacement.

King's Works, vi, 1973

Gracefield: (ABOVE RIGHT) the entrance front and service wing; (BELOW) the garden front (the conservatory linking the service wing was once an open loggia)

172

GRACEFIELD

Queen's County (now County Laois)
1817

Built for Mrs Kavanagh in the old Queen's County, Gracefield is the only 'Regency' villa Nash built in Ireland. Neale's view shows an earlier, somewhat larger house, with two windows either side of a Gothic porch. Unusual for Nash are the rounded corners to the hipped end, presumably to allow the veranda to sweep round. The garden elevation has the almost obligatory canted bay and a Gothic conservatory screening the service wing, which straggles off to join the stables. For Nash the eaves are rather skimped but still have his paired brackets. Inside, the dining-room and drawing-room open off a generously sized

hall; the upper floor is reached by a single curved flight of stairs. The rebuilt lodge at the entrance to the drive carries a Nash-like chimney pot.

J. P. Neale, *Views of Seats*, 1818–29
J. N. Brewer, *The Beauties of Ireland*, ii, 1826

ABOVE LEFT Gracefield: the main entrance gates and railings, with the rebuilt lodge
ABOVE RIGHT The garden front, before the loggia was closed in. Engraving by J. Barnett after P. Duggan
BELOW Stonelands: the entrance front, showing Nash's idiosyncratic duality of two windows in the central feature

173
STONELANDS
Dawlish, Devonshire
*c.*1817

The plain stuccoed house is attributed to Nash and has his insouciant use of duality over the Doric porch. It was built for the Hoare family of the adjoining Luscombe Castle, possibly as the Dower House. Stonelands was planned with a central core of entrance-hall and staircase-hall, with two reception rooms on each side. The entrance-hall has a shallow, barrel-vaulted and suspended ceiling carried on four Ionic columns. The decorations are otherwise very plain.

T. Edridge, 'A Garden of Fine Trees', *Country Life*, 4 April 1963

ST JAMES'S SQUARE

London
1817–1818 and 1822

This was the first West End square.
Originally laid out for the Earl of St
Albans, shortly after the 1660 Restoration,
it soon became the fashionable address.
From the Square, Wren's St James's
Church, Piccadilly, closes the view to the
north. One hundred and fifty years later,
Nash extended Charles Street to the
Haymarket and closed that vista with his
Theatre Royal. In 1817–18 he revised the
central garden for the Square's Trustees; he
enlarged, squared and replanted the
previous hexagon and installed gas lighting.
In 1822 he erected the Ionic garden shelter,
whose capitals have since been removed
but sadly never replaced.

Survey of London, xxix, 1960
J. Summerson, *Architecture in Britain, 1530–1830*, 1970

The garden shelter in St James's Square:
(ABOVE) as seen from the street; (BELOW
LEFT) with the Ionic capitals missing

THE SWISS COTTAGE

Cahir Park, County Tipperary
1810–1814

Cahir Park was probably built for the eldest
son of the Earl of Glengall. The large
cottage orné, attributed to Nash, stands on
the edge of a bluff overlooking the River
Suir, which it now serves as a fishing
lodge. Inside is a wooden spiral stair; the
living-room walls are still covered with
original French wallpaper showing pictures
of Turkish life, and its window panes are
etched with rural scenes. When visited by
the writer in 1981, the house was being
repaired and restored. Restoration was
completed in 1989. Mark Girouard
considers it to be the finest *cottage orné* in
the world.

B. de Breffny, *The Houses of Ireland*, 1975
M. Girouard, 'The Swiss Cottage, Cahir, Co.
Tipperary', *Country Life*, 26 October 1989

The Swiss Cottage: the long veranda looks down on the river valley

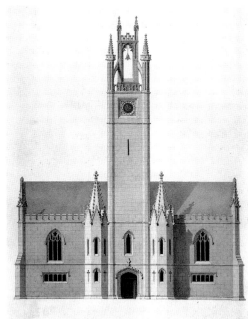

DESIGNS FOR TEN CHURCHES
1818

The Church Commissioners, under the 1818 Act for Building New Churches, invited designs for churches not costing more than £20,000 each. John Soane submitted two, Robert Smirke four and John Nash ten. As might be expected, Nash's were in every style; as Summerson remarks, 'The impression they give is that anybody in the office was allowed to have a go.' None of the sixteen was built. The two London churches that Nash did build – All Souls, Langham Place, and St Mary's, Haggerston – did cost under £20,000 each.

Summerson 1980

ABOVE AND OPPOSITE
Ten designs by Nash's office for
the Church Commissioners (RIBA)

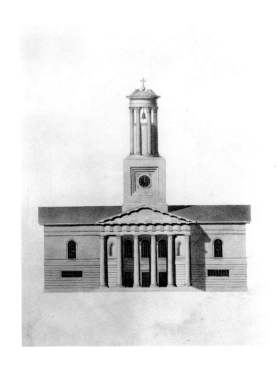

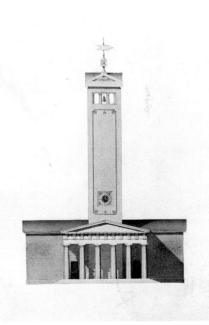

177

EXETER COLLEGE
Oxford
1818

Nash repaired the Hall and built a new entrance porch between two buttresses. Internally, two fireplaces are by him. The works were supervised by George Repton.

J. Ingram, *Memorials of Oxford*, i, 1837

178

BAGSHOT HOUSE
Bagshot, Surrey
1818

As part of his duties at the Office of Woods and Forests, Nash prepared plans for the alterations and repairs required by the Duke of Gloucester when he moved to Bagshot House. The Duke, who was a

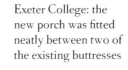

Exeter College: the new porch was fitted neatly between two of the existing buttresses

nephew of George III, had married his first cousin, Princess Mary, a sister of the Prince Regent, in 1816. The cost of the alterations, estimated at £4,000, had risen to over £7,500 by the time the work was completed. The house was demolished soon after 1861.

King's Works, vi, 1973

179

ST PAUL'S CHURCH
Cahir, County Tipperary
1818

St Paul's, the parish church of Cahir, was designed by Nash to replace the pre-Reformation one that was 'in a state of delapidation and too small'. The Gothic Revival church was built on the left bank of the River Suir on a site given by the first Earl of Glengall. The Earl was no doubt responsible for Nash being given the commission, as Nash had just finished the Earl's *cottage orné* in Cahir Park. The church cost £2,307. Internally there are three galleries under a fine plasterwork ceiling,

180

THE OPHTHALMIC HOSPITAL
Regent's Park, London
1818

The Ophthalmic Hospital, Albany Street, was founded by Sir William Adams, who had previously treated soldiers blinded in the Egyptian campaigns at the York Hospital, Chelsea. Nash designed the new hospital on a site he had leased from the Crown, and when the hospital was built he rented the site back to the government. No fee was charged by him for the design. The two wards were placed in the single-storey wings on either side of the centre block, which contained the main entrance. When the hospital closed in 1822 it became a factory for manufacturing steam guns before being largely rebuilt as a distillery for Booth's London Gin. It was demolished in 1968.

Survey of London, xxi, 1949

BELOW
The Ophthalmic Hospital: The Albany Street elevation, 1934

unusual in that they can only be entered from the outside. This is a similar arrangement to that in the earlier St Mildred's on the Isle of Wight (No. 149), where, in adding the galleries to a small nave, Nash was forced into using external entrances. The adjacent schoolhouse is also reputed to be by Nash.

R. B. MacCarthy, leaflet about St Paul's Church, n.d.
M. Girouard, 'The Swiss Cottage, Cahir, Co. Tipperary', *Country Life*, 26 October 1989

St Paul's: (ABOVE) the west end, and (OPPOSITE RIGHT) the gabled side elevation

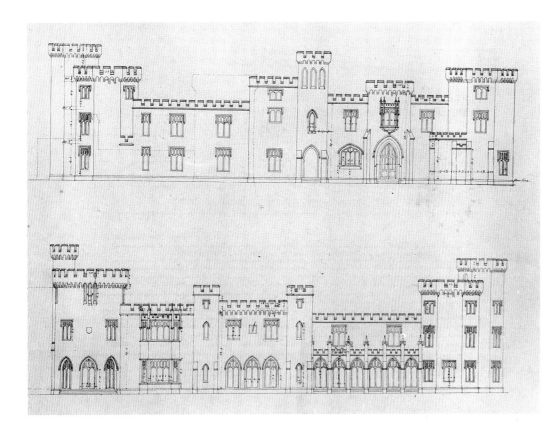

double-height kitchen in a hexagonal tower. After years of neglect all the buildings were demolished in 1960; explosives were needed to demolish them. All that remains of this once splendid residence is the two-storey summer-house by the lake in the woods.

Davis 1960

182

THE STUD HOUSE
Hampton Court Palace, Middlesex
1818 and 1821

In 1815 the Stud House was allocated by the Prince Regent to his Secretary, Sir

Shanbally: (LEFT) north, or entrance, elevation and south elevation; (BELOW) ground-floor plan. Drawings produced in Nash's office (RIBA)

181

SHANBALLY CASTLE
County Tipperary
1818–1819

Shanbally was the last of Nash's four great castles, similar in plan to Aqualate (No. 92), Caerhays (No. 117) and Ravensworth (No. 111) but more compact. It was designed for Viscount Lismore and built in the valley between the Galtee and Knockmealdown Mountains. Cut stone was used for the exteriors; inside there was fine plasterwork with Gothic details. The top-lit gallery was divided from the hall by a great pointed arch, and both were given Gothic fan-vaulted ceilings. The office wing projected in front of the house, screening the services; the outer corner contained the

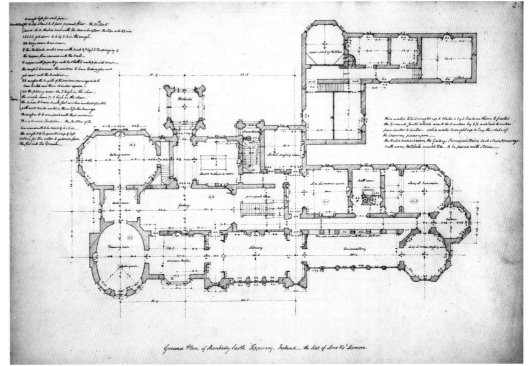

Ground Plan of Shanbally Castle, Tipperary, Ireland — the seat of Lord Vd Lismore.

The Stud House: (LEFT) Nash built his new wing across the back of the house, linking it to the kitchen block with the conservatory; (BELOW) the entrance was moved to the centre of the conservatory

Benjamin Bloomfield, who as the Clerk Marshall was responsible for the supervision of the Royal Stud. Nash's alterations were to provide suitable accommodation for the Prince on his visits to the Stud. Rooms were enlarged and extended to form dining- and drawing-rooms; two bedrooms and a dressing-room were built over them, with two garrets in the roof. The old kitchens were connected to the house by a covered way. The works were carried out in two phases.

King's Works, vi, 1973

183

THE VILLAS
Regent's Park, London
c.1818–1833

Nash's first intention of including fifty-six villas in Regent's Park was considered by the Prime Minister (Spencer Perceval) to be excessive, and the total was reduced to twenty-six. Of these only six (Hertford and South Villas, St John's and St Katharine's Lodges, Holford House and the Holme) were built in the central parkland. Outside this area were Abbey, Gloucester, Hanover and Sussex Lodges, and Albany Cottage; Grove House was sited north of the canal. The villas of Regent's Park were mainly designed by other architects, but all to Nash's approval. The remainder were designed by Nash as villas or small houses adjacent to his terraces (Cumberland, Chester, Hanover, Sussex and York), intended to provide relief from the palatial blocks, and to give movement and picturesque variation to the scene.

See plan on p.158.

E. Samuel, *Villas of Regent's Park and their Owners*, 1959
A. Saunders, *The Regent's Park Villas*, 1981

The lodge to St John's Villa, a surviving outbuilding by John Raffield

BELOW AND OPPOSITE
a St John's Villa, designed by John Raffield. Engraving by T. Barber after T. H. Shepherd for Elmes, *Metropolitan Improvements*, 1827
b St Katharine's Lodge, designed by Ambrose Poynter. Engraving by W. Tombleson after T. H. Shepherd for Elmes, q.v.
c South Villa, designed by Decimus Burton. Engraving by J. Tingle after T. H. Shepherd for Elmes, q.v.
d Albany Cottage, designed by C. R. Cockerell. Engraving by W. Tombleson after T. H. Shepherd for Elmes, q.v.

e St Dunstan's (or Hertford) Villa, designed by Decimus Burton. Engraving by J. Tingle after T. H. Shepherd for Elmes, q.v.
f The Holme, designed by Decimus Burton. Engraving by J. Henshall after T. H. Shepherd for Elmes, q.v.
g Gloucester (or Strathirne) Lodge, designed by Nash. Engraving by W. Radclyffe after T. H. Shepherd for Elmes, q.v.
h Grove House, designed by Decimus Burton. Engraving by W. Wallis after T. H. Shepherd for Elmes, q.v.

a

b

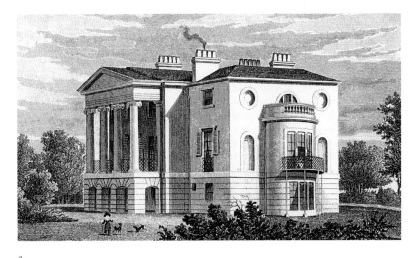

c

f

d

g

e

h

184

CUMBERLAND MARKET

Regent's Park, London
1819

Built by Nash as the hay market for
northern London, Cumberland Market did
not replace the West End Haymarket until
1830. The central market-place, marked off
with cast-iron posts linked with chains, was
surrounded by terraced houses of three
storeys and a basement; only the ground
floors were stuccoed. Under the western
side of the market lay a large commercial
icehouse holding 1,500 tons. This was
supplied by a ship constantly engaged in
bringing ice from Norway to the Thames,
where it was transferred to Regent's Canal
barges. After severe damage in the Second
World War, the whole area was
demolished in 1950.

A. Saunders, *Regent's Park*, 1969

ABOVE Cumberland Market: the Hospital Rag Carnival, which was held annually in the
Market. Painting by Charles Gerrard, *c.*1920 (Swiss Cottage Library)

BELOW The Harmonic Institution: the music shop was behind the arcade, with the entrance
to the concert hall on the corner of Little Argyll Street. Engraving by W. Wallis after
T. H. Shepherd for Elmes, *Metropolitan Improvements*, 1827

185

THE HARMONIC INSTITUTION

Regent Street, London
1819

The old Harmonic Institution, standing in
the way of the New Street, had to be
demolished. Nash's designs for the
rebuilding, commissioned by two of the
Institution's members, Welch and Hawes,
were given free of charge. The interior of
the concert room is described as having 'the
orchestra at one end facing four tiers of
boxes at the other, both framed with
Corinthian columns. Pilasters of the same
order lined the side walls, the ceiling was

arched and enriched with mosaic panels' (Elmes). The Institution also included a ballroom and a drawing-room. Behind the arcade of termini was the music shop run by Welch and Hawes. The Harmonic Institution was burnt down in 1830 and rebuilt as shops.

Elmes, *Metropolitan Improvements*, 1827
Summerson 1980

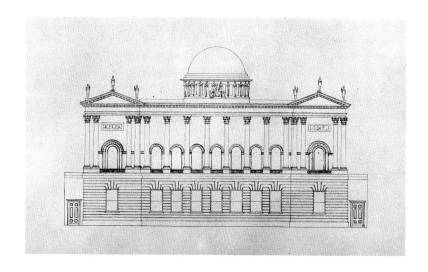

Nash's proposed design for the College of Physicians, which was never built (RIBA)

186

THE GENERAL POST OFFICE

St Martin's-le-Grand, London
1819

Nash, together with Soane and Smirke, was required by the Treasury to examine and report on the designs for the new General Post Office in St Martin's-le-Grand, submitted in an open competition held in 1819. All the designs were rejected. Eventually Smirke was given the job.

King's Works, vi, 1973

187

THE COLLEGE OF PHYSICIANS

Regent Street, London
1819–1824

Some time between 1819 and 1824 Nash designed a new building for the College of Physicians. It was to have stood in his New Street (Regent Street); for some unknown reason it was not built, and in

1825 the College moved into Sir Robert Smirke's building on the west side of what was to be Trafalgar Square. After the Second World War the College moved again and since 1964 has occupied Sir Denys Lasdun's building on the site of Nash's Someries House (No. 220) in Regent's Park.

Summerson 1980

188

AUGUSTUS STREET

Regent's Park, London
1819–1826

Augustus Street led from Cumberland Market to Augustus Square. As this was a working-class area, the leases were difficult to dispose of, so Nash at one time held all of the street and most of Augustus Square. The terrace of stuccoed, two-storey cottages ran along the east side of the street, facing the dockside wharfs. A pleasant rhythm was set up by moving the upper windows half a bay along. They had double-pitched roofs with central gutters. The architect for Augustus Street is unknown, but somebody, probably Nash, took a lot of trouble over these workers' dwellings. After wartime bombing, all were demolished.

Survey of London, xxi, 1949

Augustus Street: probably the only photographic record, of unknown date

North, or Macclesfield, Cottage and the north gate to the right of Macclesfield Bridge. Engraving by R. Acon after T. H. Shepherd for Elmes, *Metropolitan Improvements*, 1827

The remains of the bridge and cottage after the explosion (*Illustrated London News*, 10 October 1874)

Nash's proposed plan for Fort Thomas (British Library)

189

NORTH COTTAGE

Regent's Park, London

c. 1820

North, or Macclesfield, Cottage was named after Lord Macclesfield, Chairman of the Regent's Canal Company, and was built next to the Macclesfield Bridge, which crossed the canal and gave access to Regent's Park from the north. The cottage was occupied by the Park Superintendent. It was severely damaged when a barge carrying gunpowder exploded in 1874, but it was rebuilt and survived until it was demolished to make way for road widening in the early twentieth century.

Elmes, *Metropolitan Improvements*, 1827

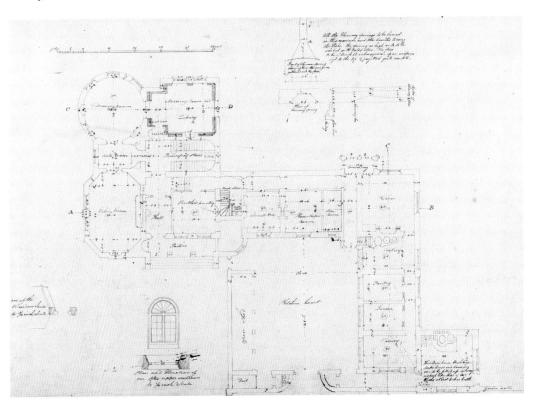

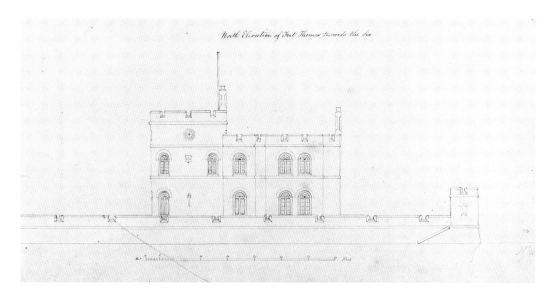

North Elevation of Fort Thomas towards the Sea

Fort Thomas:
(ABOVE)
Nash's proposed north
elevation, from the
sea (British Library);
(RIGHT)
St Thomas Villa, with
features commonly
used by Nash, such as
dormer windows and
porch with pointed
arch

191

GALLERY IN PALL MALL
St James's, London
1820

Nash is recorded in the Shide Hill Ledger (the only surviving account book from Nash's office) as having in 1822 carried out work in Pall Mall for Sir Thomas Lawrence, PRA (1769–1830). The bill was for 'Work done at the Gallery in Pall Mall' and amounted to £700 15s 6½d. There is no evidence that a gallery was ever built, and Summerson suggests that this payment might have been simply for alterations, as Lawrence, living in Russell Square, had perhaps only taken rooms in Pall Mall for use as a studio or store. Lawrence later painted Nash's portrait for Jesus College, Oxford, and Nash commissioned him to make a copy of his portrait of George IV to hang in the gallery of his (Nash's) new house at 14 Regent Street.

Shide Hill Ledger
Summerson 1935

192

14 NEWMAN STREET
Oxford Street, London
1820–1821

After the death of Nash's old friend Benjamin West (1738–1820), President of the Royal Academy, Nash was commissioned by the two sons to build a picture-gallery at the family home, 14 Newman Street. The building, which cost about £2,500, has been demolished and no record of the gallery seems to have survived.

Summerson 1980

190

FORT THOMAS
Isle of Wight
c.1820

Contained in a folio of George Ward's papers from Northwood House (now in the British Library) is a drawing of a proposed castellated house, Fort Thomas, for Sir George Thomas. The house was not built, but another, St Thomas Villa, was built at East Cowes and still exists; it has features often used by Nash.

British Library MS 18159
N. Temple, *IOW Society*, 1987

193
KINGSTON HOUSE

Knightsbridge, London

1820

The house was built around 1770 as a square, three-storey block, flanked by two detached pavilions for the kitchen and stables. In the 1820s the new owner, the Earl of Listowel, had alterations made to the Palladian house: two bay windows were added to the entrance front at first-floor level, with a balcony carried on columns forming a new *porte-cochère*. The garden

Kingston House: (RIGHT) Nash may have added the colonnade and the two bow windows above; (BELOW) the saloon, with a typical coved surround to the ceiling. Undated photographs

front was given a new covered balcony, and stucco was applied overall. A new saloon and conservatory were built over the kitchen wing and were linked to the first floor by a short corridor. Internally the saloon had a coved ceiling with paterae over a bracketed cornice. Kingston House has been attributed to Nash by Terence Davis, while Christopher Hussey considered the architect unknown, but of Nash's school. The house was demolished in 1937.

C. Hussey, 'Kingston House, Knightsbridge', *Country Life*, 20 March 1937
Davis 1966

194

14–16 REGENT STREET

London
1820–1821

Nash took up a building plot in his New Street, near Waterloo Place, to build a pair of houses for John Edwards (his cousin) and himself. They were planned, in the Parisian *hôtel* manner, around an entrance courtyard, with shops to let on both street frontages. The accommodation interlocked, with Edwards having the north wing and Nash the south; the main block was shared, with Nash's drawing offices on the ground floor, under Edwards' reception rooms. The *pièce de résistance* of Nash's house was the picture and sculpture gallery, 70 feet long, that linked the dining-room and drawing-room. At the back was yet another gallery, this time for architecture. In 1834 the house was sold and the gallery taken to East Cowes Castle and re-erected.

J. Britton and A. C. Pugin, *Illustrations of the Public Buildings of London*, ii, 1825
Prince Pückler-Muskau, *Tour in England, Ireland and France*, 1832
Summerson 1980

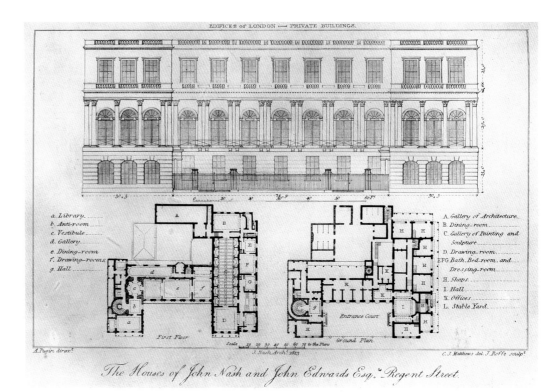

The Houses of John Nash and John Edwards Esq.ʳᵉ Regent Street

ABOVE The front elevation and ground-plan of 14–16 Regent Street, the houses of John Nash and John Edwards. Engraving by A. Pugin from J. Britton and A. Pugin, *Illustrations of the Public Buildings of London*, 1825
BELOW Nash's picture and sculpture gallery at 14 Regent Street. Engraving from J. Britton and A. Pugin, q.v.

195

CORNWALL TERRACE

Regent's Park, London
1821

Cornwall Terrace was the first terrace to be built in Regent's Park. James Burton was the builder, with his son Decimus as architect. The plans were revised several times before Nash gave his approval. After the abortive 1812 start on Park Crescent, no further building work took place in Regent's Park until 1821. The construction

Cornwall Terrace: the pediment of Clarence Terrace, at the far end, is used to stop the vista

of Regent Street was nearing completion, and contractors like Burton were looking for more work. They must have known of Nash's anxiety over the lack of progress in the Park. Did Burton indicate to Nash that he would build Cornwall Terrace if his son was allowed to design it? In the event, the terrace of nineteen houses was built and this gave the necessary impetus to the recommencing of work in the Park.

Elmes, *Metropolitan Improvements*, 1827
A. Saunders, *Regent's Park*, 1969

196
YORK GATE
Regent's Park, London
1821–1822

Nash planned York Gate as the grand entrance to Regent's Park. He designed two matching 'palaces' with Ionic façades, facing each other across the entrance road

20–21 Cornwall Terrace: the infill houses on the left, linking Cornwall and York Terraces (see No. 200), were later additions, probably by Nash

The end of Cornwall Terrace, facing Clarence Gate

York Gate, looking north: the grand entry to Regent's Park

on the axis of Thomas Hardwick's half-built chapel (now upgraded by the parish council to be the new parish church of St Mary). William Mountford Nurse and James Burton each built one of the terraces of five houses. To maintain the palace pretence the entrances were placed at the ends and in the road behind. After damage during the Second World War, both terraces were rebuilt as offices, behind restored elevations.

Elmes, *Metropolitan Improvements*, 1827
A. Saunders, *Regent's Park*, 1969

York Gate, looking south: Nash used the recently built parish church of St Marylebone as the backdrop of the entrance to the Park

LEFT Nash's façade of the Theatre Royal has suffered little change
ABOVE The stage door to the Theatre is in Suffolk Street

197
THE THEATRE ROYAL
Haymarket, London
1821

In 1819 Daniel Morris, the Crown Lessee, applied to rebuild the Theatre Royal, built in 1720 as the Little Theatre and made infamous in the 1730s by Fielding's satires. Nash and the Crown Commissioners persuaded Morris to use the adjoining site, where Nash's Corinthian portico would provide a fitting backdrop to the view from

St James's Square along Nash's extension of Charles Street (now Charles II Street). The elevation is finished in stucco, with a frieze of bull's-eye windows above the pediment and down either side. Houses in Suffolk Street were incorporated in 1837 and rebuilt to form the Royal Entrance and stage door. Three tiers of purple and gilt boxes lined the interior, which was square with a radiused back wall; the stage was framed by gilded palm trees. The interior was altered in 1880 and rebuilt in 1904.

J. Britton and A. C. Pugin, *Illustrations of the Public Buildings of London*, i, 1825
Survey of London, xx, 1940

RIGHT Nash resited the Theatre to close the view from what was then Charles Street
BELOW LEFT The plan at stalls level. Drawing by A. Pugin (RIBA)
BELOW RIGHT The interior view from the stage, as designed by Nash. Drawing by A. Pugin for *Illustrations of the Public Buildings of London*, 1825 (RIBA)

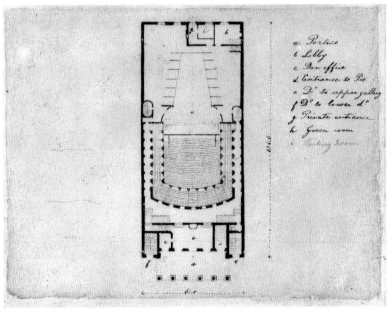

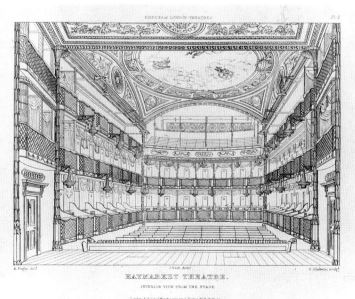

8, 9 and 11 Suffolk Street, linked by the continuous balcony, are probably by Nash

Nash's portico to 6½ and 7 Suffolk Street, the Royal Society of British Artists building

198

SUFFOLK STREET

Haymarket, London
1821–1824

This is one of the last remaining Regency streets in the West End. After the demolition of the Royal stables, the Crown decided to rebuild the area. Most of the land in Suffolk Street was speculatively bought by John Edwards, Nash's cousin, but he seems soon to have lost confidence and sold to Nash in 1822. A Select Committee report cleared Nash of any professional misdemeanour. Nash's plan was to extend Suffolk Street north to James Street (now Orange Street). This was dropped for the present cul-de-sac. Nash designed the following buildings (and all the others were approved by him): Nos 6½ and 7 (Gallery of the Royal Society of British Artists), Nos 8–11 (these match the Gallery and are probably by Nash), Nos 18–19 (the rear elevation of the Theatre Royal), Nos 20–22 (these carry a favourite Nash motif over the ground-floor windows and are probably his), and No. 23 (the return end to Suffolk Place). Immediately behind Suffolk Street, to the east, a large stable development was built by Nash in Whitcomb Street.

Survey of London, xx, 1940
Summerson 1980

BELOW The rear elevation of the Theatre Royal is in Suffolk Street
BELOW RIGHT 20–22 Suffolk Street have Nash's favourite decoration over the ground-floor windows

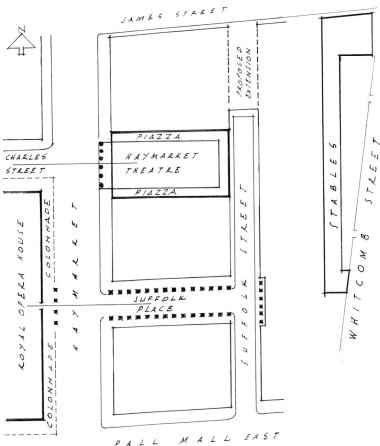

BLOCK PLAN OF THE PALL MALL END OF THE HAYMARKET. Based on drawing from Nash's office

233

LITTLE SUFFOLK STREET

Haymarket, London
1821–1824

Nash first planned an arcade in Little Suffolk Street (now Suffolk Place) with shops on both sides, centred on the main entrance to the King's Opera House opposite. The terrace he built has a shallow, central four-bay projection, bearing a pediment with Nash's motif of circle and triangles. The first-floor windows, round-headed with a shell in the tympanum, give access to a continuous balcony with fine cast-iron railings over Doric columns. A three-light window at the return end to Haymarket has Nash's other motif of shell and fan. Next door is a simple, one-bay, stuccoed elevation, with incised pilasters after Soane. The matching terrace opposite was demolished in 1915.

Survey of London, xx, 1940

Little Suffolk Street, now called Suffolk Place: a matching terrace stood on the opposite side of the road

YORK TERRACE

Regent's Park, London
1822

The York Terraces were designed by Nash as two Ionic palaces forming the wings to York Gate. His proposal for linking them across the road with a colonnade was not accepted. The main façades of both Terraces faced the Park with Ionic pavilions rising off the Doric-colonnaded ground storeys. Set back from the Outer Circle by a strip of communal garden, all the entrances were placed in the street behind. At the end of the eastern Terrace of eighteen houses, built by James Burton, Nash placed Doric Villa (two semi-detached houses masquerading as a Doric temple) and completed the range with Nos 44 to 49 York Terrace East, a Corinthian block of six houses. The matching western Terrace, also of eighteen houses, was built by William Mountford Nurse. Between it and Cornwall Terrace Nash built a double bow-fronted block of three houses similar in detail to Ulster Terrace, and shortly afterwards he filled in the gap on either side with more simply designed houses. All badly damaged by bombing in the Second World War, they have been carefully restored, some being rebuilt in facsimile with the interiors converted into flats.

Fourth Report of the Commissioners of Woods, Forests and Land Revenues, 1823
Elmes, *Metropolitan Improvements*, 1827
A. Saunders, *Regent's Park*, 1969

The Corinthian block is 44–49 York Terrace East

The rear entrances of York Terrace East are decorated with incised pilasters, a feature originated by Soane

Doric Villa (42–43 York Terrace East)

ABOVE York Terrace from across the Park lake

LEFT
The common gardens
are entered from
the colonnade

The later infill houses, linking York Terrace and Cornwall Terrace

Between York Terrace and Cornwall Terrace, Nash placed a free-standing block of three houses matching Ulster Terrace to the east; the plain houses on either side were added later by Nash

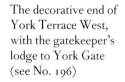

The decorative end of York Terrace West, with the gatekeeper's lodge to York Gate (see No. 196)

HANOVER TERRACE

Regent's Park, London
1822

Hanover Terrace is considered to be the most scholarly of the terraces. The twenty houses designed by Nash were built by John Mackell Aitkens in 1822. The elevation has three porticoes carried on the ground-floor arcade. Giant Roman Doric columns carry a full entablature, with decorated metopes and bearing pediments filled with sculpture. Cast-iron balustrades are set off by the stuccoed background. Hanover Mews, at the rear, separates the block from the stuccoed backs of Kent Terrace. The original stables were pleasantly designed, with grouped first-floor windows over round-headed entrances.

Elmes, *Metropolitan Improvements*, 1827
A. Saunders, *Regent's Park*, 1969

ABOVE The centrepiece of Hanover Terrace
RIGHT The stables have been replaced by garages in the pleasantly designed Hanover Mews

LEFT
The elevation facing the Park
BELOW LEFT
Hanover Terrace Mews, showing the back of Kent Terrace (see No. 248)
BELOW
The continuous arcade, with the entrances behind

NOTTINGHAM TERRACE

Regent's Park, London

1822

By placing York Gate on the axis of the newly erected parish church of St Marylebone, a vacant site in the New Road (now Marylebone Road) was left to the west; there Nash placed Nottingham Terrace, a block of ten houses with two more set back to suit the curving boundary. Provision for the terrace was made in the First Report. It is on the plan of 1826 and was presumably built at the same time as York Gate (1822). The stucco and brick elevation matched the backs of the York Gate Terraces and was most probably designed by Nash. The terrace was demolished after bomb damage and replaced by flats.

First Report of the Commissioners of Woods, Forests and Land Revenues, 1812
P. Potter, Plan of the Parish of St Marylebone, c.1832

The Marylebone Road elevation of Nottingham Terrace, before 1939

The Royal Standard flies over Nash's Race Stand at Ascot. *Preparing to start for the Emperor of Russia's Cup at Ascot*, 1845, by John Herring, sen., and James Pollard

ROYAL RACE STAND

Ascot, Berkshire

1822

The Royal Race Stand was built at Ascot Racecourse by Nash for George IV. A contemporary wrote: 'It was constructed in such a manner so as to enable every person to see the horses during the whole time of racing.' In 1824 the roof was blown off and replaced with a flat lead roof; a wooden floor was laid over it to accommodate extra spectators. Four years later the stairs were eased for the King's benefit, and refreshment rooms were added. The Stand was demolished during the reign of Edward VII.

King's Works, vi, 1973

204

HANOVER GATEHOUSE

Regent's Park, London
1822–1823

Standing on an island with the entrance road passing on either side of it, Nash's pretty baroque lodge is finished in stucco and painted stone. It has a square plan, with chamfered corners built out and stone consoles over. Both the front and the back have small bow-fronted gardens. The original Park gates to both entrance roads have been removed.

Summerson 1980

205

ST LURAN'S CHURCH

Cookstown, County Tyrone
Possibly 1822

The plain Gothic church was designed by Nash for the parish of Derryloran, where the Stewarts of Killymoon Castle (No. 74) were the grand family and were, no doubt, instrumental in Nash obtaining the commission. The plan was orthodox for the period, with the pulpit placed half-way down the north side and the vestry in the short arm behind. Nash's tower, steeple and one bay of his nave survived the church's enlargement of 1861.

Ulster Architectural Heritage Society, *Cookstown*, 1970/1

BELOW LEFT Hanover Gatehouse
BELOW St Luran's: Nash's tower, steeple and first bay survived the rebuilding

The centre section of Sussex Place has six domes

206

SUSSEX PLACE
Regent's Park, London
1822–1823

Sussex Place is the idiosyncratic member of the neo-classical Regent's Park family;
derided when first built, it is now accepted with affection. Built to Nash's designs by William Smith, Sussex Place was the second terrace to be erected in the Park. The twenty-six houses were arranged in nine parts: three flat and two curved ranges of Corinthian columns standing on the arcaded loggia, divided by canted bays capped with pointed hexagonal domes of painted metal. The bow-fronted garden, fenced with cast-iron railings, is the most spacious in the Park. The whole terrace, rebuilt behind Nash's façades, is now occupied by the London Graduate School of Business Studies.

Elmes, *Metropolitan Improvements*, 1827
A. Saunders, *Regent's Park*, 1969

Sussex Place: (LEFT) the junction of the curved wing and straight centre; (ABOVE) one of the two end pavilions

LEFT The interiors of the end stables simulate domed ceilings
ABOVE The right-hand house is original

BELOW Houses for the senior stable staff in Arabella Row

207

THE ROYAL MEWS
Buckingham Palace, London
1822–1824

It was decided that the Royal stables should
be moved from Charing Cross to the
Queen's House at Westminster in 1820.

The Royal Mews:
(RIGHT)
the main entrance: the
screen is a later
addition
(BELOW)
the Inner Quadrangle:
the balcony is a later
addition

Nash designed the new stables around a
square quadrangle, behind a forecourt off
Queen's Row (now Buckingham Gate).
The entrance archway, faced with pairs of
blocked Tuscan columns, was repeated on
all four sides of the Great Quadrangle; only
the main entrance archway carries a tower.
Inside the stables, arcades matching the
lunettes run down each side, with the flat
ceiling panelled to give the impression of
shallow domes. Staff houses were to have
been built on each side of the forecourt but,
owing to legal difficulties, the left-hand row
was not built until 1859, when the gates
and piers were also added. A pair of houses
of similar detail was built in Arabella Row
(now Lower Grosvenor Place).

King's Works, vi, 1973

LEFT
All Souls is the pivot
on which Regent
Street swings into
Portland Place
RIGHT
The nave and porch
from the north, the
only view with an
uncluttered sky

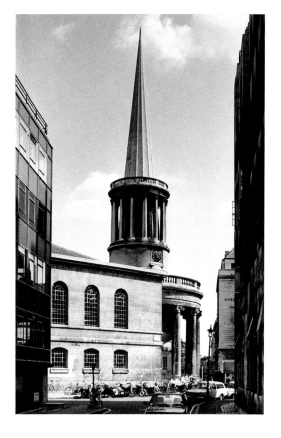

BELOW The altar arrangements are modern and
Nash's twin pulpits have been removed

208

ALL SOULS CHURCH

Langham Place, London
1822–1824

The rapid growth of the parish of St
Marylebone called for more churches.
Nash's design for a church was accepted in
1811, but the Duke of Portland objected,

and the proposed site, in the centre of Nash's planned circus at the north end of Portland Place, was abandoned. Other sites were considered, and in 1820 the offer of the Langham Place site by the Office of Woods, Forests and Land Revenues was accepted. Nash's church was to seat 1,820 people at a cost of about £18,500. The lowest tender came from Robert Streather; he was contracted in July 1823 and consecration took place in November 1824. All Souls was bomb-damaged during the Second World War. It was restored by H. S. Goodhart-Rendel, rededicated in 1951 and now attracts 1,000 worshippers or more to each of its two Sunday services.

R. Luker, *All Souls*, published by All Souls Church, 1979

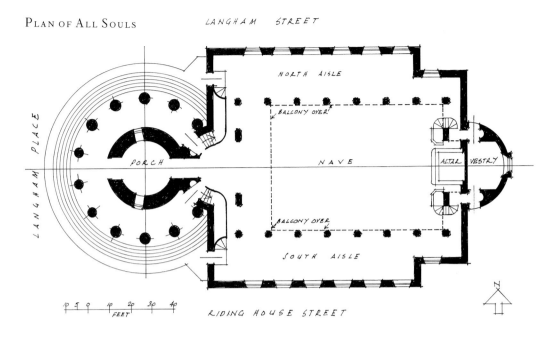

PLAN OF ALL SOULS

The nave of All Souls (the church has been recently refurbished)

CLARENCE GATE
Regent's Park, London
1823

When Marylebone (later Regent's) Park was being planned in 1811, Baker Street ran from Mayfair across the fashionable Portman estate almost to the Park boundary. In 1823, at the head of this street, between Cornwall and Clarence

RIGHT
The Corinthian portico of Clarence Terrace, rebuilt in facsimile

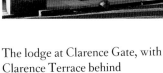

The lodge at Clarence Gate, with Clarence Terrace behind

Terraces, Nash placed a new entrance to the Park. A sturdy, yet elegant, gatekeeper's lodge makes a pleasant contrast to the palatial terraces behind.

A. Saunders, *Regent's Park*, 1969

OPPOSITE Clarence Terrace, designed by Decimus Burton to Nash's approval

210

CLARENCE TERRACE
Regent's Park, London
1823

Designed by Decimus Burton to plans approved by Nash, Clarence Terrace was built by Burton's father, James Burton. The design was for a central block with a

Corinthian portico and projecting free-standing wings linked by an open screen of Ionic columns. James Burton, presumably looking for a larger profit, filled in the space behind the screens with extra houses. Structural problems and general decay necessitated rebuilding the whole terrace with modern flats behind the facsimile elevations.

A. Saunders, *Regent's Park*, 1969

211

CARRICK TERRACE

Regent's Park, London

1823

The plan accompanying the Fourth Report of the Commissioners of Woods, Forests and Land Revenues shows terraces lining the canal on the north side of Regent's Park. One of these terraces was named Carrick and is referred to in Elmes as being marked out, but it was never built.

Elmes, *Metropolitan Improvements*, 1827

212

MUNSTER TERRACE

Regent's Park, London

1823

Munster Terrace was shown on the plan for the Fourth Report of 1823 and was referred to in *Metropolitan Improvements* as having been marked out. As with other terraces proposed for the northern side of the Park, it was never built.

Elmes, *Metropolitan Improvements*, 1827

213

WINDSOR CASTLE

Berkshire

1823

George IV decided that Windsor Castle should be brought up to date. The architects attached to the Board of Works – Nash, Soane and Smirke – together with

Jeffry Wyatt, were invited to submit designs. Wyatt's were chosen and built, whereupon he changed his name, with Royal permission, to Wyatville. Nash's drawings have been lost.

King's Works, vi, 1973

214

FOUNTAIN INN
West Cowes, Isle of Wight
1823

The architect of the Fountain Inn (now Hotel), built in 1803, is unknown, but could possibly have been Nash. Drawings dated 17 April 1823, found among papers of his friend and neighbour George Ward, show a proposed extension to the hotel of one range of buildings for stables and storage and another for a ballroom and coffee room. Neither was built, and the present single-storey dining-room was substituted.

British Library MS 18159
N. Temple, *IOW Society*, 1987

Windsor Castle: Nash's design for the Waterloo Room, which was intended to show the Lawrence portraits of the Allied leaders, *c.* 1824 (Royal Library, Windsor Castle)

Fountain Inn (now Hotel): (BELOW LEFT) on the left is the single-storey dining-room which replaced the proposed extension; (BELOW RIGHT) the front entrance

215

ST DAVID'S CHURCH
Carmarthen, Carmarthenshire
1823–1837

In 1823 it was proposed that a church be built for the Welsh-speaking community of Carmarthen. A site was chosen about 200 yards away from the present one and the foundation stone was laid. Legal difficulties made it necessary to transfer the church to its present site in 1825. The church of St David's, to Nash's design, was consecrated in 1837, two years after his death. The original nave was aligned north and south behind the tower. When in 1850 the church was found to be too small, the present nave was added, oriented east and west. Further alterations were made in the 1880s.

J. and V. Lodwick, *The Story of Carmarthen*, 1972

BELOW Fountain Inn: first-floor plan for proposed extension, which was not built (British Library)

St David's Church: the tower is by Nash; the nave was rebuilt later

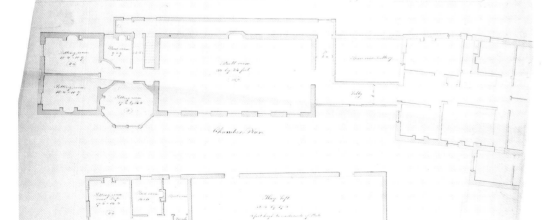

216

PARK SQUARE
Regent's Park, London
1823–1824

The northern half of the New (Marylebone) Road circus shown on Nash's early plans was replaced by the more ornate Park Square in the Fourth Report of 1823. Jacob Smith built the east side in 1823. The western block, by William Mountford Nurse, was completed the following year.

Park Square continues the line of Park Crescent across Marylebone Road

LEFT The west side of Park Square and one of the gatekeeper's lodges

Both terraces, of twelve houses each, face the communal garden. The Ionic order of Park Crescent is used again on either side of the rusticated centre. Above, an arcade of round-headed windows extends across the façade. All four end pavilions are the return fronts of adjacent terraces.

Elmes, *Metropolitan Improvements*, 1827
A. Saunders, *Regent's Park*, 1969

217

ALBANY TERRACE
Regent's Park, London
1823–1825

Albany Terrace consists of two blocks separated by Peto Place: Nos 1 to 3 form the corner of Park Square East. They were designed by Nash and built by Jacob Smith, with Ionic pilasters to match Ulster Place on the west side of the Square. The entrance porch to No. 3, in Peto Place, carries a trellised balcony and tented canopy. The second block, Nos 4 to 6, forms the end of Albany Street. The architect is unknown but Nash's influence can be seen in the assurance with which the corner is turned. This block was restored in 1988 for use as offices.

Survey of London, xxi, 1949

218

THAMES EMBANKMENT
London
Before 1824

Nash, presumably on his own initiative, designed a continuous quay extending from Westminster Bridge to London Bridge and projecting over the River Thames to the low water mark. At St Paul's the buildings between the cathedral and the quay were to have been cleared away to form a wide piazza, which would have been, in Nash's words, 'beyond measure magnificent' – perhaps an understatement. The riparian owners objected strenuously and, as with his plans for a new road from the West End to the British Museum and another to the City, the proposal was dropped.

Albany Terrace:
(ABOVE)
Nash's original railings and lamp standards, similar to those used on most of the squares and gardens;
(LEFT)
Nash designed the left-hand block and probably the right-hand one

Nothing happened until, in 1825, Colonel Trench presented a similar scheme and was unfairly accused of plagiarism. Nash's drawings have not been found.

Colonel Trench, MP, *The Thames Quay*, 1827

219
ST ANDREW'S PLACE
Regent's Park, London
1823–1826

Nash designed the eight houses of St Andrew's Place to form a terrace, with bow-windowed ends stopping an Ionic colonnade, to match Ulster Terrace on the opposite side of Park Square. The cul-de-sac is closed with a Corinthian porticoed

ABOVE
St Andrew's Place is now a pedestrian precinct
RIGHT
St Andrew's Place and the return end to Park Square East on the right

SOMERIES HOUSE
Regent's Park, London
1824

Someries House was designed for the Adult Orphan Asylum by Nash, whose services were given free of charge. The Asylum took in and educated the orphaned daughters aged between 14 and 19 of clergymen and officers. Set in a large garden, the square building of five bays to each side was placed diagonally across the northern corner of St Andrew's Place and the Outer Circle. The main elevation had an arcade of round-headed windows, matching Park Square Terrace on the

BELOW
Someries House, left, and St Andrew's Place. Engraving by W. Radclyffe after T. H. Shepherd for Elmes, *Metropolitan Improvements*, 1827

mansion, divided into two houses. The builder was Jacob Smith. On the Park corner, Nash's Someries House has been replaced by the Royal College of Physicians (designed by Denys Lasdun, 1964), which recently took over and restored the terrace; at the same time the precinct was pedestrianized.

Elmes, *Metropolitan Improvements*, 1827
A. Saunders, *Regent's Park*, 1969

ABOVE
The Corinthian portico at the end of St Andrew's Place is the terminal feature of the cul-de-sac and can just be seen on the left of the illustration opposite

opposite corner. Greatly altered, it was eventually demolished and replaced by Sir Denys Lasdun's Royal College of Physicians in 1964.

Elmes, *Metropolitan Improvements*, 1827

The backs of the houses in Park Village East seen from Park Village West; Regent's Canal once ran between them

THE PARK VILLAGES
Regent's Park, London
1823–1834

The branch canal leading to the markets left a narrow strip of land inside the eastern boundary; on the other side of the canal was a small triangle of land north of the new barracks in Albany Street. Both pieces were too small to interest developers, so in 1823 Nash took up the leases himself and built two picturesque villages, recalling earlier ones, as he wrote, '. . . in another part of the Kingdom', presumably Blaise Hamlet (No. 133). Building these villages for his own amusement occupied his time until his retirement in 1834, when James Pennethorne took over the practice and completed both villages. They became the models for later suburban development.

Only the two houses on the right-hand side of the street are by Nash

Park Village East, looking south towards Augustus Street

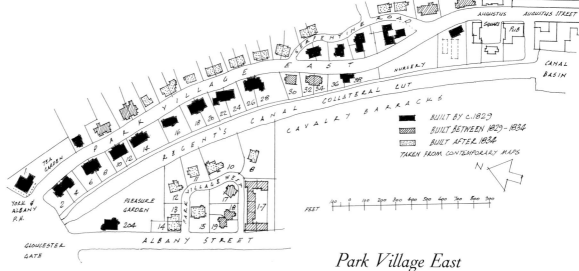

BELOW
Park Village East from
Regent's Canal, which
once ran between the
Villages. Engraving
by W. Radclyffe after
T. H. Shepherd for
Elmes, *Metropolitan
Improvements*, 1827

BELOW LEFT
18–20 Park Village
East, shortly before
demolition, 1941
BELOW
The junction of Park
Village East and
Serpentine Road.
Artist unknown,
*c.*1840 (Swiss Cottage
Library

Park Village East

The northern end of Augustus Street, from
Augustus Square to Gloucester Gate,
became Park Village East. Nash laid out a
gently winding road, looped on one side to
form an island of eight houses. In all a
total of fifty houses lined both sides of the
roads. Most of those on the western side
still exist; the others were destroyed by the
railway widening of 1900–6 and by
bombing in the Second World War. Very
few records of the demolished village exist
other than contemporary maps and some
watercolour sketches.

6 and 8 Park Village
East, with the gables;
10 and 12 with the
fretted eaves fascia

BELOW
36 and 38 Park Village
East are built back to
back
BELOW RIGHT
26 and 28 Park Village
East, named
Piercefield Cottage
and Wyndcliff
Cottage

LEFT Casina Lodge (8 Park Village West): the
duality of two windows above the entrance porch
was unusual but not unknown in Nash's designs
ABOVE 10 Park Village West

BELOW The south entrance to Park Village West

Park Village West

Park Village West, the smaller of the two
villages, is triangular in shape, with its
apex occupied by an earlier Nash house
(208 Albany Street). The site was divided
into two parts by a loop road off Albany
Street. Seventeen villas were built; some
were single houses, others paired. A
miniature terrace was even introduced. No
two houses were the same, or even in line
with their neighbours, producing a

13 and 14 Park Village West (the latter, left, is entered from Albany Street)

picturesqueness only equalled by Blaise Hamlet (No. 133). No. 15 was badly damaged by war bombing and is now a modern replica; its neighbour, No. 16, is a post-war pastiche.

Survey of London, xxi, 1949
A. Saunders, *Regent's Park*, 1969
Summerson 1980

18 and 19 Park Village West

Tower House (12 Park Village West) is designed to be seen from two directions

BELOW 18 Park Village West

222

CAMBRIDGE TERRACE

Regent's Park, London
1824

Cambridge Terrace is a plain block, built by Richard Mott, with ten houses facing Regent's Park and two more in Chester Gate. The Park elevation has two wings and a recessed centre. The wings are decorated with incised piers in the style of Soane. The porches, with rusticated Doric columns or piers, are unusual for Nash. Badly damaged by wartime bombing and later neglected, Cambridge Terrace was restored in 1988 for use as offices. The mews behind has been replaced with modern housing.

Elmes, *Metropolitan Improvements*, 1827
A. Saunders, *Regent's Park*, 1969

ABOVE LEFT AND ABOVE Cambridge Terrace, recently restored: the recessed centre and projecting porch reflect Nash's early Welsh houses, Llanfechan and Llanaeron (Nos 7 and 28)

263

THE KING'S ROAD

London

1824

The King's Road was originally a private road used by Royal families to travel to Hampton Court. The eastern end of the road, between Buckingham House and Sloane Square, crossed an area of open ground known as the Five Fields. The Grosvenor estate wanted to develop the area but the illness of George III prevented an agreement on the layout being reached. After the King's death, Nash suggested: '. . . the road should be made exactly straight in the manner of an avenue, in the middle space, ground twenty feet wide on each side of the King's Private Road planted

BELOW Ulster Place faces on to the Marylebone Road

ABOVE King's Road: Nash laid out the centre section with treelined gardens on both sides

with a row of trees and the intermediate spaces filled up with a plantation.' This led to the planning of Eaton Square and the development of Belgravia and Pimlico.

King's Works, vi, 1973

224

ULSTER PLACE

Regent's Park, London

1824

The terrace of Ulster Place faces Marylebone Road and forms the return end of Park Square West. It is a plain Ionic terrace of seven houses, now converted into twenty-six flats. The continuous cast-iron balcony front is carried round the ends to stop against the projecting blocks of the Square. The terrace is set back from the main road by a carriageway and a belt of trees; the view along the forecourt is terminated by the stuccoed gatekeeper's lodge of Park Square. Ulster Place was designed by Nash and, presumably, built by William Mountford Nurse, who was responsible for the surrounding terraces of Park Square West and Ulster Terrace.

A. Saunders, *Regent's Park*, 1969

225
CLARENCE MARKET
Regent's Park, London
1824

Clarence Market was originally intended to serve as the vegetable market. It was

BELOW Clarence Market (now Clarence Gardens), 1955

The statue of the Duke of Kent, installed in Park Square by Nash

eventually built as terraced artisan housing, with a nursery garden in the centre, and renamed Clarence Gardens. Undistinguished architecturally, the brick and stucco elevations with their pleasantly proportioned windows took a back seat to the light, spacious environment. The market was demolished in 1951 and replaced by council housing.

A. Saunders, *Regent's Park*, 1969

226
PARK CRESCENT and PARK SQUARE: THE GARDENS
Regent's Park, London
*c.*1824

On either side of the New (Marylebone) Road, Nash laid out gardens with meandering walks, lawns and shrubs; a passage under the road links the gardens and is still in use. Both gardens had two gatekeepers' lodges, faced with plain piers, stylized pediments and Greek Doric columns *in antis*. The gardens are still enclosed by Nash's panels of cast-iron railings between open-work obelisks, several of which carried gas street lamps. Nash's final work in the Park, in 1832, was to install S. S. Gahagen's bronze statue of the Duke of Kent, erected to face down Portland Place.

Elmes, *Metropolitan Improvements*, 1827

Ulster Terrace, on the right, matches St Andrew's Place on the other side of Park Square, with its end pairs of bow windows

The east side of Brunswick Place (now Upper Harley Street), with Ulster Terrace on the left

227

ULSTER TERRACE
Regent's Park, London
1824

The Ionic order first appearing in Park Crescent, then Park Square, now turns the corner into the Outer Circle as the colonnade of Ulster Terrace. This terrace was designed by Nash to match St Andrew's Terrace on the opposite side of Park Square. The eight houses in the terrace, built by William Mountford Nurse in 1824, are now a mixture of flats and offices.

Elmes, *Metropolitan Improvements*, 1827
A. Saunders, *Regent's Park*, 1969

228

BRUNSWICK PLACE
Regent's Park, London
1824

Nash did not intend to have any openings on to Regent's Park between Park Square and York Gate, but after complaints from the residents of Harley Street and Devonshire Place he reluctantly agreed, on condition they made good the lost rents for any houses that had to be omitted. In the event only Brunswick Place (now called Upper Harley Street) was left open. Between the ends of Ulster Terrace and Ulster Place Nash placed four large houses in two pairs (Nos 1–4), matching the Terrace ends with a small house (No. 5) built back-to-back with a mews stable. On the west side, Nos 6 and 7 are smaller and more ornate, with the only examples in Regent's Park of Nash's shell-and-fan device. Nos 1–4 are now flats and Nos 6 and 7 are doctors' consulting rooms; only No. 5 remains a private house.

A. Saunders, *Regent's Park*, 1969

6 and 7 Brunswick Place (now Upper Harley Street), on the corner of York Terrace East

BELOW
Cambridge Terrace and the Colosseum. Engraving by R. Acon after T. H. Shepherd for Elmes, *Metropolitan Improvements*, 1827

229

THE COLOSSEUM
Regent's Park, London
1824–1827

Built to a design by Decimus Burton, the Colosseum stood on the east side of Regent's Park, at the south end of Cambridge Terrace; Nash made several amendments to the design, including a reduction in its size. It was designed to show the panoramas painted by E. T. Parris, from Thomas Hornor's drawings made from the ball above the dome of St Paul's Cathedral in 1822. Hornor, who instigated the enterprise, was a topographical artist who had worked mainly in the Vale of Neath, South Wales, where he had painted views of an earlier Nash house, Rheola (No. 148). In January 1829 the Colosseum opened to the public; a year later it closed, with Hornor and his backer fleeing the country. The building was demolished in 1875 and replaced by the present Cambridge Gate flats.

B. Weinreb and C. Hibbert (eds), *The London Encyclopedia*, 1983

Hippisley House was built on the waterfront next to the Royal Yacht Squadron. Engraving by G. Brannon, 1825

230

HIPPISLEY HOUSE
West Cowes, Isle of Wight
1825

Hippisley House was a Gothic villa built by the waterside for Sir John Coxe-Hippisley. The elevation had two gabled bays between pinnacled buttresses, with canted bay windows to the ground floor. The entrance was in the side road. A pavilion was built in the grounds behind, for use as a ballroom. The pavilion was later converted into Castle Rock House, then incorporated in the Royal Corinthian Yacht Club. An annexe of the Royal Yacht Squadron now occupies the site of the demolished villa.

R. Ackermann, *Views of Country Seats*, i, 1830

The Corinthian columns of Chester Terrace seen through the entrance arch

The pavilion and
arched screen of
Chester Terrace

BELOW
Five pavilions of
Chester Terrace break
up the long front

231
CHESTER TERRACE
Regent's Park, London
1825

Built by James Burton, Chester Terrace is
nearly 1,000 feet long and divided into nine
parts. A projecting portico of eight
Corinthian columns marks the centre, with
similar porticoes at each end; further
porches of six columns break up the long
ranges. Nash's design had the ends brought
forward as wings, but Burton separated

ABOVE
Chester Terrace from
the Park

them to allow for extra houses to be
squeezed in behind. After much
acrimonious argument, Nash made the best
of the *fait accompli* and linked the pavilions
to the terrace with the now acclaimed
arches. The forty-two houses are still
residential and Nash's war-damaged mews
has been replaced by flats.

A. Saunders, *Regent's Park*, 1969

269

Chester Gate: across the road is Chester Terrace, with Nash's decorated blank end wall

5 Chester Gate, on the corner of Chester Terrace Mews

232

CHESTER GATE
Regent's Park, London
*c.*1825

Originally named Cambridge Place, Chester Gate lies between Chester Terrace and Cambridge Terrace, linking Albany Street with the Outer Circle. At the east end a narrow entrance between two blocks of artisan dwellings and shops gives on to an open space. A small house masks one side of Chester Terrace Mews, with Nash House on the other side. The end of Chester Terrace is relieved by the green of

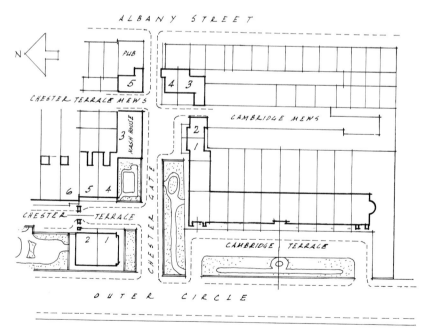

BLOCK PLAN OF THE CHESTER GATE AREA ABOUT 1870

ABOVE Chester Gate, with Cambridge Terrace on the right: the gardens were removed for road widening

LEFT 3 Chester Terrace, with the incised pilasters borrowed from Soane

the gardens and trees, once matched by another garden, across the end of Cambridge Terrace. All the buildings and the open area were designed by Nash and built by Richard Mott.

A. Saunders, *Regent's Park*, 1969

The end of Chester
Terrace forms one
side of Chester Place

233

CHESTER PLACE
Regent's Park, London
1825–1826

Chester Place is part of a little-known and
charming backwater of tree-lined streets
and gardens behind Cumberland Place.
Nash's terrace of twelve houses has a
simple elevation, marked out with Doric
pilasters between bays. The only accents
are attic storeys at the centre and ends. The

ABOVE Gloucester Gate, or East Gate: in the background is the York and Albany Public House (see p.258). Engraving by T. Barber after T. H. Shepherd for Elmes, *Metropolitan Improvements*, 1827

BELOW When the road was widened the two lodges were joined together

Chester Terrace is seen from Chester Terrace Mews through the Doric archway

back elevations line Albany Street and form a group with the public house, Prince George of Cumberland. The terrace remains residential.

See plan on p.280.

A. Saunders, *Regent's Park*, 1969

234

GLOUCESTER GATE LODGES

Regent's Park, London
1825–1826

Gloucester Gate, known to Elmes as the East Gate, formed the entrance to Regent's

Park from the north. The pedimented lodges on either side of the road had their entablatures carried across the roadway on four cast-iron Roman Doric columns. In 1878 the entrance road was widened, the crossing entablature dismantled and the South Lodge moved and rebuilt against the North one.

Elmes, *Metropolitan Improvements*, 1827
Summerson 1980

BUCKINGHAM PALACE

London
1825–1830

Nikolaus Pevsner wrote of the Royal Palace: 'When Nash performed the change from house to palace he succeeded in keeping it a country house.' Nash was sixty-nine when he received George IV's instructions, and was already heavily involved with Regent's Park and Regent Street. The King made it a condition that Buckingham House (later named the Queen's House), where he had been born, was to be retained; in the end only its shell was built into the new Palace. Entered from

ABOVE Buckingham Palace as completed to Nash's design, with the Marble Arch. c.1830

The garden screen wall of Buckingham Palace

the new *porte-cochère*, the old entrance-hall was kept, along the back of which Nash placed his usual gallery; beyond that there was a range of rooms, with the Bow Room opening on to the Garden Terrace. New wings enclosing the courtyard replaced the old ones: the north wing was given over to the Royal Private Apartments and the household staff occupied the south one. Open Doric arcades surrounded the courtyard on three sides, and the fourth, protected by an iron railing, was entered through the Marble Arch. In the centre of the garden front the half-round, full-height bow carrying a drum and plain dome was flanked on either side by two pavilions with attics. Giant Corinthian columns rose off the rusticated ground floor. From the terrace, terminating in glazed temples, Nash's landscaped grounds stretched down to the serpentine lake. Summerson considers Nash's internal designs dignified and rich, with each room full of character. Over the ground-floor gallery Nash placed the top-lit picture-gallery, with the Music Room

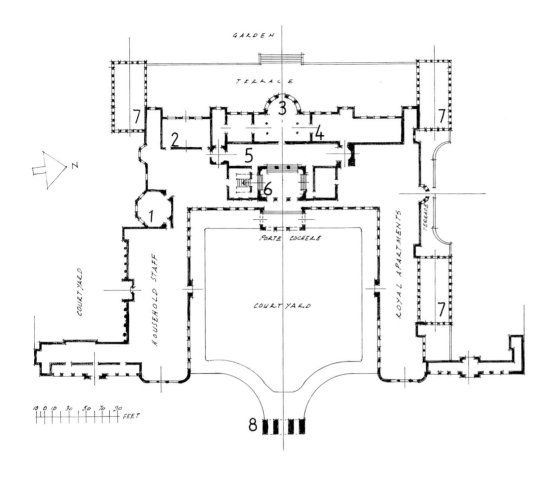

1 Library   5 Gallery
2 Stateroom   6 Grand Hall
3 Bow Room   7 Pavilion
4 Staterooms   8 Marble Arch

between the White and Blue Drawing Rooms, overlooking the garden. On the courtyard side are the Throne Room and Green Drawing Room. The State Dining Room, later redecorated by Blore, is at the south end.

George IV died before the building's completion. Nash was dismissed and Edward Blore took over. He removed Nash's harmless dome, closed the courtyard with a new east wing and eventually dispatched the Marble Arch (No. 259) to the other side of Hyde Park. Later Sir James Pennethorne, a relative of Mrs Nash and previously Nash's assistant, added the Ballroom Suite. Finally, in 1911, Sir Aston Webb laid out the *rond point* and the Victoria Memorial, and two years later he encased

BELOW Buckingham Palace from St James's Park in 1827, before the building of the Marble Arch. Engraving by J. Allen
BELOW RIGHT The Grand Staircase

Buckingham Palace: the Throne Room

Blore's north wing in Portland stone. A stucco-covered lodge still exists by the Royal Mews; other lodges at Hyde Park Corner were apparently demolished when the roads there were altered.

Summerson 1980

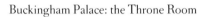

RIGHT
The Music Room
BELOW
The White Drawing Room
BELOW RIGHT
The Blue Drawing Room

The Picton Monument. Artist unknown

236

THE PICTON MONUMENT

Carmarthen, Carmarthenshire
1825–1827

General Picton's death at the Battle of Waterloo was commemorated by a Doric column surmounted by his statue, recorded by Spurrell as being sixty feet high. It was erected by the Town of Carmarthen at a cost of £3,000 to Nash's design. Nash revisited the town in 1828, when he was presented with a gold box. The monument was demolished shortly afterwards.

W. Spurrell, *Carmarthen and its Neighbourhood*, 1879

RIGHT
The garden elevation of Worcester Park. Engraving from G. F. Prosser, *Illustrations of Surrey*, 1826

RIGHT
The entrance front of Worcester Park, as seen in an old photograph: the rounded corners were also used at Gracefield (see No. 172)

237

WORCESTER PARK

Surrey
Before 1826

The site of Worcester Park was originally part of the gardens of Nonsuch Palace. William Taylor bought the Georgian house in 1750; his son, also William, had it 'much enlarged and improved under the superintendence of Nash' (Prosser). It would seem likely that Nash added the two porticoed wings and enlarged the ground-floor windows. The date of the work is not known but must be before 1826, the date of Prosser's book. It may possibly be as early as 1802, when Nash was making a design for the neighbouring Nonsuch Park.

G. F. Prosser, *Select Illustrations of the County of Surrey*, 1826

Clarence House: in 1875 Nash's two-storeyed porch was replaced by the balcony, and the fourth storey was added

238

CLARENCE HOUSE
St James's, London
1825–1828

After his marriage in 1818 the Duke of Clarence, later William IV, was given permission to enlarge his quarters in St James's Palace. Nash's plans were approved. Nash placed the entrance in the centre of Stable Yard, with the dining-room and breakfast-room on either side of the hall. Across the back he ran a corridor the length of the house. The first floor was similar, with a drawing-room on either side of the ante-room. Nash's works were severely altered during the extensions of 1875. His two-tier entrance porch was demolished and the entrance was moved to the Mall front. Internally only the ceilings to the drawing-rooms and the chimney pieces have survived. In 1830, when the Duke became William IV, he stayed on in the house, preferring it to Buckingham Palace. It is now the home of the Queen Mother.

C. Hussey, *Clarence House*, 1949

Clarence House: Nash's entrance was under the balcony

239
CUMBERLAND PLACE
Regent's Park, London
1826

Cumberland Place is a block of four houses, built by William Mountford Nurse between Chester Terrace and Cumberland Terrace and projecting in front of them to interrupt the length of their façades and to give movement to the street. Each end elevation has a large bow window as a *point de vue* to the terrace carriageways. Nash designed the block to simulate a large

Cumberland Place: (LEFT) the bow window forms a *point de vue* from Cumberland Terrace; (ABOVE) the entrances at the back, in Chester Place, retain their original ironwork

Cumberland Place: the Park façade, behind which
are four houses

mansion. This impression was aided by
placing the entrance porches at the rear.
After war damage Cumberland Place has
now been restored to its original condition
– except for the addition of the
overpowering dormer windows.

A. Saunders, *Regent's Park*, 1969

BLOCK PLAN OF
CUMBERLAND
PLACE AND
SURROUNDING
BUILDINGS
ABOUT 1870

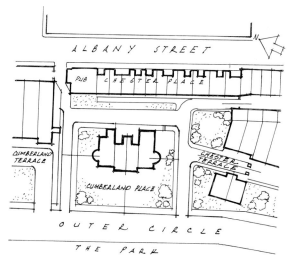

PARK TERRACE
Regent's Park, London
1826

By 1823 Sussex Place was complete and Clarence Terrace had been started. Behind them the same builders, James Burton and William Mountford Nurse, were constructing Park Terrace. The terrace consisted of thirty-two houses, most with shops on the ground floor and living accommodation over. At the southern end the only three houses that have not been rebuilt have bow façades facing the back of Sussex Place. Behind Clarence Terrace were another twelve houses, now demolished. The architect is not known, but the terrace was part of Nash's overall design for the Park, and he was responsible for the siting and general appearance.

P. Potter, Plan of the Parish of St Marylebone, c.1832

LEFT Three houses remain at the south end of Park Terrace

LEFT
The northern end
of Park Terrace
RIGHT
The backs of the three
southernmost houses
of Park Terrace

The north block of
Cumberland Terrace

BELOW
The carriageway is
visually stopped by
Cumberland Place
(see No. 239)

241

CUMBERLAND TERRACE

Regent's Park, London
1826

The grandest and most spectacular building
in Regent's Park, Cumberland Terrace was
designed by Nash to be seen from the
Royal *guinguette*. The terrace is composed
of three main blocks linked by Ionic
triumphal arches leading into small courts.
The side blocks have strongly projecting
end pavilions faced with Ionic porches on a
rusticated ground floor. The main block is
similar, but with an additional centre
pavilion, from which another Ionic porch

The linking archway and courtyard behind

RIGHT
At the north end of
Cumberland Terrace
Nash placed a pair of
smaller houses

advances. Built by William Mountford
Nurse in 1826, Cumberland Terrace
originally contained thirty-three houses and
is some 800 feet long. The buildings were
restored after the Second World War. Only
twelve of the houses remain in single
occupation, the remainder being divided
into flats.

A. Saunders, *Regent's Park*, 1969

PLAN OF CUMBERLAND TERRACE
ABOUT 1870

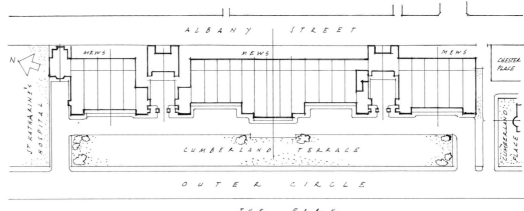

242

GLOUCESTER LODGE
Regent's Park, London
*c.*1826

Gloucester, or Strathirne, Lodge was built for Sir Brook Taylor, the diplomat brother of the Master of neighbouring St Katharine's Hospital. Originally named Strathirne Lodge, the building dates from about the same time as the Hospital and Gloucester Gate, but before Gloucester Terrace (1827). The architect is not recorded but was most probably Nash, who designed the lodge as an Ionic version of his Doric Villa at York Terrace, which it closely resembles. Gloucester Lodge is now a pair of houses.

Elmes, *Metropolitan Improvements*, 1827
E. C. Samuel, *The Villas in Regent's Park and their Residents*, 1959

Gloucester Lodge
is now divided
into two houses

Gloucester Lodge is on the left, next to the Gloucester Gate Lodges (see No. 234); beyond the lodges is St Katharine's Hospital; between the lodges and St Katharine's Hospital, Gloucester Terrace was eventually built. Engraving by S. Lacey after T. H. Shepherd for Elmes, *Metropolitan Improvements*, 1827

243

ST MARY'S CHURCH
Shoreditch, London
1826–1827

Nash designed St Mary's Church in Haggerston for the Commissioners responsible for Building New Churches. The design was as controversial and abused by the critics as had been All Souls, Langham Place. The plain, attenuated tower, topped with a square lantern, must have made a striking landmark. The west front, built in Bath stone, had octagonal towers carrying ogee domes. Inside the brickwork body of the church the gallery was, unusually, carried round all four sides. Built by Robert Streather, the builder of All Souls, St Mary's was destroyed by bombing in 1941.

Elmes, *Metropolitan Improvements*, 1827

THE UNITED SERVICE CLUB

Pall Mall, London
1826–1828

Nash was appointed to build a larger replacement for the original club on the eastern corner of Waterloo Place and Pall Mall. The stuccoed building comprised two storeys and a basement. Two façades had Doric porches, and the third, facing Pall Mall, was given a Corinthian portico. In 1858 Decimus Burton added the ornate frieze, altered the ground-floor windows, and replaced Nash's cast-iron railings with a stone balustrade. He also removed the

St Mary's: one of two London churches built by Nash (see also All Souls, No. 208). Engraving by W. Deeble after T. H. Shepherd for Elmes, q.v.

GROUND-FLOOR PLAN OF THE UNITED SERVICE CLUB

1 Hall
2 Dining-room
3 Bar parlour
4 Offices
5 Coffee room
6 Dining-room
7 Morning-room
8 Area

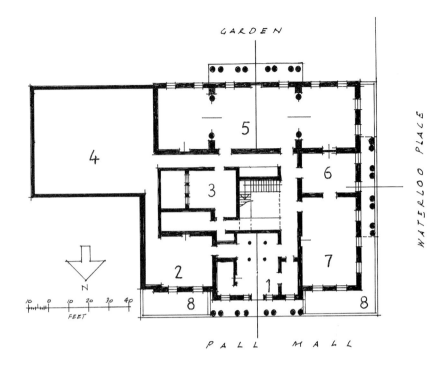

The United Service Club: the ornate decoration was added later by Decimus Burton

The United Service Club: the garden porch

Pall Mall looking east, with the United Service Club in the centre: Nash extended Pall Mall through to the new square and St Martin-in-the-Fields

west porch and added the attic storey. In 1912 the building was extended eastwards along Pall Mall. The Club closed in 1976; the building is now occupied by the Institute of Directors.

Survey of London, xxx, 1960

245

THE WEST STRAND IMPROVEMENTS
London
1826–1831

Nash's starting point was the church of St Martin-in-the-Fields; he placed the block

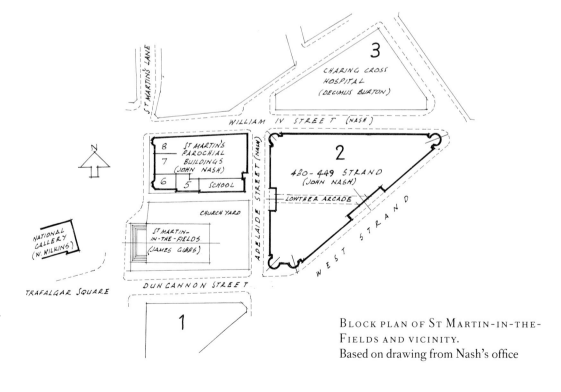

BLOCK PLAN OF ST MARTIN-IN-THE-FIELDS AND VICINITY.
Based on drawing from Nash's office

containing the new parochial buildings parallel to its north wall. North of this he laid out William IV Street, which ran from St Martin's Lane to the Strand. To the south of the church, Duncannon Street was formed to run from Trafalgar Square to the Strand. Across these streets Nash placed Adelaide Street. This grid formed three triangular sites: 1) now occupied by South Africa House, this site was reserved by Nash for public buildings, although in the event commercial hotels and housing took over; 2) Nos 430–49 the Strand (Nash); and 3) Decimus Burton's Charing Cross Hospital. This was the last of Nash's grand plans to be built with William Herbert as builder. Two further schemes were envisaged: an extension of St Martin's Lane northwards to a new square in front of the British Museum, opening up views of Hawksmoor's St George's Church; and a new road from Leicester Square through Holborn to the City. Unfortunately neither was carried out.

Summerson 1980

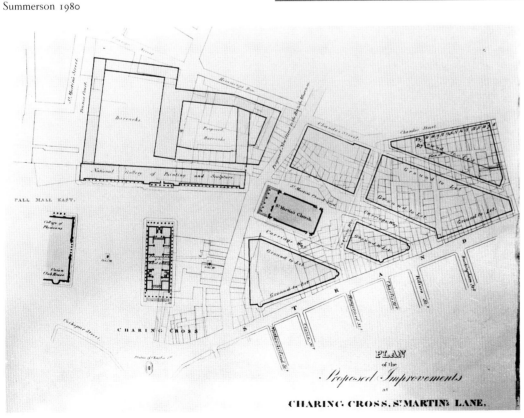

ABOVE Looking west along Duncannon Street, with St Martin-in-the-Fields in the centre: Nash cut Duncannon Street through to the future Trafalgar Square and sited the new National Gallery

LEFT Nash's plan for improvements at Charing Cross, 1826: the rectangular building in the centre is Nash's proposed Royal Academy, which was never built; the National Gallery on the north side was eventually designed by William Wilkins

246

THE NATIONAL GALLERY

Charing Cross, London
1832

After Nash's proposal to house the newly formed national collection of paintings in

247

THE ROYAL ACADEMY OF ARTS
Charing Cross, London
1826

Nash's plan showing what was to be Trafalgar Square had in the centre a building, based on the Parthenon in Athens, allocated to the Royal Academy of Arts, then occupying part of Somerset House. Nothing came of this proposal, the Academy eventually sharing Wilkins's National Gallery building until its move to Burlington House in 1868.

King's Works, vi, 1973

248

KENT TERRACE
Regent's Park, London
1827

The only 'grand' terrace not facing the Park, Kent Terrace is entered from Park Road and backs on to Hanover Terrace.

William Kent's Great Stable at Charing Cross had been turned down, Kent's building was demolished and the site allocated to a new National Gallery. In his design for the competition organized by the Office of Woods, Forests and Land Revenues, Nash proposed a gallery 460 feet long with a central Corinthian portico facing down Whitehall. William Wilkins's design was preferred and today occupies the site on the north side of Trafalgar Square.

King's Works, vi, 1973

Kent Terrace is the only outward-facing one of the Park terraces; (RIGHT) over the doors is Nash's favourite piece of decoration

Gloucester Terrace
is now confusingly
called Gloucester Gate

Nash had to persuade the Commissioners that this arrangement would benefit the neighbourhood by socially upgrading the north end of Park Road, where, with gardens on three sides, it faced the bucolic cottages of Alpha Road, now demolished. The terrace of twenty houses was built by William Smith, who afterwards went bankrupt. Nash, always interested in things new, made it one of the first buildings to be roofed with zinc. The terrace is still residential.

A. Saunders, *Regent's Park*, 1969
P. Potter, Plan of the Parish of St Marylebone, *c.*1832

249

GLOUCESTER TERRACE

Regent's Park, London
1827

Now confusingly known as Gloucester Gate, the terrace was built by Richard Mott. Nash designed it as a block of eleven houses with Ionic pilasters between bays. The centre and ends are emphasized by

Ionic porches carrying attics, with only the end ones having pediments. The mews behind is entered from Albany Street. The stables have been rebuilt or altered to form housing. The terrace itself remains residential.

A. Saunders, *Regent's Park*, 1969

RIGHT
Leamington Spa:
Holly Grove, a green
strip with a
carriageway on either
side
BELOW
Pairs of villas line the
crescent, shown as an
oval on the plan on
the opposite page

250
LEAMINGTON SPA
Warwickshire
1827

Nash was commissioned by Edward Willes
to develop his Newbold Comyn estate,
then on the outskirts of Leamington Priors
(later Spa). Nash, still engaged with his
Metropolitan Improvements, divided the
commission with his long-standing factotum
James Morgan. They laid out a strip of
park on either side of the River Leam, and
a linear garden, Holly Grove, to the north.
The river was crossed by a new bridge

designed by the partners. Roads were built to form crescents, squares and terraces that were divided into building plots, interspersed with public gardens. The present-day layout north of the river still resembles their plan, whilst to the south their scheme seems to have been abandoned. Some houses and terraces recall Nash's Regent's Park buildings, but no firm proof of his authorship has yet been found.

J. Nash and J. Morgan, Plan of Newbold Comyn, 1827 (unpublished)
L. F. Cave, *Royal Leamington Spa*, 1988

Leamington Spa:
(ABOVE)
some villas in Holly Grove recall the Park Villages in Regent's Park;
(RIGHT)
the original layout of Leamington Spa designed by Nash and J. Morgan, 1827

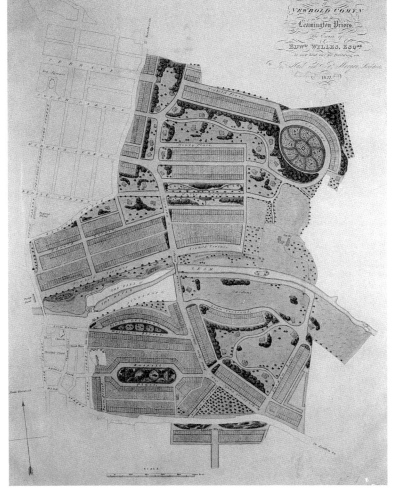

251

HOLY TRINITY CHURCH

Bembridge, Isle of Wight
1827

Holy Trinity Church was a plain Gothic design, about which very little is known

Holy Trinity Church is shown between the two trees; Hill Grove is the domed house to the left. Engraving from G. Brannon, *Vectis Scenery*, 1832

The entrance lodges to Hanover Lodge: the stripped classical pediments recall the Park Square lodges

Hanover Lodge, with St John's Lodge beyond

apart from Brannon's simplified drawing. It stood near Nash's classical house, Hill Grove (No. 153), and as Summerson comments, it must have been 'disgracefully cheap'. It was demolished and replaced by the present church in 1845.

G. Brannon, *Vectis Scenery*, 1832
Summerson 1980

252

HANOVER LODGE
Regent's Park, London
*c.*1827

The house designed for Sir Robert Arbuthnot has recently been attributed to Decimus Burton, since drawings bearing his name were found. It had previously been considered a design by Nash. Certainly the frontal elevation, consisting of a recessed centre and projecting porch, had been used by Nash at Llanaeron (No. 28), the Warrens (No. 65), and in the Park itself at Cambridge Terrace (No. 222). The pair of entrance lodges in Park Road recalls Nash's stylized lodges in Park Crescent and Park Square. It would seem probable that Nash made a preliminary sketch and handed it over to Burton for completion.

A. Saunders, *The Regent's Park Villas*, 1981

253

HOSPITAL OF ST CROSS
Winchester, Hampshire
1827–1829

The Hospital of St Cross, in the water meadows of the River Itchen, was founded

Hospital of St Cross: tall chimneys mark the Brethren's lodgings; the courtyard is open to the south

by the Brethren of the de Blois (1136) and Beaufort (1145) Foundations. The Hospital is built on three sides of a courtyard: the twelfth-century Chapel, on the east side, faces the fifteenth-century almshouses, the Hall closes the north side, and the southern side was left open. The restoration was begun by a fellow pupil of Nash's, Samuel Pepys Cockerell. After Cockerell's death in 1827 Nash completed the work, spending some £750, which was quite a large sum at that time.

Summerson 1980

254

PARISH BUILDINGS OF ST MARTIN-IN-THE-FIELDS
Charing Cross, London
1827–1830

The Vicarage of St Martin-in-the-Fields was demolished in the Royal Mews clearances in

1825, and Nash planned new parochial buildings on the island site north of the church. The new Vicarage, on the corner of St Martin's Place, was given a canted bay window and projecting porch. The two attic storeys are later additions; they make a nonsense of Nash's cornice line, which matches that of the church, and diminish the pediment on the Vestry Hall, further along the footpath. The row is completed by St Martin's National School, built on land donated by George IV, with a simple, elegant façade of giant Ionic columns on the rusticated ground floor. An Application for Aid, dated 13 October 1827, for building the school to a design – presented gratuitously to the Parish – by John Nash, is in the files of the National Society. A further application for aid was made in December 1829, when the design was estimated to cost £4,650.

See plan on p.286.

The National Society Archives (unpublished)
Survey of London, xx, 1940

ABOVE
St Martin-in-the-Fields Vicarage, Vestry Hall, and School, with 430–449 the Strand in the background; the two top floors of the Vestry are later additions.
LEFT
St Martin's School

St Martin's pedimented Vestry Hall, with the
Vicarage on the corner

Carlton Mews: (ABOVE) the first-floor stables with grooms' quarters above,
and (BELOW) the horses' access ramp to the stables. Photographs dated 1951

255

CARLTON MEWS

St James's, London
1827–1829

Carlton Mews was designed by Nash as
stable accommodation for Carlton House

Terraces. The first phase consisted of
coach-houses at ground level, with stables
above, which were reached by ramps and
galleries. The next phase was a courtyard
with the same stable accommodation on
three sides, plus an additional storey for
grooms' quarters above. The galleries to
the brick-built mews had iron railings and
were supported on cast-iron brackets. Each

lessee built his own stable to Nash's master
plan. In the 1930s the stables were
converted into mews houses, forming an
unexpected and delightful enclave. Carlton
Mews survived both world wars, only to be
demolished to make way for Government
offices.

King's Works, vi, 1973

Carlton House Terrace: (ABOVE LEFT) the western Terrace; (ABOVE RIGHT) the entrance fronts and the Duke of York's Column; (RIGHT) the final solution was a broad flight of steps up to the Duke of York's Column

256
CARLTON HOUSE TERRACES
St James's, London
1827–1833

The two Terraces form a backcloth to the Royal Processional route of the Mall and were built on the sites of Carlton House and Warwick House. The difference in ground levels from front to back gave the Park elevation an extra storey to the Mall elevation. These lower ground floors, faced

Carlton House
Terraces, with the
Mall in the foreground

The entrance fronts,
with the Nash device
over the windows

with cast-iron Doric columns, were used
for kitchens and offices, with the roofs
forming private terraces. Above rise two
storeys faced with Corinthian colonnades
and carrying an attic storey with a central
pediment filled in with ornament by
Bernasconi. The nine houses in each
terrace were built as individual units by
several architects; all had to conform to
Nash's master Park elevations. Nash built
eight of the houses himself. In the western
block he built No. 5 for Lord Caledon
(Nash's client at Caledon House, County
Tyrone), the interiors of which are still
extant and are good examples of Nash's
work; No. 7 for William Henning; and No.
9 for James Alexander. In the eastern block
No. 10 was built for Sir Matthew Ridley,
No. 12 for the Marquis of Cholmondeley

BELOW Carlton Gardens: the flight of steps was added afterwards

and No. 13 for the Marquis's mother, the Dowager Marchioness. Major-General Balfour took No. 14, and the Marquis of Tavistock took No. 15.

King's Works, vi, 1973
Survey of London, xx, 1940
Shide Hill Ledger

257

CARLTON GARDENS
St James's, London
1827–1833

In about 1825 it was proposed that Marlborough House should be demolished and a third block of the Carlton House Terraces built in its place. This idea was abandoned and Nash laid out the remaining piece of the Carlton House gardens with seven houses: two pairs faced each other across the oval grassed centrepiece, with the others in a single block on the north

3 Carlton Gardens:
the projecting porch is
a later addition

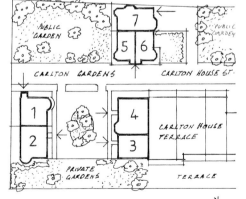

PLAN OF CARLTON
GARDENS.
Based on drawing
from Nash's office

1 Sir Alexander Grant
2 William Huskisson
3 Charles Arbuthnot
4 W. G. Coesvelt
5 Count de Salis
6 Henry Baring
7 Charles Herries

2 Carlton Gardens: the elevation to St James's
Park

side of Carlton House Street, surrounded
by private and public gardens. No. 4 was
replaced in 1923 with a huge, out-of-scale
house; in 1960 the northern three houses
were demolished to make way for an office
block.

Survey of London, xx, 1940

258
THE STATE PAPER OFFICE
Whitehall, London
1828

The Treasury decided, in 1828, to rebuild the State Paper Office in Whitehall. The attached architects – Soane, Smirke and Nash – were invited to submit designs and estimates. Nash, in his report, made the point that his building would be fireproof, with a flat roof of cast-iron beams and brick infill arches, an early example of filler joist construction. Soane's design was chosen, presumably because it was in his 'district' in the Office of Woods, Forests and Land Revenues. The building was demolished in 1862.

King's Works, vi, 1973

259
MARBLE ARCH
London
1828

Originally designed and built as the entrance to the forecourt of Buckingham Palace, the design for Marble Arch was most probably based on the Arc du Carrousel in Paris, which Nash would have seen on his visits. The first intention was to build the Arch in Bath stone, later changed to Ravaccione marble; the relief carvings on the north face are by Richard Westmacott, the southern ones by Edward Hodges Baily. S. Parker designed the centre cast-iron gate. Chantrey's equestrian statue of George IV, intended for the top, is now in Trafalgar Square. The Arch was almost completed in 1830, when Edward Blore took over the completion of Buckingham Palace from Nash. It became redundant as an entrance when the east wing was added to the palace, and it was taken down and put in storage. It was eventually re-erected at Cumberland Gate, Hyde Park, in 1851; it acquired the name Marble Arch, which was later adopted by the locality.

King's Works, vi, 1973

The Marble Arch, relocated north of Hyde Park

260
KING'S COLLEGE
Regent's Park, London
1828

In 1828 King's College applied to the Commissioners for a site on the Inner Circle of Regent's Park. Nash's plan of the Park, dated 1828, shows the Inner Circle laid out as gardens. Attached to the plan is an overlay block plan with four right-angled blocks placed around a quadrangle containing a circular chapel. The proposal to have students in Regent's Park was received with such uproar by the inhabitants that the idea was immediately abandoned and King's College was built in the Strand.

Summerson 1980

Statue of George III: (RIGHT) Nash's design for the base of the Copper Horse, c.1830; (LEFT) the base as built was possibly by Wyatville

261

STATUE OF GEORGE III

Windsor Great Park, Berkshire
1830

The equestrian statue, also known as the Copper Horse, stands on a hilltop looking down the Long Walk in Windsor Great Park. Nash prepared a design for a classical base but it was not built. The present base of rough boulders is probably by Wyatville.

King's Works, vi, 1973

262

ST JAMES'S CHURCH

East Cowes, Isle of Wight
1831–1833

For his own parish at East Cowes, Nash designed an inexpensive plain Gothic church and tower. The body of the church

St James's Church: the tower was designed by Nash, who with his second wife lies buried in the white tomb at its base

was later taken down and a larger one built against his tower, at the foot of which Nash and his wife are buried.

Summerson 1980

263

RESIDENCE FOR LORD BELFAST

West Cowes, Isle of Wight
1832

George Hamilton Chichester (1797–1883), Earl of Belfast, was the son of the second Marquis of Donegal. He lived at 108 Pall Mall and later at 23 Arlington Street, London, before acquiring an address in West Cowes. Nash's diary for 1832 has two references to work for Lord Belfast at West Cowes. So far his address has not been identified.

John Nash's Diary, 1832

The Strand: (ABOVE LEFT) the junction of the Strand and William IV Street; (ABOVE) the Doric-columned opening in Adelaide Street was the entrance to the Lowther Arcade; (OPPOSITE LEFT) the twin pepper pots, on the corner of the Strand and Adelaide Street

264

430–449 THE STRAND

London

1830

The triangular site bounded by the Strand, William IV Street and Adelaide Street was part of Nash's West Strand Improvements. It was developed by William Herbert, with shops and living accommodation over. A covered passage, the Lowther Arcade, ran from Adelaide Street to the Strand and was later famous for its toy-shops. Central pavilions with giant Corinthian columns or pilasters were repeated on three fronts. With consummate ease Nash used domed, cylindrical towers to turn the three unequal corners. In the 1970s Frederick Gibberd and Partners restored all of Nash's work except for the Strand centrepiece and then spoiled it with monstrous roofs.

See plan on p.286.

S. Cantacuzino, 'The fall and rise of a Regency terrace', *The Architectural Review*, March 1979

Aroid House:
the third pavilion at
Buckingham Palace
was removed and re-
erected at Kew Palace

eastern terraces – Gloucester, Cumberland, Chester and Cambridge – into segments by planting copses and plantations, between which fresh vistas would be unfolded as one advanced up the Broad Walk.

Summerson 1935
Summerson 1980

265

REGENT'S PARK GARDEN

London
1832

The Regent's Park garden referred to in Nash's diary for 1832 was possibly

intended for the centre of the Inner Circle, replacing the buildings of King's College proposed in 1828 and abandoned shortly afterwards. At about the same time as the garden was designed Nash proposed extending the Broad Walk northwards across Regent's Park to meet the Outer Circle, where an obelisk would be erected. He also wanted to divide the view of the

266

AROID HOUSE

Kew Gardens, Surrey
1836

Aroid House was originally one of three garden pavilions that Nash built at Buckingham Palace. They are unusual in having Tuscan piers along the sides and Ionic columns at each end. The building was moved to Kew Gardens in 1836 on the instructions of William IV, who is reputed to have chosen the site himself.

King's Works, vi, 1973

UNDATED WORKS

267

HOUSE FOR LORD GAGE

Date unknown

Sir John Summerson, in his 1935 book on Nash, refers to a house for Lord Gage that is mentioned in Knight's *English Cyclopedia* (Biography) and adds that there is no evidence of one having been built. No other reference has been found.

268

COLBY LODGE

Amroth, Pembrokeshire
Date unknown

Colby Lodge was built for a member of the Colby family of Ffynone and is attributed to Nash, possibly because the work was supervised by one of his Clerks of Work. The two stuccoed blocks, set at right angles, are unhappily built to conflicting scales. The property is now owned by the National Trust.

Davis 1966

269

COWDRAY PARK

Midhurst, Sussex
Date unknown

William Poyntz, MP, of Grosvenor Place, London, and Midgham House, Newbury, Berkshire, seems to have acquired Cowdray Park sometime before his death in 1809. George Repton's RIBA Sketchbook shows a rustic column and simple capital, marked William Poyntz, that was possibly intended for Cowdray. Poyntz's third daughter, Isabella Henrietta, married

Cowdray Park: (BELOW) drawings of rustic column and capital, from George Repton's RIBA Sketchbook; (OPPOSITE LEFT) design for a conservatory for Lady Cork, from George Repton's Brighton Sketchbook

Colby Lodge: the present entrance

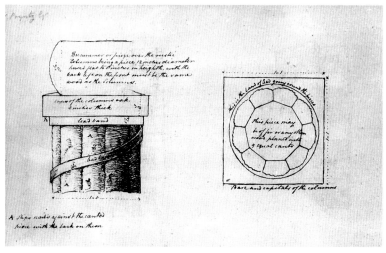

Edmund Boyle, eighth Earl of Cork and Orrery, of Marston House, Frome, Somerset, in 1795. She later (presumably after she became Dowager Countess) commissioned Nash to design a heated conservatory. The intended site is not known.

Repton, RIBA Sketchbook
Repton, Brighton Sketchbook

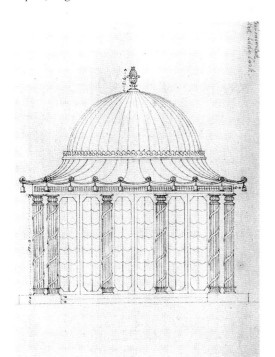

Albury Park:
(RIGHT) the conservatory roof is carried on Nash's standard iron truss, from George Repton's Brighton Sketchbook;
(BELOW) the causeway was dressed up as a bridge to form an eye-catcher, from George Repton's RIBA Sketchbook

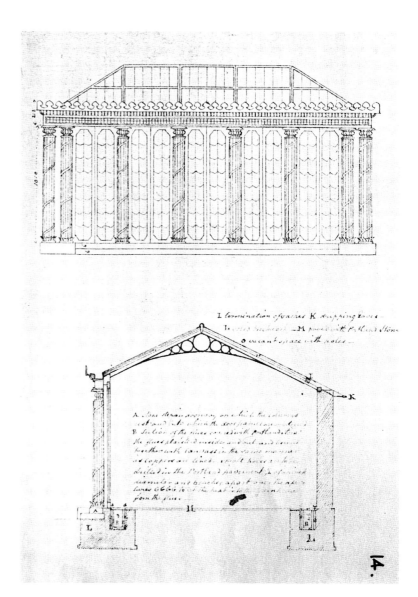

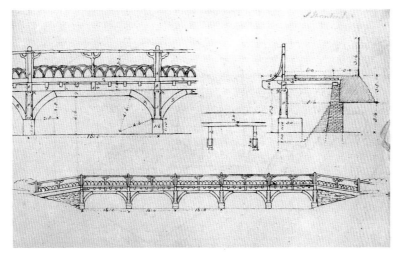

270

ALBURY PARK
Albury, Surrey
Date unknown

George Repton's Sketchbook at Brighton contains a design for a heated conservatory with open-work iron columns and entablatures. The iron roof trusses match those used at the Barnsley Park orangery (No. 101). The RIBA Sketchbook shows a rustic five-arched bridge designed to close the view at the end of the lake. Both designs are marked 'Samuel Thornton Esq, Albury Park'. No trace of either the conservatory or the bridge has been found on the site.

Repton, RIBA Sketchbook
Repton, Brighton Sketchbook

271

COTTAGE AT STOKE EDITH
Herefordshire, or

PRESTWOOD HALL
Kinver, Staffordshire

Date unknown

The Hon Edward Foley, MP, had estates at Stoke Edith, in Herefordshire, and

Prestwood Hall, near Kinver in Staffordshire. Humphry Repton worked on both and produced a *Red Book* for Prestwood Hall in 1791 and one for Stoke Edith sometime before 1794. In his *Memoir* Repton refers to being introduced to Nash by Edward Foley in 1790 but does not say at which house the introduction took place. Neither is it known for which house the cottage shown in George Repton's RIBA Sketchbook was intended. The drawing is marked 'Mr Foley' and is possibly the result of an earlier collaboration between Nash and Humphry Repton at one of Foley's estates.

G. Carter, P. Goode, K. Laurie, *Humphry Repton, Landscape Gardener*, 1982

End elevations of a classical gymnasium at Belmont, from George Repton's RIBA Sketchbook

The cottage for Mr Foley, which might have been designed either for Stoke Edith or for Prestwood Hall, from George Repton's RIBA Sketchbook

Belmont: design for a gatehouse, from George Repton's RIBA Sketchbook

BELMONT

Clehonger, Herefordshire
Date unknown

Dr John Matthews retired from practising medicine in London while still in his thirties and built his country house, Belmont (designed by James Wyatt), in 1790. Among his neighbours were Uvedale Price at Foxley, George Cornewall of Moccas and the Hon Edward Foley at Stoke Edith, all clients of Nash. It is not known how many estate buildings Nash erected at Belmont, nor when. Two almost certainly built by him exist: Dewsall Lodge, similar to the Circular Cottage at Blaise Hamlet (No. 133); and Woodman's (now Lake) Cottage, both considerably altered. Neither is shown in George Repton's Sketchbooks, where other designs marked 'Matthews' include a gatehouse, gymnasium and three cottages. Nigel

Dewsall Lodge, similar to Circular Cottage at Blaise Hamlet: the pent roof was once continuous and the roof was thatched; the back extension is later

Elevation of Spring Grove, declared derelict in 1964 and demolished, from George Repton's Brighton Sketchbook

Design for an estate farmhouse or large cottage at Belmont, from George Repton's RIBA Sketchbook

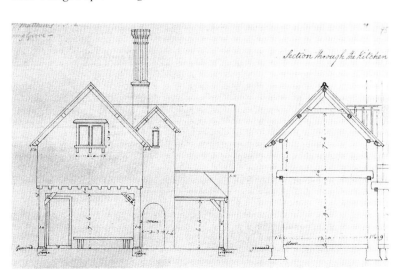

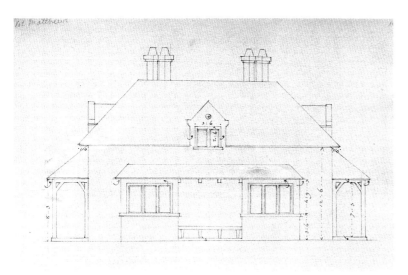

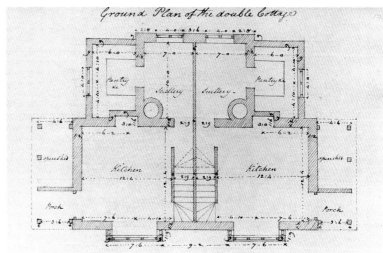

Temple identified one cottage as No. 2 Spring Grove and the other two as the pair forming Belmont Post Office; both were demolished in the 1960s. Humphry Repton worked here before 1794, and since he had been introduced to Nash in 1790 it is likely that some if not all of the buildings date from then.

N. Temple, *John Nash and the Village Picturesque*, 1979

Belmont: elevation of the double cottage, probably Belmont Post Office, demolished since 1964, from George Repton's Brighton Sketchbook

Ground-floor plan of the double cottage, from George Repton's Brighton Sketchbook

RIGHT
Barton Manor: design for a *ferme ornée* on the Barton estate

273

BARTON MANOR
East Cowes, Isle of Wight
Date unknown

The Barton Manor estate adjoined the eastern boundary of the Osborne estate. Barton Farm was a cottage designed by Nash, but to judge from its accommodation of drawing-room and dining-room, both with canted bay windows and columned loggias, it was intended to be more of a *ferme ornée* than a farmer's cottage.

Repton, RIBA Sketchbook

274

CRAWFORDSBURN
Near Bangor, County Down
Date unknown

The estate of Crawfordsburn was owned in Nash's time by John Crawford, the uncle of the second Earl of Caledon, for whom Nash worked at Caledon and Carlton House Terrace. The design is one of a series that started with Tern Lodge at Attingham Park (No. 55). A drawing for a similar lodge exists in the library at Caledon. The estate is now a magnificent country park, with the lodge still serving as a gatehouse at the main entrance.

N. Temple, *Society of Cymmrodorion*, 1985

ABOVE Mrs Jennings' house. Drawing attributed to Joseph Nash (Royal Library, Windsor Castle)
ABOVE RIGHT Proposed bridge across the Long Walk. Artist unknown (RIBA)

Crawfordsburn: the lodge

275

WINDSOR GREAT PARK (BRIDGE and COTTAGE)

Berkshire
Date unknown

An estate plan in the Public Record Office shows that a piece of land on each side of the Long Walk in Windsor Great Park was owned (until 1828, when it was sold to the Crown) by somebody called Foster, who claimed to have road access across the Long Walk linking the two pieces. As this was the only private land straddling the Long Walk, it was presumably the site that had been previously owned by Mrs Jennings, for whom Nash is reputed to have designed the triple-arched Norman bridge (attribution on stylistic grounds by Dr Tim Mowl). A drawing in the Royal Collection shows an exotic Chinese house, also possibly by Nash, described as being for Mrs Jennings in Windsor Great Park. A drawing of 'Mrs Jennings Villa' was included in the sale of Nash's effects in 1835. Neither structure was built.

The Royal Library, Windsor Castle
The Public Record Office, London
J. Lever (ed.), *Catalogue of the Drawings Collection of the Royal Institute of British Architects*, 1973

276

26 SOHO SQUARE
London
Date unknown

No. 26 Soho Square was the house of George Ward, a neighbour and client of Nash's in the Isle of Wight. Nash, who lived in London, would have been the obvious choice of architect for extending Ward's London house, and there are drawings for the alterations in a folio of Ward's papers from Northwood House (now in the British Library). The major additions of stables and kitchens, if carried out, have long since disappeared, and the proposed curved back wall to the house was not built.

British Library MS 18159
N. Temple, *IOW Society*, 1987

277

SOMERSET HOUSE
Coleraine, County Derry
Date unknown

The early eighteenth-century villa overlooking the River Bann was built for the Richardson family. The house had two storeys with one bow end, and the canted bay in the centre of the west front contained the main entrance. In the posthumous sale of Nash's drawings, one lot was described as being for 'Mr Richardson, Somerset House, nr Coleraine'. There is no documentary evidence that this is the house or that Nash was replaced by another architect.

Nash Sale Catalogue, 1835

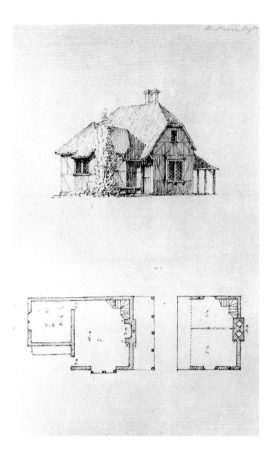

Somerset House: behind the house, greatly overgrown, are remains of a stable block with circular windows

ABOVE Foxley: design and plan of the half-timbered cottage

278

FOXLEY
Yazor, Herefordshire
Date unknown

Designed for Uvedale Price for his Herefordshire estate at Foxley, the cottage must date from after 1795, when Nash first worked for Price at Aberystwyth. Drawings of the cottage are in George Repton's RIBA Sketchbook. The cottage cannot now be found.

Repton, RIBA Sketchbook

279

TOWNLEY HALL

Burnley, Lancashire
Date unknown, but before 1805

Included in the 1835 sale of Nash's drawings were alternative designs for something at Towneley [sic], near Burnley, presumably for Charles Townley (1737–1805), the famous collector of antique statuary. Nash's design was made before 1805, as Townley's successor, Peregrine Townley, then employed Jeffry Wyatt.

Nash Sale Catalogue, 1835

RIGHT
Elevation of Mr Goodrich's house: the bay window lit the parlour and Mr and Mrs Goodrich's bedroom above. From George Repton's Brighton Sketchbook
BELOW
Plan for chamber floor of Mr Goodrich's house, probably Spring Hill House, from George Repton's Brighton Sketchbook

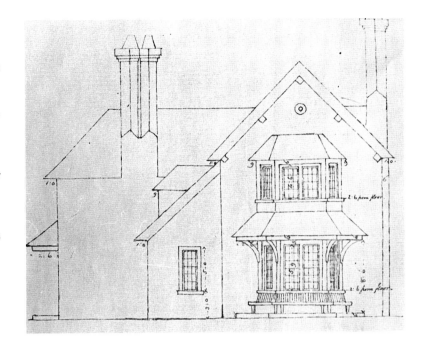

280

MR GOODRICH'S HOUSE

Isle of Wight
Date unknown

George Repton's Brighton Sketchbook contains plans and an elevation of a small house with a two-storeyed canted bay window, a variation on the front of Blaise Castle dairy (No. 43). The ground floor had a dining-room, 'Parlor' and a storeroom for Mr Goodrich; the chamber floor had two bedrooms with servants' garrets behind. Offices and the kitchen were in the basement. No such cottage has been found. Temple tentatively suggests that if it was built it could have been Spring Hill House, East Cowes, known to have been occupied by the Goodriches in 1813. A convent now stands on the site.

N. Temple, *IOW Society*, 1988

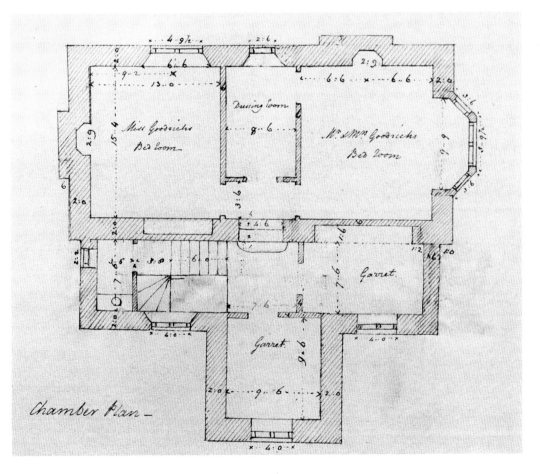

Chamber Plan —

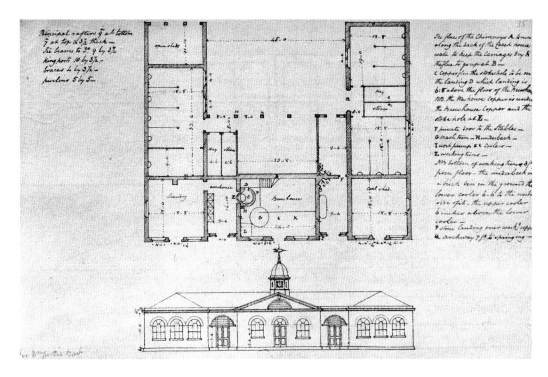

GELLI-TAL-SARN
Cardiganshire
Date unknown

Nash's plain stuccoed extension block was placed across the end of the earlier Tal Sarn farmhouse, and the farmhouse became the service wing. It is remarkably unaltered: only the side glazing to the Venetian windows has been replaced. Two of Nash's favourite details occur, paired brackets under the eaves and diagonally set

LEFT Cliff House: the stable block, from George Repton's Brighton Sketchbook
BELOW Gelli-tal-Sarn: the louvred sidelights were originally glazed

281

CLIFF HOUSE
Ramsgate, Kent
Date unknown

Sir William Curtis of Cullands Grove, Lord Mayor of London, was a member of the Prince Regent's circle and therefore known to Nash. Besides Cullands Grove, Middlesex, he acquired another country estate, Cliff House, Ramsgate. Both of George Repton's Sketchbooks contain work for him: the Brighton one shows a stable block, probably for Ramsgate, where preparations were being made for a possible visit by the Prince Regent; the RIBA Sketchbook has a detail of a cornice, presumably for the same stables.

Repton, Brighton Sketchbook
Repton, RIBA Sketchbook

Gelli-tal-Sarn: the new wing was placed at right angles to the old farmhouse

The gatehouse at Gelli-tal-Sarn

chimney stacks. The posts to the porch, quatrefoil in plan, are made of cast iron. The design of the octagonal rustic gatehouse was to be used again, with variations, at Charborough Park in Dorset (No. 126), and Holwood House in Kent (No. 60). T. Lloyd has recently discovered a similar design at Llanstinan (Pembrokeshire). Gelli-tal-Sarn is situated in the Aeron Valley and was once occupied by Dylan Thomas.

GLASLOUGH CASTLE
County Monaghan
Date unknown

In the immediate vicinity of Caledon House are two other estates with buildings attributed to Nash: Glaslough Castle and Tynan Abbey (No. 168), both probably the results of introductions by Lord Caledon. Glaslough Castle, also known as Castle Leslie, is a Victorian mansion incorporating an earlier house. The arched entrance and gatehouse are considered to have been designed by Nash; the outsized Gothic window used as an eye-catcher on entering the estate was a device used by him at Attingham Park (No. 55) and the boathouse at Corsham (No. 54).

Lord Killanin and M. V. Duigram, *The Shell Guide to County Monaghan, Northern Ireland*, 1962

Glaslough Castle: the finials to the arched entrance resemble those of Killymoon (see No. 74)

80–82 Chapel Street: the creeper-covered house on the left was the original Dower House

284

80–82 CHAPEL STREET
Cookstown, County Tyrone
Date unknown

Local attributions give Nash as the architect of the Dower House, which was built for the Stewarts of Killymoon Castle (No. 74) in the main street of nearby Cookstown. It is now two houses, with the central bow forming part of the left-hand house. The right-hand house was probably an extension. They are finished in harling, or Irish roughcast, with slated roofs. Both the doorcases have transoms on quarter-round, fluted, wooden columns. The glazing bars in the fanlights are missing.

Ulster Architectural Heritage Society, *Cookstown*, 1970/1

285

FENAGHY HOUSE
Ballymena, County Antrim
Date unknown

The present Fenaghy House was built for the Cunningham family in 1857. At the entrance to the estate still stands an early nineteenth-century gate lodge, much rebuilt. Its open porch, flanked with cruciform slit windows, and the miniature gables-cum-dormer windows breaking the eaves line survive to show its parentage stemming from Oak Cottage at Blaise Hamlet (No. 133) through several others that Nash left scattered around the countryside. Fenaghy is reasonably near to Shanes Castle and could have been designed by Nash or by contemporary architects trained in his office, like the Paine brothers.

Ulster Architectural Heritage Society, *West Antrim*, 1970

BELOW Fenaghy House: the gate lodge

ABOVE Woodpark Lodge: remains of octagonal towers and linking loggia

286

WOODPARK LODGE
Killylea, County Armagh
Date unknown

Woodpark Lodge was the gatehouse for the Killylea Castle estate before being rebuilt as a square Georgian house for the Blackwood family, later the Lords Dufferin, who added the battlements, canted bays and linking arcade in the early 1830s. Woodpark was burnt out one hundred years later and today only the derelict shell remains. The late T. G. F. Patterson, local historian and curator of the Armagh Museum, considered that Nash designed the alterations in about 1830.

CONJECTURAL WORKS

Evidence exists of some projects which were apparently designed by Nash but which have so far not been traced. Among Nash's architectural drawings sold after his death were some 'Statues of Cardinal Wolsey and Henry VI. Christ Church. Ox'. These were possibly for plinths or bases, but nothing has been found. Untraced works mentioned in the Shide Hill Ledger include some building work in Marylebone Street, London (1823), and a candelabrum base for the Very Reverend James Hook at Worcester Cathedral (1826), who was Nash's client at St Mildred's Rectory, Isle of Wight (No. 81).

In Wales a number of houses attributed to Nash were probably designed by local builders copying the fashionable architect from London. Later his name was added to auction advertisements in order to attract a higher price. Thomas Lloyd has recently drawn attention to the remains of a circular lodge at Llanstinan in Pembrokeshire, similar to Gelli-tal-Sarn (No. 282) but with ogee windows, and to yet another lodge at Cwmgwili in Carmarthenshire that could have been designed by Nash. Mr Lloyd also points out that Nash, having worked for Richard Foley at Haverfordwest (No. 24),

ABOVE Yaverton Rectory, Isle of Wight
BELOW LEFT Swainston Manor, Isle of Wight
BELOW RIGHT This design is possibly the first of the Claudean series (see No. 72)

might well have been involved with nearby Ridgeway, the house of Richard Foley's brother John Herbert, and with Abermalais, built in Carmarthenshire at about the same time by another brother, Admiral Thomas Foley. Both these houses were unfortunately demolished.

In England, Dr Nigel Temple considers it possible that Nash might have had a hand in the alterations at Swainston Manor, Isle of Wight, which acquired a pair of bow windows similar to those added by Nash to neighbouring Westover (No. 151). At the eastern end of the Isle of Wight, Yaverton Rectory could well have been designed by Nash.

No doubt other buildings with a claim to be by Nash will come to light. Several of the smaller estate buildings recorded in G. S. Repton's Sketchbooks have still to be identified, including a cottage in the style of Cronkhill (No. 72), possibly intended for the unbuilt village at Atcham (No. 52).

CLIENTS AND PATRONS

In the list below Nash's works are followed by their catalogue numbers

Abergavenny Town Council — Abergavenny, Monmouthshire 27

Adams, Sir William — Ophthalmic Hospital, London 180

Adult Orphan Asylum Committee — Someries House 220

Agnew, Edward — Kilwaughter Castle, Co. Antrim 108

Alexander, James — 9 Carlton House Terrace, London 250

Ashburton, Lady — Sandridge Park, Devonshire 90

Belfast, Lord — Residence at West Cowes, Isle of Wight 263

Bembridge, Parish of — Holy Trinity Church, Bembridge, Isle of Wight 251

Berwick, Lord — Atcham, Shropshire 52
Attingham Park, Shropshire 55
Cronkhill, Shropshire 72

Blachford family — Osborne Cottage, East Cowes, Isle of Wight 83

Blackburne, John — Hale Hall, Lancashire 96

Blicke, C. T. — 15 Regent Street, London 194

Bloomfield, Sir Benjamin (with Office of Woods, Forests and Land Revenues) — The Stud House, Hampton Court Palace, Middlesex 182

Board of Works — Carlton Gardens, London 257
Carlton House Terraces, London 256
Carlton Mews, London 255
Green Park, London 152
Hyde Park 97
King's Mews, London 170
Marble Arch, London 259
Royal Mews, London 207
St James's Park, London 161
Windsor Castle, Berkshire 213

(with the Prince Regent) — Cumberland (or Great) Lodge, Windsor Great Park, Berkshire 155

Botfield, Thomas — Hopton Court, Shropshire 134

Boughey, John Fenton Fletcher — Aqualate Hall, Staffordshire 92

Bowen, John — Cardigan Priory 44

Brethren of St Cross — Hospital of St Cross, Winchester, Hampshire 253

Bulkeley, Henry — Temple Druid, Pembrokeshire 37

Burrell, Bt, Sir Charles Merrick — Knepp Castle, Sussex 122

Burrell, Walter — West Grinstead Park, Sussex 121

Burton, Robert — Longner Hall, Shropshire 77

Cahir, 12th Baron (later Earl of Glengall) — Swiss Cottage, Cahir Park, Co. Tipperary 175

Cahir, Parish of — St Paul's Church, Cahir, Co. Tipperary 179

Caledon, 2nd Earl of — Caledon House, Co. Tyrone 116
5 Carlton House Terrace, London 256

Caledon, Parish of St John — St John's Church, Caledon, Co. Tyrone 113

Cardigan, 6th Earl of — Deene Park, Northamptonshire 75

Cardigan Magistrates — Rheidol Bridge, Aberystwyth 18
Tre-Cefel Bridge, Cardiganshire 21

Cardigan Town Council — Cardigan Gaol 22

Carmarthen, Church Council of St Peter's — St Peter's Church, Carmarthen 3

Carmarthen, Parish of — St David's Church, Carmarthen 215

Carmarthen Town Council — Carmarthen Gaol 12
Picton Monument, Carmarthen 236

Chichester City Council — Market House, Chichester, Sussex 103

Clarence, Duke of (with Board of Works) — Bushey House, Middlesex 107
Clarence House, London 238

Colby, Captain John — Ffynone, Pembrokeshire 19

GAZETTEER

Nash's works are listed below by the counties as they were known in his day, with the modern names given in brackets. The works are followed by their catalogue numbers.

ENGLAND

BERKSHIRE Cranbourne Lodge, Windsor Great
Park 157
Cumberland Lodge (Great Lodge),
Windsor Great Park 155
George III, Statue of, Windsor Great
Park 261
Royal Race Stand, Ascot 203
Royal Lodge, Windsor Great Park 137
Windsor Castle 213
Windsor Great Park (Bridge and
Cottage) 275

BRISTOL Harfords Bank 135

BUCKINGHAMSHIRE Bulstrode House 73
Chalfont House 62
Shardeloes 23

CHESHIRE High Legh Hall 56

THE BRITISH ISLES

*Nash's architectural practice took him from Wales to England and Ireland,
with a solitary excursion into Scotland. Visits to the sites were made by horse-
drawn carriages over rough country roads and tracks, with the few exceptions of
John McAdam's newly surfaced trunk roads. In one year alone, Nash told
Farington, he had travelled eleven thousand miles at a cost of £1,500 for
chaise hire. In addition he regularly commuted from London to his country
house on the Isle of Wight.*

*The county names and boundaries shown on the map are those of the early
nineteenth century. Present-day county names are given in brackets in the
Gazetteer.*

SLIGO

61 127
128

ROSCOMMON

GALWAY

132

TIPPERARY

175, 179
181

CORK

115

• site of Nash building
● more than one building at site
▦ London

0   50 miles

DERRY

ANTRIM

277

285

142

108

TYRONE

74, 106, 205, 284

113, 116

283

286

168

ARMAGH

DOWN

MONAGHAN

QUEEN'S COUNTY

72

KIRKCUDBRIGHTSHIRE

46

DURHAM

111

20

YORKSHIRE

162

279

LANCASHIRE

159

98

96

56

FLINTSHIRE

71

CHESHIRE

105

CAERNARVONSHIRE

124

STAFFORDSHIRE

120

25

92

52, 55, 72, 77

47

SHROPSHIRE

271

69

WARWICK-SHIRE

75

HUNTINGDON-SHIRE

14

18, 38

140

26

134

35

NORTHAMPTON-SHIRE

100

SUFFOLK

156

CARDIGANSHIRE

114

110

21

RADNOR-SHIRE

4

86

250

66

28, 29, 30

282

93

40

119

WORCESTER-SHIRE

22, 44

82

131

7

HEREFORD-SHIRE

99

278

271

19

17

84

50

37

CARMARTHENSHIRE

BRECONSHIRE

272

OXFORD-SHIRE

41

BUCKINGHAM-SHIRE

PEMBROKESHIRE

10

33

68, 164, 177

32

11

36

13

27

23

51

MIDDLESEX

24, 31

GLOUCESTER-SHIRE

62

42

163

268

16

148

130

MONMOUTH-SHIRE

15

87

101

BERKSHIRE

78

73

107

266

158

49

58

2

3, 5, 6, 8, 9, 12, 215, 236

34

137, 155, 157, 213, 261, 275

182

48

60

GLAMORGAN

BRISTOL

43, 133

135

203

178

118

76, 237

KENT

63

45

WILTSHIRE

SURREY

270

DEVONSHIRE

SOMERSETSHIRE

HAMPSHIRE

64

253

88

94

122

SUSSEX

129

269

121

112

65

103

165

109

104, 125

39

53

153, 251

67, 173

85

95

89 ISLE OF WIGHT

126

151

79

59, 83, 190, 262, 273, 280

70, 214, 230, 263

81, 149

138, 154

CORNWALL

80

90

117

LONDON

Nash's plans for London were almost entirely confined to the north-western outskirts, where the open countryside of Marylebone Park was developed into the residential area of Regent's Park. Linked to this by his New Street, later named Regent Street, were his redevelopments in the built-up areas of St James's and Charing Cross. Nash's plan to build a new street from Charing Cross to the British Museum was, alas, turned down.

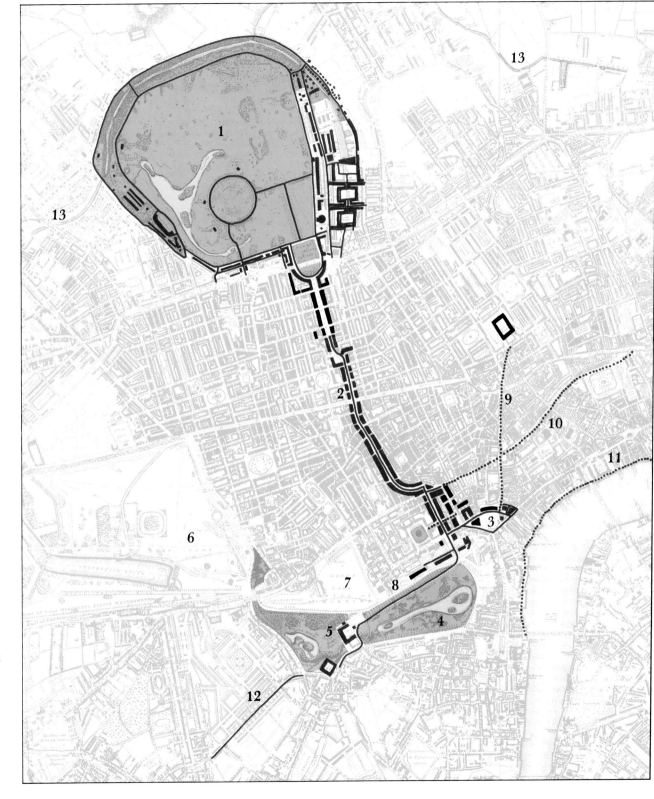

1 Regent's Park
2 Regent Street
3 West Strand
4 St James's Park
5 Buckingham Palace
6 Hyde Park
7 Green Park
8 St James's Palace
9 road to British Museum
10 road to the City
11 Thames Embankment
12 The King's Road
13 Regent's Canal

◼ Nash's completed
buildings

◼ existing buildings
incorporated by Nash
into his design

— Nash's roads

•••••• Nash's proposed
roads never built

▢ Nash's open spaces

GLOSSARY OF ARCHITECTURAL TERMS

antefixae	The upright ornamental pieces used to conceal the ends of the roofing-tile joints at the eaves
barge boards	Boards, sometimes decorated, that follow the slopes of a gable
battlement	A parapet indented alternately with raised portions
bay window	A window projecting from the wall face, either square or, if the sides slope, canted; if curved, it is a bow window
blocking course	A course of stonework above the cornice
bow window	*See* bay window
bracket	A plain or shaped cantilevered support, used, for instance, under the eaves
capital	The top part of a column or pilaster
castellated	Dressed with battlements
colonnade	A row of columns linked at their heads by a horizontal beam, entablature or series of arches
colonnette	A small column
console	Ornamental bracket
Corinthian	*See* Order
cornice	The projecting band at the top of a wall or the top section of an entablature
cottage orné	An ornamental cottage, typical of the Picturesque movement, built on an estate as an eye-catcher and originally of no practical use; a hybrid term, as the word 'cottage' is not a French word
crenellation	*See* battlement
curtain wall	The lengths of wall built between the towers of a castle or the wall surrounding a castle
dentil	A small square block, resembling a tooth, used in some classical cornices
doorcase	The whole wooden framework surrounding a door
Doric	*See* Order
dressings	Decorative stones or bricks used around an angle or opening to emphasize it
embattled	Having a battlement
entablature	In classical architecture the horizontal structure above the columns, subdivided into three sections: the architrave (the lowest), the frieze (above the architrave) and the cornice (on top)
fanlight	A window, usually semicircular, immediately above a door
ferme ornée	An ornamental farm building designed to embellish an estate or for use in playing at farming and the rustic life
frieze	The central portion of an entablature
gable	The triangular section of wall under a pitched roof
gablette	A small gable
grisaille	Monochrome painting in grey
guinguette	Parisian open-air café or dance-hall, later a pleasure house
hipped roof	A roof whose ends slope at the same angle as the main roof
in antis	When the columns are in line with the side walls of a portico
Ionic	*See* Order
label	A square moulding over a window or door to throw off rainwater
lattice window	Window with diamond-shaped panes
loggia	An open gallery, usually behind a colonnade
lunette	A semicircular opening, usually a window
machicolation	In castellated architecture, a parapet projecting in advance of the wall face, with holes in the floor for defensive purposes
metope	The square space in a Doric frieze

mullion	A vertical post in a window frame	quatrefoil	In Gothic architecture, four segments linked to resemble the petals of a flower
ogee	An S-shaped curve	quoins	Dressed stones used on corners, usually long and short alternately
Order	One of five classical styles (Doric, Ionic, Corinthian, Tuscan and Composite) of column, all strictly governed by their own proportions	relieving arch	An arch built into the wall over a lintel to relieve the load on it
oriel window	A bay window built out from the wall above ground level	rusticated	Stones laid with deep, wide joints, used to give texture and the impression of stength
patera	A small, flat, circular or oval applied ornament	rustic order	A pseudo-classical order built out of rustic timbers, usually with the bark left on
pediment	Classically, the crowning part of a portico – usually triangular, sometimes segmental – contained within the divided cornice	screen wall	A non-structural partition or wall used to divide space
pent roof	A sloping roof rising against the main wall	*tempietto*	A small temple
piano nobile	The main floor of a building when above the ground floor	tracery	In Gothic architecture, the intersection in various ways of the mullions in a window
pier	Solid masonry support, with same function as a column	transom	The main horizontal member in a window, or the dividing member between door and fanlight
pilaster	A shallow, usually square, pier projecting from a wall	Tuscan	*See* Order
porte-cochère	A covered porch for wheeled vehicles	tympanum	The triangular or semicircular face of a pediment between the horizontal and the raking cornices
portico	Centrepiece of a house or church, with classical columns and a pediment; it can be one or more storeys high		

PHOTOGRAPHIC ACKNOWLEDGEMENTS

The author's literary executor and the publishers are grateful to all museums, institutions and private owners who have given permission for works in their possession to be reproduced and to those who have kindly provided photographs. They have endeavoured to credit all known persons holding copyright and reproduction rights for the illustrations, and apologise for any omissions or errors which may have arisen as a result of the author's death.

References are to page numbers (t=top, m=middle, b=bottom, l=left, r=right).

Reproduced by gracious permission of Her Majesty The Queen 175tr, 175br, 182m, 182b, 250t, 301tr, 309tl; Abergavenny Museum 49br; NMR Wales, Aberystwyth 39br, 122b; Batsford/RCHME 84tl; British Architectural Library/Royal Institute of British Architects 62tr, 63tl, 65tr, 68b, 69tl, 70tl, 82t, 82br, 91tl, 97b, 100tr, 108bl, 110tr, 111r, 113bl, 116t, 116m, 116b, 123t, 123mr, 123bl, 123br, 136bl, 137ml, 137bl, 143tr, 146t, 146b, 162bl, 164tl, 164tr, 164b, 188b, 206bl, 207t, 214, 215, 218t, 218b, 223t, 231bl, 231br, 304r, 305b, 306, 307br, 308mr, 309tr, 310t, 316br; Royal Pavilion, Art Gallery and Museums, Brighton 26, 27, 82bl, 83tl, 83tr, 100bl, 100br, 109br, 113tl, 150bl, 153b, 154tr, 154br, 155t, 187tl, 187tr, 201b, 202bl, 202br, 203t, 305l, 305r, 307bl, 308tl, 308tr, 311t, 311b, 312t; Buckinghamshire County Council 89br; The Earl of Caledon 147tr, 147bl; National Library of Wales, Cardiff 40t, 43b, 44t, 44b, 178t, 178b, 179; Carmarthen Museum 40b; Crown Copyright/RCHME 298tl, 298tr; © Donald Davies/NMR Wales 46t, 46b; Devon Library Services 95b, 118b; National Library of Ireland, Dublin 139tr; Martyn Gregory 125t; Harrow School, Middlesex 63tr, 63b; Hereford Archaeological Unit 70tr, 70br; Hereford CRO/RCHME 115tl, 115tr, 115mr, 126t, 126bl, 126br; Historic Monuments and Buildings Branch, Department of the Environment, Northern Ireland 208tl, 208tr;

Isle of Wight Record Office 117b, 188t, 291b; reproduced by kind permission of the Principal, Fellows and Scholars of Jesus College, Oxford 12; Howard Jones/NMR Wales 59t; I. Wyn Jones 38bl; A. F. Kersting 240t; Peter Laing 11; Liverpool Libraries 124t; Liverpool Record Office 124b, 125br; Walker Art Gallery, Liverpool 49tl; Thomas Lloyd 38t, 53tr, 53b, 59b, 66t, 111l, 168t; British Library, London 224b, 225t, 251b; courtesy of the Trustees of the British Museum, London 15, 86t, 187bl; Christie's, London 48t, 240b; Country Life, London 136t, 152t, 181tr, 226t, 226b; Courtauld Institute of Art, University of London 74bl, 74br, 75l, 80b; Marylebone Library, London 185t, 185b, 224tr; Museum of London 180t, 192t; Public Record Office, London 204bl, 204br, 287b; Savills, London 62tl; Sir John Soane's Museum, London 205m, 205r; Society of Antiquaries, London 61tl, 61tr; Swiss Cottage Library, London 222t, 257br; reproduced by permission of the President and Fellows of Magdalen College, Oxford 98tl, 98ml; Newport Library, Isle of Wight 76tm, 76tr; M. Pinhorn/RCHME 277mr; RCHME 87tl, 103bl, 107tl, 107tr, 120t, 121tl, 121bl, 142b, 154tl, 154bl, 163tl, 163br, 217b, 223b, 227t, 227b, 257bl, 265b, 275br, 276, 295tr, 295mr; J. Summerson/RCHME 142t, 183t; Surrey County Council 69tr, 277tr; Dr Nigel Temple 39t, 87b, 127t; Warwick County Record Office 291tr; Lady West 192b.

The following plans were redrawn by the author from the sources given below: plans by I. Wyn Jones 43, 50, 84t, 86, 102, 119, 150, 157; plans by John Summerson 77, 120, 275; plan from Hereford Record Office 71; estate plan from Grovelands Priory 72; estate plan from Sundridge Park 84b; plan by G. S. Repton (BAL/RIBA) 155; Davies's 1834 map of London 158; National Trust plan 170; Public Record Office plan 176; drawings from Nash's office (BAL/RIBA) 205, 233, 285, 286, 299; plan by R. Luker (courtesy of Robert J. Potter and Partners) 247; Ordnance Survey map of 1870 (courtesy of David & Charles Ltd.) 270, 280, 283; plan in the *Survey of London*, xxx 285.

INDEX

Page numbers in *italics* refer to illustrations